Mall Maker

Mall Maker

Victor Gruen, Architect of an American Dream

M. Jeffrey Hardwick

UNIVERSITY OF PENNSYLVANIA PRESS

Philadelphia

10   9   8   7   6   5   4   3   2   1

Published by
University of Pennsylvania Press
Philadelphia, Pennsylvania 19104–4011

Library of Congress Cataloging-in-Publication Data
Hardwick, M. Jeffrey.
   Mall maker : Victor Gruen, architect of an American dream / M. Jeffrey
Hardwick.
      p.   cm.
   ISBN 0-8122-3762-5 (cloth : alk. paper)
   Includes bibliographical references and index.
   1. Gruen, Victor, 1903– 2. Expatriate architects–United States–Biography.
3. Architects–Austria–Biography. 4. Stores, Retail–United States–History–20th
century. 5. Shopping malls–United States–History–20th century. I. Title.
NA737.G78 H37   2004
725.21/092–dc22   2003060192

To my parents,
Mark and Helen Hardwick
Thank you

Contents

The Gruen Effect

It is our belief that there is much need for actual shopping centers—market places that are also centers of community and cultural activity. We are convinced that the real shopping center will be the most profitable type of chain store location yet developed, for the simple reason that it will include features to induce people to drive considerable distances to enjoy its advantages.

—Victor Gruen, 1948

Gruen's most convincing argument is himself and what he has done.

—Richard Hubler, *Los Angeles Times*, 1964

In 1997 the University of Minnesota hosted a conference to figure out that ubiquitous American institution, the mall. The location was significant, since America's first enclosed mall had opened its doors in nearby Edina forty-one years earlier. Participants took an officially sponsored field trip to ponder Club Snoopy and Legoland at the Mall of America; they looked upon the apotheosis of American consumerism; they agreed on little. Journalists, architects, historians, and sociologists saw different cultural meanings in the 5.2-million-square-foot mall. Grandiose or monstrous? Liberating or oppressive? Entertaining or stupefying? The thinkers could not settle on a simple answer. The panelists offered diverse and often opposing views about America's immense shopping palace. Did it really mean anything to Americans, or was it just one more place to shop? Had the mall compromised the essence of democracy—people gathering together and voicing their concerns—or had it merely redefined public space and personal expression as shopping? And, perhaps, was there an unrealized potential for political or economic mobilization at the mall? Was it the cause or a symptom of Americans' love affair with consumption?

The conference participants often contradicted each other. They presented searing critiques about the significance of fountains, ficus trees, parking lots, suburban life, food courts, and shopping itself. One theologian saw a shopping trip to the mall as akin to a medieval pilgrimage. A European architect celebrated America's commercial frenzy as the triumph of incongruity and complexity. In the end, they agreed on only one thing—the disturbing prevalence of a major retail theory. Dubbed the Gruen Transfer or Gruen Effect, the theory holds that shoppers will be so bedazzled by a store's surroundings that they will be drawn—unconsciously, continually—to shop. The experts pointed to this theory as explaining mall shopping's powerful and pernicious hold on America's collective psyche. Journalists covering the conference latched onto this unity of opinion. Reporters began their stories by unveiling the Gruen Effect as if by exposing it to light the theory perhaps would evaporate. The reporters, like the panelists, took comfort in the notion that one theory might explain why Americans consume so much and enjoy consuming.

One Minneapolis journalist breathlessly revealed the inner workings of the theory to his readers. "In fact, you've already been Gruenized repeatedly and probably don't know it." He summarized how architects strategically manipulate the public with trees, lights, fountains, and colors to make them mindlessly purchase more goods. Mall design is all about "the removal of those impediments to the consumer impulse," he explained. "The displays are everywhere, the air is dry and clogging, the credit card is in your hand as you march like a POW toward the next display of goodies." The entire shopping mall experience was as if "the guards won't let you stop, even for a moment, the process of having fun."[1] That invisible design strategies could manipulate the public's desires was deplorable. For the reporter, the success of American malls was explained by the Gruen Effect. For the rest of us, the theory captures a phenomenon we know all too well. The Minneapolis conference commented on an inevitable experience of late-twentieth-century American life—shopping in a covered, contained, store-filled mall. Although this event is now so common that it feels like a natural process, the Gruen Effect, shopping malls, and even the all-American love affair with shopping owe much of their feeling and form to the work of one man—architect Victor Gruen, who had unleashed his vision upon the country forty years earlier as the designer of Southdale, that first mall in Edina.

Gruen, the so-called philosopher and father of the shopping center,

became the Minneapolis conference's scapegoat. All the sins of the
shopping mall were laid at his feet. He was held responsible for single-
handedly shaping the stereotypical cultural wasteland of suburbia. But
as with so many apocryphal morality tales, seeing Gruen as a wholly
evil figure responsible for the malling of America, the collapse of an earlier communal culture, and America's consumption mania seems like a
rush to judgment. Gruen's theory about shopping captures only one
aspect of his extraordinarily rich architectural career. And yet, for better or worse, Gruen did help reshape America into a country obsessed
with shopping.

At first glance, Gruen—a fervent socialist and a Jewish refugee from
Vienna who escaped Hitler's occupation—seems an unlikely villain in
the drama of American consumerism. In the early 1960s, *Fortune* magazine marveled that Gruen had a puzzling background "completely
remote from the U.S. commercial scene." Within the world of store
design, Gruen was extremely fortunate. From the moment he landed in
New York City in 1938, he found enthusiastic clients. Beginning with
Fifth Avenue boutiques, Gruen helped invent a new aesthetic for retailing. Taking his store modernization theories across the country during
World War II, Gruen spread and standardized the new commercial aesthetic. In the postwar years, the successful retail architect would turn to
designing paradoxical projects: immense suburban shopping centers
and ambitious urban renewal projects.[2]

Gruen's American architectural career spanned the years between the
dream of the 1939 New York World's Fair and the nightmare of the 1968
urban uprisings, an era that witnessed large-scale suburbanization, massive changes in retailing, the triumph of the automobile, white flight,
and the economic deterioration of America's downtowns. As a result of
his architectural projects, it is no overstatement to say that he designed
and built the popular environments of postwar America. Americans of
all classes and races have encountered Gruen's architectural dreams.
Gruen created the spaces that postwar Americans lived in, moved
through, and longed for.[3]

Chain stores, department stores, shopping centers, and downtown
plans—Victor Gruen was a powerful influence on all these areas. He also
substantially shaped the ways that merchants, architects, planners, and
politicians conceived of and realized these projects. Commercial architecture, and retailing itself, also changed substantially over the course
of Gruen's career and his influence was felt at every turn. From the
1930s to the 1960s, retail strategies were standardized across the nation

as chain stores used design to focus consumers' attention on the goods. Gruen was crucial to the spread of this aesthetic. Without it, retailers would not have begun using identical strategies for selling the same goods from Buffalo to San Diego. By the end of his American career in the late 1960s, Gruen had ushered in a new era of consumerism in America. In its institutions, on its landscape, in Americans' hearts, shopping had come to redefine what it meant to be an American. The popularity of retailing also transformed the American city. As retail projects increased in size and scale, 1950s malls and urban renewal plans soon took over larger and larger tracts. Quite literally, more and more of America was devoted to buying and selling.

Early in his American career, Victor Gruen realized that the retail environment could entertain Americans better than any show, exhibition, or performance. In all of his designs, he relied on visual surprises to amuse visitors, create consumers, and produce profits. His theory was simple: the more time people spent enjoying themselves in the commercial environment, the more money they would spend. Using artificial lights, giant show windows, and fancy facades for his stores—grand fountains, twirling sculptures, and rose gardens for his shopping centers—Gruen attempted to seduce and produce a larger audience for retailers. Thrift, frugality, or prudence—even during the Great Depression—did not have a place in Gruen's glittering world. With his commercial successes, he altered the ways Americans lived in and thought about their cities. While Gruen cannot single-handedly be credited with all the clanging of cash registers and swiping of Visas in the last half century, more than any other invention Gruen's realized vision of the mall has been the venue where Americans have acted out their love affair with shopping. Shopping, because of Gruen, has become a distracting and fulfilling experience, a national pastime.[4]

Gruen built his thirty-year American career on a foundation of commercialism, and the creation of spaces for merchandising formed the heart of all his projects. Extraordinarily ambitious, Gruen could not rest on his successful store designs. Throughout his career, he turned his eyes toward ever larger projects, eventually setting his sights on the creation of entire new cities and expanding his influence into territory usually reserved for city planners. Thus, Gruen's name has been associated also with the ambiguous legacy of the urban renewal efforts of the 1960s.

Gruen had lofty social goals for the spaces he created. The architect hoped to combine the reform of retail and the reform of America; "good planning & good business are in no way mutually exclusive," he once declared about his approach to architecture.[5] These selling spaces, he promised, could unite Americans and create new communities. Through his retailing work, Gruen desired to stop commercial sprawl, give Americans a richer public life, and produce retailing profits. In the land of buying and selling, Gruen saw the means by which he could fashion large-scale projects to improve the American environment. But balancing these different agendas was never an easy act for him to sustain.

"An Architect of Environments," *Fortune* knighted Gruen in a celebrity profile of 1962.[6] Individual buildings did not matter to him. What did matter was a project's entire context. He wanted to control the development on two, three, five hundred acres of land. At one point, Gruen, obliquely describing himself, called for a new Renaissance man, the environmental architect.[7] He referred to himself as an "environmental designer."[8] At the end of his American career, he even started a Los Angeles think-tank, the Victor Gruen Foundation for Environmental Planning. "Victor was preoccupied with the environment rather than building," one partner recalled about Gruen's priorities.[9] Retailing, according to Gruen, could produce a new Renaissance that married commercialism and culture, business and beauty. Yet Gruen often compromised his sweeping visions to meet his clients' economic concerns. In these compromises, Gruen hit upon new forms for retailing, created new spaces for public life, and experienced his greatest disappointments.

In this account of twentieth-century retailing, Victor Gruen looms large. He was a significant historical actor, even if the outcomes of his actions occasionally flew in the face of his stated goals. His ideas, so meticulously developed, were adopted by merchants, developers, and other architects, and in ways even Gruen could not have anticipated. Often, Gruen was appalled at what clients did to his grand plans. To remedy these problems, he turned to larger and larger projects where he would have more control.

As Gruen was a prolific architect, so he was a prolific writer, and he was never a better salesman than when selling himself in his writings. He offered his opinions on everything in America from the importance of artificial lighting for impulse sales to the need to bring civic space into the growing suburbs. His forceful and flashy ideas found their greatest expression in his popular writings. He published three influential books, *Shopping Towns USA* (1960), *The Heart of Our Cities* (1964), and *Centers for the Urban Environment* (1973). He had also penned at least 250 articles by 1968 and, in addition to these writings, presented thousands of speeches.[10] Gruen was a constant proselytizer, explaining his grand visions for improving retail and transforming the city to citizen's groups, architects, academics, politicians, and his own employees. He was nothing if not opinionated. Frequently, he put down in words what was beyond his reach in architecture. He recommended strategies for turning profits, stopping commercial sprawl, and remaking downtowns. He also had a knack for staying ahead of the curve in architectural ideas by borrowing from others. Yet Gruen also had his blind spots. At a time when Americans were becoming more segregated in their residential patterns, Gruen rarely addressed race. While his writings often envisioned profound dreams of perfect cities, his built projects changed the way Americans lived their daily lives—not always for the better.

Through his work, Gruen changed as well. He became Americanized while working to change American retailing, though he never was content with the ways of Americans. Despite his work, he denounced suburbia, attacked the middle class, and even criticized his own successes. He was a deeply conflicted man, and the paradoxes in his career loomed large. He specialized in retailing but did not enjoy shopping, celebrated the values of pedestrian cities but loved driving around L.A., argued for the value of stable communities but continually traveled between New York, Los Angeles, and Vienna.

In this biography, I focus on Gruen's American architectural career, from 1938 to 1968. Born in Vienna in 1903, Gruen arrived in Manhattan in 1938. Moving to Los Angeles two years later, he founded his American architectural firm in 1951. The year 1968 saw him back in Vienna.[11] In the span of only three decades, Gruen's architectural work had reshaped the landscape of more than two hundred American cities and suburbs. I describe the origins of Gruen's major projects, the growth of his career, and the philosophy behind his architectural creations.

But much more is at stake here than the historical record of one architect's career. By also exploring the relationship between Gruen's work and American culture and by historicizing the birth of the mall, I hope to reach beyond the popular notions of the "malling of America," the privatization of public space, postwar suburbanization, and downtown decline. By explaining the ways in which Gruen's commercial projects reshaped public life for Americans—for better or worse, I hope to make the conversation about consumerism and suburbia a little less shrill. With his writings and designs, Gruen created a new, appealing stage and scale for retailing. He literally defined the prevalent vocabulary for retailing in America. (Before he had even built a shopping mall, Gruen authored a dictionary of shopping center terms.)[12] He informed merchants and architects how to use art, courtyards, and parking lots to make their businesses more beautiful and profitable. This is Gruen's legacy—building and refining the arena of American retailing and turning shopping into America's favorite pastime.

CHAPTER ONE

Escaping from Vienna to Fifth Avenue

You must make this window-shopper push your door open
and make him take a step, the one step, which changes him
from a window-shopper into a customer. A good store front
tries to make his step as easy as possible for him, and tries not
to let him even notice that he takes such an important step.
—Victor Gruen, 1941

Seeing is selling.
—Libbey-Owens-Ford Glass Company, 1941

"A good storefront is one of your best salesmen," designer Victor Gruen once informed merchants. "On its dignity and good taste people will base their opinions of your entire business." Snazzy displays, he promised, could stop a person in his tracks and transform a mere passerby into a breathless customer. Gruen, barely a year in America, devoted much time to speculating about how best to fashion "sales appeal." Strategic lighting, neon signs, show windows, glass facades, and ingenious floor plans could transform an ordinary store into what Gruen sensationally called "a machine for selling." He wholeheartedly believed in his own skill at creating irresistible spaces and goods. These fabulous environments, Gruen promised, would excite, persuade, and ultimately control consumers' emotions, responses, and pocketbooks. Later this consuming fever would be referred to as the Gruen Effect, a tribute to Gruen's persuasive retail theories.[1]

At first glance, Victor Gruen—a Viennese Jewish refugee, named Gruenbaum until 1941—seems an unlikely protagonist for the triumph of a new style for American retailing. Yet his initial rise in retail circles was meteoric. Within two years of arriving in New York, he had designed exhibitions for the 1939 World's Fair, helped produce two Broadway plays, and written magazine articles on modern store design. Gruen offered more than advice—he also put his theories into practice. Beginning with few American contacts, Gruen capitalized on his new designs for two high-profile Fifth Avenue boutiques, created a shockingly new retail experience, and helped usher in a new era of retailing that would spread far beyond Manhattan's avenues. And as Gruen pulled American retailing in a new direction, he drew on his past experiences of living and working in Vienna.

Gruen had not wanted to move to New York. He had loved his life in Vienna. "[I] never really left Vienna . . . it was a haven," he later remembered. For thirty-five years he had lived in the vibrant Austrian city on the Danube, enjoying successes in theater and architecture, an active political life, and a rich social life. However, when Hitler seized power in March 1938, Gruen, like other Viennese Jews, had few options.[2]

Victor Gruenbaum was born in 1903, the only son of a "typical Viennese liberal family" with a "well-staffed household." His father worked as a lawyer for theatrical clients. Adolf Gruenbaum also had a bit of the showman in him and was a popular lecturer in Viennese social clubs.[3] The Gruenbaum family lived in Vienna's Central District I in the heart of old Vienna. Turn-of-the-century Vienna was the birthplace of modernism. The city was famous for the art of Gustav Klimt and Oskar Kokoschka, the music of Gustav Mahler and Arnold Schoenberg. Modern psychoanalysis, with Sigmund Freud, Wilhelm Reich, and the younger Erik Erikson, had been developed in Vienna. The group of writers known as Young Vienna—including Arthur Schnitzler, Stefan Zweig, and Robert Musil—also explored the mores of middle-class Viennese. In architecture, modernists like Josef Hoffman, Adolf Loos, and Otto Wagner revolutionized the design of houses, stores, and public buildings in Vienna by combining sleek ornamentation and modern materials. At the craft guild and retail store Wiener Werkstatte, modernists also designed a new kind of decorative arts.

Gruen grew up in the dying embers of this vibrant aesthetic life. By the time he was a young man, Viennese citizens had turned toward more political activities, though a new generation did continue to invent new aesthetic forms to better people's lives.[4] In the midst of coffeehouses, theaters, restaurants, stores, hotels, and apartments, Gruen believed he was living in Europe's "center of intellectual and cultural life."[5] In 1917 he graduated from the prestigious Realgymnasium in central Vienna and in keeping with his generation and circumstances immediately began to pursue an advanced degree. He concentrated on architecture at the Vienna Academy of Fine Arts,[6] where modernist Peter Behrens, famous for his machine-inspired buildings in Berlin, taught. Gruen quickly developed a strong interest in Vienna's most famous turn-of-the-century modernist architect, Adolph Loos. Loos represented for Gruen the perfect blend of modernism and commitment to architectural ornament through using attractive materials.

In 1918 Gruen's father died suddenly and the young student left school to support his mother and sister. As his personal life was thrown into disarray, so was his beloved Vienna. After the end of World War I, the Austro-Hungarian Empire collapsed. Vienna, as Austria's capital city, felt the reverberations of this swift decline. Thousands of desperate refugees from Eastern Europe filled the city. Unemployment skyrocketed, and adequate housing was in short supply. The Viennese endured "chaotic social and economic conditions . . . followed [by] years of hunger and suffering," Gruen later recalled.[7] He was luckier than most, finding employment with his godfather's architectural and construction firm, Melcher and Steiner. He worked there for eight long years, feeling "little satisfaction" from the projects. As a young man still in his twenties, Gruen found architecture too "practical," especially for Vienna's bleak times. To defeat "the basic sadness of this time," he poured his energies into two other outlets: the cabaret theater and Socialist politics. Both interests remained with him throughout his life. He would always play showman and idealist, entertainer and reformer, sometimes on a grand scale.

As a child, Gruen had accompanied his father to rehearsals of plays and musical comedies, "letting theatrical life of Vienna soak into my bones."[8] Working in the architectural firm by day, Gruen performed in Vienna's coffeehouses by night. His short performances, a vaudeville mix of music, slapstick, social critique, and drama, offered something for everyone. Gruen's passion for theater soon combined with his commitment to Socialism, and he devoted his energies to working on Politisches Kabarett, a theater group that staged overtly political and controversial one-act skits.[9] Nothing escaped the criticism of the Politisches Kabarett. "I was in the thick of the revolutionary movement—acting and writing social commentaries for the little theaters, very anti-Hitler, anti-Dolfuss, anti-clerical," Gruen nostalgically recalled.[10] The acts were also famous for skewering the mores of the Viennese bourgeois. Most of all, the plays, as much as their staging in coffeehouses, created an intense relationship between actors and audience. Gruen adored this sense of the cabaret as a gathering place for the liberal Viennese community. For Gruen, there existed no distinct line between educating people about Socialist politics and entertaining them with jokes or songs—and he would also tread this ambiguous line in his later architectural work.[11]

Gruen continued to work for the architectural firm and even earned his Austrian architectural license, but his passions remained elsewhere. In one particular play, Gruen voiced his discomfort with the architectural profession. Through a back-and-forth dialogue between an architect and a government official, he satirically portrayed the architect's idealism being stifled by codes and regulations.[12] Architecture seemed too practical for this outgoing, idealistic Socialist. At the cabaret, Gruen saw more immediate results for Socialism and himself by entertaining people.

Gruen's identity as a socialist was much stronger than his identity as a Jew. Though he had grown up in a decidedly Jewish part of Vienna, and nearly half his high school class had been Jewish, Gruen nevertheless remembered receiving "severe beatings by the other students" because he was a Jew.[13] Like many of his generation, he had little use for religion. He was more committed to secular causes than religious ones. "Victor was much more of a Viennese than a Jew," one architectural partner later explained.[14] Decades later, Gruen tallied and ranked his various identities throughout his life: "adorer of the female, Socialist, humanist, environmentalist, architect, businessman, philosopher." Jew was not among them. However, being Jewish led Gruen to Socialism. The rise of Socialism in Vienna was strongly connected to urban Jews; or rather, Jews in Vienna were much more likely to be Socialists than their Protestant neighbors. One historian of Vienna estimates that three-quarters of all Viennese Jews regularly voted with the Socialist party.[15] In this respect, Gruen was not unique.

His interest in Socialism began while he was still a teenager. At the age of thirteen, he joined a scout troop of "budding socialists with red scarves." He remembered the group as "increasingly political" and "consciously anti-monarchist." On one occasion, the troop refused to parade in front of Kaiser Karl, Austria's ruler.[16] Gruen's commitment to Socialism lasted well beyond his school days. He proudly remembered himself as having been a passionate Socialist up until 1938, and he and his first wife, Lizzie Kardos, were "staunch comrades in the Socialist movement." Gruen met and fell in love with Lizzie through their involvement with the theater. They were married in 1930, celebrating with a costume party with theater friends and members of the Social Democratic Party.[17]

To uplift the working class, Viennese Socialists pursued concrete civic improvements, and adequate housing became the party's rallying cry. From 1919, when the Socialists won citywide elections, to 1934, when the Austro-fascists seized the city government, Socialists constructed housing for 20,000 residents. That was one-tenth of the city's residential property. One of Gruen's early assignments for Melcher and Steiner was the construction of a municipal housing project, and he soon assumed responsibility for managing the entire project because his overweight supervisor could not climb the building's stairs. Caught up in the Austro-Marxist building boom, Gruen also proposed a reform-minded architectural project of his own. In 1925 Gruen and two former art students (a later architectural partner, Rudi Baumfeld, and Ralph Langer) entered a competition to design one of the government's apartment buildings. The team received third prize. Called "people's palaces," these were apartment buildings on a monumental scale. With hundreds of dwelling units for individual families, the buildings also stressed communal spaces. With kitchens, bathhouses, dining rooms, and schoolrooms, the Socialist-built apartments were designed both to house people and to unite them. This was Gruen's sole project for the Socialist city government; the rest were commercial ventures.

Viennese Socialists placed great faith in large-scale planning efforts, pursuing what one writer remembered as "the human engineering needed to create the egalitarian society of the socialist dream."[18] The Socialists' bedrock belief was in an improved environment that could uplift the working class. Historian Steven Beller characterizes the Socialists' project as "creating an enclosed and protected living framework in which the worker family could be assisted to a higher standard of civilization and new humanity."[19] The Viennese Socialists' belief in an environment's power to determine people's social, cultural, and political character would eventually become central to Gruen's American architecture, although in a vastly different realization. Throughout his career, Gruen sought to build his version of a better future, economically and socially, through a reform of cities' physical environment.

When the Socialists were removed from power in the violent battles of 1934, the proto-Fascist government cracked down on Socialism and closed the cabaret. So Gruen channeled his energy into architecture. With his wife Lizzie's help, he redecorated his family's flat to make space for his own architectural firm. From 1934 to 1936, Gruen undertook apartment renovations and interior design. He later claimed to have renovated as many as five hundred apartments. After 1936, he focused on more public architectural expressions, and soon landed

FIGURE 1. Two of Gruen's Vienna store designs. From Talbot Hamlin, "Some Restaurants and Recent Shops," *Pencil Points* 20 (August 1939).

retail clients in Vienna's posh First District. Over two years, Gruen designed seven stores for Viennese merchants. One London review of his design for Bristol's Parfumerie for the elegant Ringstrasse praised Gruen's work as "one of the most modern and interesting shops in Vienna." "Attractive shops" for "Vienna's most exclusive shopping district," was how one American publication summed up the designer's Viennese retail designs. Gruen's store designs played with innovative materials and lighting. For Bristol's, Gruen placed mirrors on three walls and the ceiling to create the illusion of a more spacious interior.[20] Little did the enthusiastic reviewers realize that Gruen's new retail career would soon end in Vienna.

On March 12, 1938, Austria invited Hitler across the border. Viennese Fascists joined Germany with enthusiasm. Fascists also turned on Viennese Jews with vehemence. Jews were forced to scrub Vienna's streets, sidewalks, and buildings. Many Jewish leaders were immediately rounded up and sent to the concentration camp at Dachau. Suicides in

Vienna increased, as many Jews saw little hope for the future and took their own lives rather than face humiliation and torture at the Fascists' hands. Gruen, like many Viennese Jews, was caught unprepared. He later told how the Fascists immediately confiscated his car, seized his firm, and briefly jailed him. When he was released he went immediately into hiding at his mother-in-law's house. Gruen—ever the optimist and perhaps unwilling to believe that his beloved native city could turn against him—waited longer to leave Austria than was wise. After Germany annexed Austria, Gruen set about destroying evidence of his connection with the Social Democratic Party. He spent a long night feeding the stove with some of his plays, writings, and books, later declaring, "my past goes up in flames."[21] As his past turned to ashes, Gruen also worried about his present safety and possible future.

Soon after Hitler's troops marched into Vienna, Gruen, Lizzie, and their theater friends gathered together. Over a late-night dinner, the group pledged that if they managed to escape from Vienna they would reunite and perform their plays again. To preserve their material, the group typed up multiple copies of their skits. They then mailed the plays between pages of Fascist newspapers to sympathetic theater friends in Paris, London, and New York. After making this pact with their friends, Victor and Lizzie worked to save themselves.

Lizzie sought to secure the couple a permit to leave Austria. This was a legally simple, albeit expensive and emotionally difficult process. For the Gruens, as for many European Jews, the more difficult issue was finding a country to accept them. One month after Germany's invasion, the Gruens had a lead. Ruth Yorke, a New Yorker, was working to find the desperate couple an American sponsor. Gruen had met Yorke on a train from Paris to Vienna five years earlier. The two had become close friends while Yorke lived in Vienna and pursued an acting career. Yorke even hired the young architect to redesign her Viennese flat. After Yorke returned to New York, the friends maintained a lively correspondence. All the while, Yorke anxiously urged Gruen to leave Vienna. In late April, she found the Gruens an American sponsor, Harry Lowry of New York City. Lowry immediately provided assurance of financial support to the American consul in Vienna. In a letter to Lowry, the consul assured him that the Gruens "will be shown every possible assistance . . . and that their case will be sympathetically considered when they call." At the beginning of the next month, Germany granted the Gruens permission to emigrate to America. They paid a hefty tax to leave their native land and were now bankrupt. Many other Jews were not so lucky. Of the 175,000 Jews living in Vienna in 1938, the Germans killed 65,000 in the Holocaust.[22]

The Gruens escaped from Vienna on June 9, leaving behind a city that had turned on its own Jewish citizens. A theater friend disguised as a Nazi storm trooper escorted the Gruens to Vienna's airport. There the couple caught their first airplane flight, to Zurich, Switzerland. On the plane, Gruen thanked God for letting him escape with his life. He also denounced the German Fascists who had ruined his Viennese life and declared that for him the country no longer existed. "Goodbye, Vienna!" one refugee remembered celebrating his escape. "We were not sad to leave that fascist city. Goodbye!" Even the quintessential Viennese Sigmund Freud, fleeing the same week as Gruen, was thankful, if a little ambivalent, about his escape. "The triumphant feeling of liberation," Freud wrote, "is mingled too strongly with mourning, for one had still very much loved the prison from which one has been released."[23]

After fleeing Vienna, the Gruens spent a leisurely month in Europe, visiting with theater friends in Zurich, Paris, and London. They then booked passage to New York. Victor and Lizzie boarded the steamer *Statendam* in Southampton, England, traveling tourist class.[24] "A happy week," Gruen later recalled about his escape from Europe. A "strange kind of emigration," one German Jewish writer remembered of his own similar voyage to New York. "We did not sit in the steerage on our bundles; we were tourist class passengers on some of the giant boats and the adventure started like a vacation journey without return ticket."[25] The Gruens also had an uneventful and pleasant journey across the Atlantic. They played ping-pong, ate at the captain's table, and tipped the staff with their few remaining dollars. Gruen, however, did receive one piece of advice that he later recalled with nostalgic precision. A "Yankee" told him how to succeed in America. "Don't try to wash dishes or be a waiter—we have millions of them out of work, but if you are an architect, and a good one, we don't have many," the stranger advised.

Never given to extreme modesty, Gruen bragged to his new acquaintance about his "practical" architectural background designing stores. He consciously left out his more romantic and political experiences with theater, Socialism, poetry, and philosophy.[26] As the ocean liner carried Gruen away from Europe's storm clouds and toward New York, he looked to America's shores to forge a new life for himself.

Four months after the German takeover of Austria, the Gruens sailed into the Port of New York. Ruth Yorke, their only friend in the city, picked them up at the dock in a little convertible and whisked them away for a whirlwind tour of New York City.[27]

As a thirty-five-year-old refugee, Gruen arrived in New York speaking no English, carrying only his Viennese T-square and a few of his plays.[28] He felt boundless optimism. "I have nothing with me, no problems, everything is ahead, the world is open," he later recalled.[29] In later life, Gruen rarely spoke about his refugee experience. "Victor rarely looked at the past," one friend explained.[30] Gruen described his natural demeanor as "living in the present—with an intense interest in planning the future."[31] Throughout his life, Gruen would have an impressive ability to ignore present difficulties and focus on the future. In 1938, Gruen saw that future in New York.

New York seemed fantastic—the largest city in America. Its population of seven and one half million made it five times larger than Vienna.[32] Compared to the oppression and poverty of Vienna, even during the Depression New York promised peace and prosperity for the Gruens. They had left behind a city racked by two decades of dire economic conditions. The Empire State Building, Rockefeller Center, and the Chrysler Building, all less than a decade old, dominated Manhattan's skyline. The master builder of New York, Robert Moses, spearheaded the planning and building of giant public works like the Triborough Bridge and the Westside Highway. But skyscrapers, bridges, and highways did not attract Gruen. He felt instead the pull of two very different New York attractions—the flashing lights of the Great White Way and the bucolic calm of Central Park. Built for nearly opposite reasons, Broadway's brashness and the park's peacefulness shared one important aspect: they were loved and used by the public. On a larger scale than Vienna's parks or theaters, Broadway and Central Park welcomed all New Yorkers. The two places—one built with public funds and the other erected by private capital—provided entertainment for all comers. In his later retail projects, Gruen would try to unite these two seemingly contradictory experiences.

Gruen desperately needed to earn a living. He was broke and the couple was temporarily staying in a borrowed apartment. "The pressure to establish himself and make a living were uppermost," one partner later remembered.[33] Many Jewish refugees found the move to America extremely difficult. Upon immigration to the United States, many educated Jewish émigrés did not find an American audience eager for their talents. Anti-Semitism was rife, and a number of professions were openly hostile to outsiders' ideas. Surprisingly, one of the most stereo-typical American spheres—consumer culture—would benefit immensely from the exiles' concepts. Of course, which ideas Gruen offered and how those ideas were translated into the American context would determine his future success or failure. Would Gruen's satirical plays about the Viennese middle class delight Broadway audiences? Or would his store designs that were celebrated on Vienna's Ringstrasse stand out along Fifth Avenue?[34]

Luckily, Gruen soon landed promising work. He was hired to work on two of the more ambitious architectural projects in Depression-racked America: World's Fair exhibitions and Fifth Avenue stores. The two projects fit Gruen's American mood; both were hopeful, optimistic. The work also brought him into the heart of America's upbeat dreams for its future. With a common goal of presenting objects in a dramatic light, the stores and exhibitions valued smooth design using new technologies.

When Gruen arrived in New York City, the most conspicuous architectural project in New York was being built not on Manhattan but across the East River in Queens. The 1939 World's Fair, built on a gigantic ash dump made infamous in F. Scott Fitzgerald's *Great Gatsby*, was the pet project of Grover Whalen and Mayor Fiorello LaGuardia. The mayor had practical reasons for promoting the World's Fair in the middle of the Depression. With the fair, he saw a way to make much-needed improvements in highways, parks, and bridges and to promote the city of New York.[35] The World's Fair's planners did not attempt to compete with Broadway's lights or Manhattan's heights. Rather, the fair's corporate exhibitors offered an idealized version of the future American city. "These buildings are themselves a glimpse into the future, a sort of foretaste of that better world of tomorrow," explained the fair's president.[36] In its combination of corporate money, new technology, progressive art, and social planning, no place else could have immersed Gruen so quickly in America's hopes for overcoming the Depression. While the fair supposedly commemorated George Washington's 150th birthday, its corporate-sponsored exhibitions presented an appealing future made possible through new technologies. As both subject and backdrop, new technology suffused the Fair's exhibitions. Television, Lucite, air conditioning, diesel engines, color film, fluorescent lighting, and nylon stockings were all unveiled there.[37] Americans were truly impressed. The fair showed how technological marvels could be fun and futuristic, planned and playful, profitable and progressive.

Gruen found work at the heart of the World's Fair with two Manhattan design firms, Ivel and G. Whittbold. Though he played only a minor role as draftsman, both firms worked for large corporations, such as General Motors, Ford, Coca-Cola, General Electric, and Planter's Nuts, to help corporate America fashion an exciting image of America's possible future. The designers freely experimented with new technologies like fluorescent lighting and plastics, while the exhibitions themselves offered endless novelties. Televised baseball games, curving highways, giant cash registers, modern kitchens, streamlined automobiles, miniature soda factories, an opera of performing railroad cars, and models of new cities entertained visitors. Radiantly optimistic in the midst of the dark Depression, the fair literally illuminated new possibilities for living.

The fair's popular displays also heralded the arrival of a new profession that allied companies and art—industrial design. Beginning with their work at the fair, industrial designers would now work as the artists of corporate America, and many—including Norman Bel Geddes, Raymond Loewy, Walter Dorwin Teague, and Donald Deskey—would go on to become the best known in America. If corporations doubted the value of designers before the fair, those doubts were put to rest by the exhibitions' popular and critical success.

Gruen was thus among distinguished company, and even in his lowly capacity worked on one of the fair's more futuristic exhibitions, General Motors, Futurama, designed by Bel Geddes. Combining Coney Island's entertainment with a museum's edification, Futurama displayed a miniaturized modern American city, which proved to be the fair's biggest hit. Visitors rode on a guided tour over an immense, realistic model of the American city—showing both the old city of 1939 and the remade city of 1960. An omniscient narrator pointed out the public benefits of this meticulously planned city. Of course, Futurama's future city was premised on the dominance of General Motors own technology: automobiles. Highlighting superhighways, skyscrapers, parking garages, apartment buildings, amusement parks, and parkland, Futurama presented a perfectly ordered metropolis. Futurama had none of the dilapidated buildings, commercial blight, or congested roads of the American city seen right outside the fairgrounds. Just as the World's Fair had transformed the giant ash dumps of Flushing into a pleasant park, so too designers could transform all of America into a fair.

The Futurama ride ended dramatically. Visitors were dropped off in front of a life-size future intersection. The intersection illustrated how city planning would separate cars and pedestrians. As Bel Geddes explained the visitors' final view, "On the elevated sidewalks, the city crowds are walking, gazing in the shop windows, lounging on the building roof gardens. . . . Cars are moving in the streets." Gruen later credited Futurama with selling the public on highways and cars. He believed that the show had set "the scene for the [1950s] national highway program."[38] For Gruen, Futurama and the fair created an impressive vision. The Vienna he had left was a compact city of few cars, limited indoor plumbing, and no major highways.[39] The exhibition, on the other hand, heralded a new way of life in which planners and corporations could work and improve the existing city. The popular and critical success of the industrial designers' exhibitions also ushered in a new era in American architecture.

Gruen arrived in New York during a time of drastic change for American architecture. Since the mid-nineteenth century, architecture in New York had been a gentleman's pursuit. The profession, long the domain of elite WASPs, was dominated by connoisseurs, dilettantes, and wealthy men. Indeed, architectural critic Lewis Mumford disparaged American architecture from 1910 to 1930 as the "Genteel Reaction." As early as 1918 architectural historian Fiske Kimball voiced another concern. He fretted about the future direction of American architecture. He saw a battle for America's soul between a classically inspired "nationalist" revival and a functionalist European modernism.[40] Kimball, who had written extensively on American classicism during the nineteenth century, saw the revival of classicism as a retreat into the past. And European modernism, for Kimball, seemed to leave American architects behind.

During the 1930s refugee architects and designers fleeing the spread of German Fascism pulled American architecture toward modernism. The now-legendary Mies van der Rohe, Walter Gropius, and Marcel Breuer all arrived in the United States in this period and began designing in a decidedly modern and European style. Through their teaching positions at Harvard and the Illinois Institute of Technology, in Chicago, these émigré architects quickly turned elite academic institutions away from their romance with classicism.[41] As these exiles influenced the direction of academic architecture, Gruen and others changed the course of popular architecture.

At the time of Gruen's entry into the field of store design, the field barely existed. Gentlemen architects did not build their careers on lowly retail work. A yawning gulf divided architecture from store design. Houses, museums, train stations, skyscrapers, and even large department stores fell within architects' purview, but individual stores were seen as too crass, too commercial, and too small. Yet just as corporations began to turn to industrial designers to stylize their products during the depression, so too retailers turned to store designers for help. As "machines for display," storeowners sought to place their goods in the best possible light to sell more and attract more attention.[42]

Morris Ketchum, Gruen's first partner, described how "a new generation of architects" turned to retail design as the Depression forced them to drum up new clients. Before the 1930s, a store's "final design and equipment were left to owner and contractor, architects were not involved," Ketchum explained.[43] Morris Lapidus, another colleague of Gruen's in the 1930s, declared: "I had no desire to be a store designer; to my mind that was not architecture. There were hardly any architects engaged in the store field at the time; stores were designed by draftsmen who did not need degrees in architecture."[44] Although Lapidus belittled commercial architecture, he soon excelled in it and became one of its most prolific practitioners. Gruen acutely felt the difference between a designer and an architect. He once wrote to *Architectural Forum* correcting an article that referred to Gruen and a partner as "architects." He wanted to set the record straight; "We always have made it a point to be called Designers," Gruen informed the magazine.[45] He would not become a licensed architect—and promote himself as one—until the late 1940s.

Additionally, Gruen's Viennese experience in no way prejudiced him against retail design. As much as New York architects had spurned retail, Viennese architects had relished it. In Vienna retail design did not have the lower-class or immoral connotations that tainted it in the United States; indeed, it enjoyed respect. The most famous Viennese architects worked on store designs. For instance, Adolf Loos, one of Gruen's heroes, had designed a men's clothing store.[46] The innovative Viennese architects who founded the Wiener Werkstaate eventually went into the retail business, even opening their own department store. The famous Viennese modernist and leading member of the group, Josef Hoffman, did not see it as below his architectural training to design advertisements, receipts, signage, and displays for the department store. In New York, Gruen's Viennese work would serve him well; with seven store commissions to his name, he was nearly an expert in the emerging field of retail design.

In 1941 fellow store designer Morris Lapidus used Gruen's store designs to illustrate the best in contemporary retailing for a landmark *Architectural Record* article.[47] Lapidus, like Gruen, had turned to retail more by chance than by design. The two architects stepped into the largely vacant field of retail design and created a completely new aesthetic. In his second autobiography, *Too Much Is Never Enough*, Lapidus captures the atmosphere of the architectural profession, the interaction of a Jew with the profession's traditions, and the emergence of commercial architecture in the late 1930s.

Lapidus begins by recalling a chiding lecture he received from the venerable A. D. F. Hamlin, dean of Columbia's prestigious School of Architecture. The dean explained that "no one would ever become rich practicing architecture." Lapidus saw all his classmates as "gentlemen who were entering a gentlemen's profession." They were all from Ivy League colleges and moneyed families. Lapidus was "the outsider, a prisoner of my own deep-rooted sense of inferiority." The son of Russian Jews, his only friend in school was a German immigrant with whom he endlessly discussed the "differences between Americans and Europeans."[48] Lapidus was hoping to earn a living through architecture, not become an American gentleman of leisure.

By Lapidus's own account, his Jewish identity and outsider status compelled him toward "odd," "modern," and "rebel" designs.[49] As his Columbia peers looked back to classicism for inspiration, Lapidus, a self-described "ghetto youth," turned to his New York City environment.[50] For domes, he copied subway stations; for a cemetery gate, he looked to automobile parkways; for a garage ornament, he chose a chrome radiator grill for inspiration. He questioned the appropriateness of Gothic styles, like Cass Gilbert's 1913 design for the Woolworth Building, for skyscrapers (or, as Lapidus called them in Yiddish, *himmel kratzer*). Lapidus swore "to experiment with these modern styles. I wanted to get into the twentieth century." All of these quirky designs won Lapidus hesitant praise at Columbia; he triumphed because of his unique, "rebel" eye.

After graduating from Columbia, Lapidus aspired to design mansions, skyscrapers, and museums. He found little work because of the Depression, and slowly turned to retail work out of necessity. After designing exhibitions for the World's Fair and completing a few New York specialty stores, Lapidus began working for chain stores. Opening on Main Streets in Knoxville, Memphis, and Atlanta, the chains wanted their branches to be shockingly new, modern, and urbane. Lapidus served them well, using neon signs, brilliant colors, woggle displays, Swiss-cheese ceilings, and blinding light. He later nicknamed his eclectic style "an architecture of joy," and it caught on in Knoxville as it had in New York.[51]

Throughout the late 1930s and the 1940s, Lapidus and Gruen traveled in the same professional circles. Gruen, like Lapidus, succeeded and assimilated within the architectural profession largely by parlaying his outsider status into a strength and working on commissions that were seen as beneath traditional architects. As Jewish architects working in a profession long dominated by the Protestant establishment, Gruen and Lapidus both gravitated to retail design and earned their early reputations specializing in that area. As Gruen's background pushed him toward retail, his Viennese past also led to a number of commissions. Indeed, Gruen entered the whirl of American consumer culture through his ties with other transplanted Viennese.

Upon arriving in New York, Gruen remained close to other Viennese refugees. He actively participated in the exile community, once lecturing (in German) on modern architecture for a refugee organization. On another occasion in 1940, he helped organize a benefit show for recently arrived Jewish refugees in Jersey City.[52] Gruen's theater friends had made their way to New York and were eager to begin performing again. Along with some German refugees, the exiles founded the Refugee Artists Group to pursue their theatrical careers in America.[53]

The Group turned to sympathetic New York stars to realize their dream of performing again. Gruen arranged a Group performance for Beatrice Kaufman, wife of the popular playwright, George, after which she signed on as the Group's biggest fan and benefactor. Kaufman lined up a star-studded list of sympathetic New Yorkers. The composer Richard Rodgers, the singer Al Jolson, and the novelist Edna Ferber all donated money to the refugees' cause.[54] Irving Berlin helped the Group polish their songs for American audiences. Charles Friedman, coauthor of the hit labor musical *Pins and Needles*, helped with final production.[55] Feeling sympathy for the refugees' plight and wanting to make a political statement about U.S. immigration policies toward Jewish refugees, the liberal New York stars gave freely of their time and money. Gruen even traveled to Princeton to see his fellow exile Albert Einstein. Einstein wrote a stirring letter of support for the Group. "This new type of theater concerns itself with the political and psychological problems," Einstein proclaimed, "that should be presented to the American public in its battle against the forces of fascism and race hatred."[56] With such strong endorsements, the Refugee Artists Group took their talents to Broadway.

Not surprisingly, the refugees' greatest hurdle proved to be the English language. They hired a speech coach and began taking daily English lessons, working hard to lose their accents and master the basics of English. Opening in June 1939, the Group staged their first show, the aptly titled *From Vienna*. Directly transferring their style from Vienna to Broadway, they staged cabaret pieces cutting between drama, music, and comedy. Playing in the donated Music Box theater, the performance became a minor sensation. Positive, if not glowing, reviews greeted the refugee's reunion. "The town relished them—went to see them . . . all summer long," the *New York Times* enthused. The press reacted to *From Vienna* by focusing on the Group's travails and survival more than on the performances. Articles stressed how the actors were "beginning a new life and new careers in a new land."[57] The play lasted at the Music Box for eleven weeks and the Group decided to launch another performance.

Reunion in New York, the Group's second, more ambitious show, opened in February 1940. In this performance the Group tried to move beyond immigrant tales and engage American popular culture. Once again, however, the press doggedly focused on the refugees' personal stories rather than on the performance. When the critics did turn their attention to the play, the reviews were mixed. The critics most enjoyed skits that stuck closely to the immigrants' own stories. Indeed, the show's most popular skit was "English in Six Easy Lessons," where two actors spoofed their own attempts to learn English. Bringing Vienna's cabaret style and substance to Broadway proved difficult, if not impossible. *Reunion in New York* did not last long and was the Group's final performance.[58]

If Gruen's theatrical work did not directly transfer to America, he hoped his architectural experience would. The day after his job on the World's Fair ended, the unemployed Gruen went window shopping on Fifth Avenue. While strolling along, he bumped into Ludwig Lederer, an acquaintance from Vienna. Lederer was from a family of established Viennese merchants and had operated stores in Vienna, Paris, and Berlin before the Anschluss.[59] Lederer hoped to open an American branch of his high-end leather goods store on Fifth Avenue and only needed a designer. He hired Gruen on the spot.

Since Gruen did not hold an American architectural license, he teamed up with an American who did, Morris Ketchum. Gruen and

Ketchum had shared a desk in the modernist Edward Durrell Stone's architectural office. There they had worked on World's Fair designs for Coca-Cola and Planter's Nuts.[60] Nearly Gruen's exact opposite, Ketchum grew up in an old Protestant family from New York. He received classical training in architecture, first at Columbia and then in France. When he met Gruen, Ketchum had already completed one store design with another Viennese modernist, Paul Frankl. Their design for the Mosse Linen Store on Fifth Avenue had earned modest praise for being "clean and orderly and attractive." Gruen and Ketchum's partnership would last barely a year, in which they would design only four Manhattan stores. These few collaborations, however, launched both of their prolific careers as retail architects.[61] They would both go on to design some of the first postwar shopping centers.

For their first job together, Gruen and Ketchum were lucky enough to design not one but two swanky boutiques for Fifth Avenue at Fifty-Fifth Street. Both stores were officially styled by Ketchum with Gruen acting as designer. When Lederer de Paris and Ciro's Jewelry of London opened in 1939, the Avenue had been undergoing major transformations. The monumental Rockefeller Center, constructed throughout the Depression from 1931 to 1940, brought offices, retail businesses, and entertainment to the Avenue. National chain stores featuring less expensive goods operated below Forty-Second Street; Woolworth's and Kress faced each other at Thirty-Ninth Street. At Thirty-Eighth Street the smaller chains A. S. Beck and Lerner's dress shop courted customers. Farther north, the Museum of Modern Art opened on Fifty-Sixth Street off the Avenue in 1939 and introduced high culture. High-priced boutiques soon began opening nearby and elevating the Avenue's shopping. Two blocks down from the Plaza Hotel and across the street from the stately turn-of-the-century Gotham Hotel, Lederer and Ciro were among the first expensive specialty stores to move into the Fifties. The next year Tiffany & Company opened its Fifth Avenue store a block up from Lederer and Ciro. During the late 1930s and early 1940s, upper Fifth Avenue became the most expensive and elite retail street in the world.[62] "It is on the specialty store that New York's reputation as a shopping capital depends," one journalist later reminisced about Fifth Avenue. He imagined the emotional grip high-priced Fifth Avenue stores had on New Yorkers. The stores gave "every New Yorker and every visitor an occasional feeling of intoxication—the realization that he is part of a big crazy town where no wild purchase is inconceivable."[63] In this heady retail world, Gruen

FIGURE 2. Ciro facade, Fifth Avenue, New York, 1939. Victor Gruenbaum, designer, Morris Ketchum, architect. From Talbot Hamlin, "Some Restaurants and Recent Shops," *Pencil Points* 20 (August 1939).

and Ketchum sought the spotlight with startlingly unique facades, floor plans, and materials.

For Lederer de Paris, the partners devised an ingenious lobby or "arcade" stretching across the store's entire Fifth Avenue facade. "Set in a typical Fifth Avenue block of flush shop fronts, this shop gains tremendously because of the contrast afforded by its recessed display space," *Architectural Forum* explained.[64] Measuring seventeen by fifteen feet with twelve-foot ceilings, the arcade featured six tiny (three-and-a-half feet high) glass cases that looked more like interior showcases than exterior show windows. The displays were installed at eye level to break up the bright walls. The designers placed another small display case on a pedestal in the center of the arcade for gloves and handbags; this case lit by a spotlight hidden in the ceiling glowed. An opaque gray glass, called suede-finished Carrara, simulated marble walls.[65] The ceiling of corrugated green glass hid fluorescent lights that poured a diffuse green light over the entire arcade. All in all, Gruen and Ketchum's front was a remarkable shiny rectangle, undecorated but for a few small display cases showcasing examples of the merchant's elegant Paris products.

Next door at Ciro of Bond Street, the designers played with the same motifs. Instead of a rectangular arcade, the jewelry store's lobby formed a perfect circle. Whereas Lederer's front opened to the sidewalk, Ciro's had an eight-foot entrance with a more imposing facade of glass tiles and showcases. The designers placed narrow show windows on the arcade's circular walls. The jewelry, spotlighted from above and against a midnight blue velvet background, sparkled in the display cases. Smooth cream-colored stucco formed the walls. For both stores, the partners had fashioned a covered space—an arcade or shopping lobby— off the sidewalk for the public to browse and window-shop in a leisurely way. Gruen and Ketchum believed the arcade was the perfect customer trap.

The stores' opening brought the partners instantaneous praise and— better still—more commissions. Critics praised the stores as "distinguished examples of modern luxury shop design" that "show with what excellent effect new materials and new handling of old materials are being used."[66] Two more high-end retail commissions immediately followed, Steckler's on Broadway and Paris Decorators on the Grand Concourse in the Bronx.[67] Employing innovative store layouts, brand-new materials, strategic lighting, and shocking facades, the partners fashioned a retail experience that surrounded the viewer with glittering goods. The *New Yorker, Architectural Forum, Pencil Points*, the Museum of Modern Art, and numerous trade journals applauded the store designs. Calling Lederer a "New Departure" and Steckler's "a World's Fair marvel at night," the Museum of Modern Art spotlighted the stores in a guidebook to modern architecture.[68] One retail journal applauded the stores for being "two inspirations within the reach of many." The store designs propelled Ketchum from an unknown to what *Architectural Forum* called "one of the most brilliantly imaginative designers in this field."[69]

The designers' trademark was their arcade front, which they used on all four of their New York storefronts.[70] *Women's Wear Daily* described how Lederer's "highly novel arcade store front" was "the first of its kind."[71] In essence the arcade was a generous lobby with banks of show windows on either side and occasionally a display case at its center. By

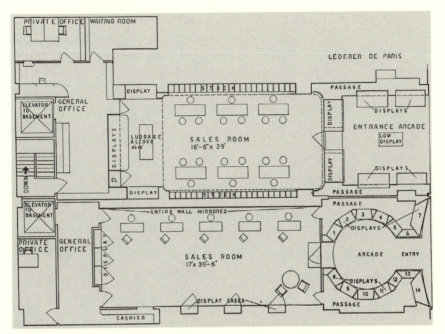

FIGURE 3. Plan of Gruen and Ketchum's Fifth Avenue stores, Lederer's and Ciro's, with their impressive arcade space. From *Store of Greater New York*, August 1939.

carving out depth from what had been flat windows, the arcade created a middle space that extended the store's threshold and placed the wares on the sidewalk. The arcade acted as a "FISH-BOWL technique" that "recently drew a crowd on opening night that resembled the pressure at a Hollywood premiere," one reviewer raved.[72] Of course, the potential customer was the fish swimming toward the baited hook of goods. Just as department stores employed large plate glass windows along an entire block, smaller specialty stores used the arcade to create more display space.

"The arcade front," Gruen explained in 1940, "was born out of the desire to gain additional show window length."[73] Ketchum explained that arcades "extend a hospitable welcome to window shoppers." Morris Lapidus also loved the arcade; its "zigzag, sawtooth, angled, [and] stepped" show windows provided merchants with "more windows and more space for display."[74] By 1944 Lapidus, who consistently used the design, imagined doing away with storefronts completely. "The ideal

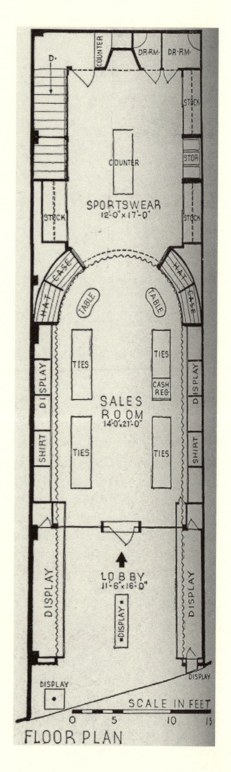

FIGURE 4. Floor plan of the Steckler store with its prominent arcade lobby. From "Stores," *Architectural Forum* (December 1939): 429.

store front," he dreamed, "would be an arcade for display leading directly to the selling area."[75] As the arcade gave merchants more display space, the form further popularized window displays focused on a few items.

"To catch the interest of the window-shy shopper is the task of the designer," Gruen reminded merchants.[76] One of the tenets of modern window display since the turn of the century held that spotlighting a few objects made the goods more tempting.[77] The focus would be on the goods. But, Gruen went on, "the gaudiness of materials and trimmings often kill the effect of exhibited goods."[78] A retailing textbook told merchants that to "dramatize the goods" a window should have "one central theme or idea."[79]

FIGURE 5. Photograph used in a retail textbook to illustrate poor store design with "bargains of all sorts jammed into the windows." From R. G. Walters, John W. Wingate, and Edward J. Rowse, *Retail Merchandising* (Cincinnati, Ohio: South-western Publishing, 1943), 264.

Not everyone embraced sparse window displays, however. Many retailers still wanted to fill their windows with piles of goods and signs. A national survey of show windows conducted in 1937 found that only higher-end retailers employed "selective" displays.[80] One industrial designer warned merchants as late as 1947 that "if there is no focal point in a mass display of merchandise, the eye can wander rapidly over everything and rest on nothing—passing without interest."[81] But with window displays, many merchants were reluctant to sacrifice numbers for notoriety, inventory for impressions. Arcades provided these reluctant merchants with an easy solution. By creating more show windows, the arcade allowed a retailer to place a variety of products on display and focus each window on fewer goods. "We never put too many things [in the showcases] . . . the elegance is not in quantity," an owner of Lederer's recalled about his displays.[82] Gruen even fantasized about the ultimate in glamorous display methods, imagining future stores arranged like museum exhibitions. Spotlights would light single objects to accentuate their preciousness and patrons would focus on the individual items.[83] Gruen and Ketchum hoped that their sleek arcades would attract customers through another illusion as well.

Unlike the show window's transparent view onto wares, the arcade beckoned people into the store's illusions and reflections. In an arcade, the gloves, handbags, bracelets, and rings literally surrounded the viewer. "The whole ensemble," one magazine observed, "presents a uniform attractive invitation to enter and buy." The arcade blurred the boundary between inside and out, store and street. One did not merely peek into a sensuous world; the arcade brought the passerby into the whirl of brightly lit goods. "There is no forbidding blank wall, no visible division between the front windows and the interior," one retail magazine marveled.[84]

Gruen and Ketchum sought to make the barrier between arcade and store even more invisible. They continued materials, colors, and lighting from outside to in. For Ciro's floor, the partners used a new material called Monocork, a mixture of cork and cement, and continued it from the sidewalk into the store. In the Steckler shop the partners extended the wall, floor, ceiling, lighting, and display cases from the arcade into the interior.[85] Transparent plate glass doors with clear plastic handles (both recent innovations) gave Gruen and Ketchum the perfect material to let shoppers see into the store's interior. "Since the door is also made of glass," *Women's Wear Daily* admired about Lederer's, "the illusion of an unbroken merchandise display is created."[86] Gruen and Ketchum even had to decorate Lederer's doors with discreet logos to prevent people from crashing through the closed doors.[87] For a later shoe store, Gruen realized the arcade's ultimate promise. He completely did away with the store's front doors by sliding them into the walls. The design, *Chain Store Age* admiringly observed, would remove "all obstructions to easy entrance" and easy purchases.[88] The arcade design did have one failing, though; it traded sales floor for sidewalk.

As arcades grew, stores shrank. When Gruen and Ketchum used an arcade on the Steckler store, they reduced the sales floor by one-third. For a shoe store, Gruen used a full quarter of the store on a twenty-five-foot arcade.[89] While designers saw the trade-off as worthwhile, some merchants remained skeptical. Morris Lapidus supported the partners, insisting that traditional show windows actually deterred window shoppers. He substantiated this conclusion with scientific "traffic counts." When shoppers were bumped and jostled on the sidewalk, Lapidus explained, they avoided looking in show windows. Lapidus reassured merchants that with an arcade the exterior actually functioned as an interior. "The shopper should have a feeling of being in the store once he has passed the building line," Lapidus argued.[90]

In 1940, Gruen hinted at his inspiration for arcades. In an article about store modernization, he designed two outrageously exaggerated arcade fronts. Shown in perspective, the arcades completely dominated the storefronts. In the first store, the arcade began at the store's entrance and dramatically swept past the building line to incorporate the sidewalk. One thick column supported the entire arcade. Large, curving show windows jutted into the arcade. In the second design, the store wrapped around a corner site. Here, Gruen swept the arcade up into a curving, lighted gallery. In the article's layout these two drawings framed a photograph of one of Gruen's Viennese designs. The Lowenfeld's store, Gruen proudly explained, used a "canopy leading back to two-foot recessed windows where 'lookers' are not jostled by passersby."[91] The solid "canopy" stretched out over the sidewalk and lit up the exterior with two rows of lights. The lesson drawn in this and a related article was clear: Gruen's New York designs were an improvement on high-class Viennese shops. As Gruen hyped his arresting store designs, architectural critics cast a bemused eye at retailing's brash new look.

Writing in the *New Yorker*, the architectural critic Lewis Mumford saw less dignified origins lurking behind the arcades. He looked for the arcade's origins not in Vienna but in downtown Manhattan. He admit-

FIGURE 6. Gruen and Krummeck's drawing of a fanciful arcade wrapping around a corner site with show windows for attracting customers. From Victor Gruen and Elsie Krummeck, "Face to Face," *Apparel Arts* (June 1940): 53.

ted that Gruen and Ketchum's arcades were "two bright new modish attempts to capture attention" and that these "New Stars on the Avenue" were "the logical conclusion of the merchant's attempt to lure customers into his store." But he thought that Fourteenth Street nickelodeons and peepshows, not European designs, were the arcade's real predecessors. He suspected that tawdry downtown inspirations lurked behind the uptown facades.

In Gruen and Ketchum's designs, Mumford saw a feverish attempt to pursue the customer. He found the trickery morally repugnant, like the sexual temptations of a downtown peepshow. The new facades drew in customers like "a pitcher plant captures flies or an old-style mousetrap catches mice." Mumford also saw a fatal flaw in Gruen and Ketchum's attempt to seduce customers. As Gruen celebrated the arcade's ability to break the building line and bring the sidewalk into the store, Mumford saw that conceit as the design's horrible flaw. For in a rare accommodation to Manhattan's grid, Mumford predicted that few merchants would imitate the arcade because it would rob Fifth Avenue "of its special character of being one long display window."[92] Little did Mumford know that Gruen and Ketchum were receiving more commissions from the acclaim over their Fifth Avenue designs.

Whereas Gruen and Ketchum worked to design enchanting stores, Mumford leaned in another direction. His tastes in retail ran more to the sedate store. In an earlier *New Yorker* column, "New Facades," Mumford wrote a year-end review of New York stores. "QUIETLY," he began, "and the word quietly has happy implications—Fifth Avenue has been having its face altered . . . not [through] new buildings so much as new show windows and shopfronts." For Mumford, the perfect shop did not employ the ballyhoo of contemporary commercialism; he preferred the quiet, classically inspired shopfront.[93] Any hint of decoration was too gauche and decadent for his eye. Whether it was an "unnecessary touch of delicate scalloped carving," "teasing antics," "funeral parlor pomp," or "overbold" lettering, overt ornamentation assaulted his senses. He reprimanded an architect for using "pseudo-modern" stone decorated with "a fat bundle of fasces" and railed against another store where the "design slips from modern into neo-romantic rococo," resembling shapes "usually reserved for goldfish pools for Renaissance gardens." The ornamented marketplace, according to Mumford, created a hedonistic architecture symbolizing a hedonistic society. Over-decorated stores produced a deceitful design that corrupted both architectural and human purity.[94]

Mumford wanted commercial architecture to resemble high art; another New York observer held no such illusions. New York stores "belong to another world," the architectural historian Talbot Hamlin breathlessly exclaimed. Like Mumford, Hamlin was an unlikely observer of the retail world's fashions. Architectural critic for *Pencil Points* and son of the dean of Columbia University's Architecture School, Hamlin was better known for his writings on early nineteenth-century American architecture. Whereas Mumford expressed distaste over the temptations of Gruen and Ketchum's designs, Hamlin took a more cynical view. The sole purpose of store architecture was to hawk goods, he said. "If ugliness can attract them [shoppers] better than beauty, or incoherence better than harmony, it is just too bad." Shops "are of necessity creatures of fashion," he resolved, "and must follow 'merchandising' habits of the time." Retail architecture's one function, for Hamlin and Gruen, was to help merchants move their wares. Whether ornate or spare, modern or classical, whatever style charmed shoppers was not too surprising to Hamlin.

For all his cynicism over retail design, Hamlin still had his standards.

And Gruen and Ketchum's stores broke one of Hamlin's cardinal rules—the partners had disregarded their Fifth Avenue context. Lederer's milky gray-white glass, Ciro's black, white, and gold, and Fifth Avenue's weathered limestone all seemed too chaotic; the ensemble's colors struck a "discordant note." While Hamlin acknowledged that store design was primarily about advertising, not art, he still insisted that stores fit into their contexts.[95]

Even though critical, Hamlin and Mumford themselves were strangely attracted to the new retail designs. They lavished much attention on describing and interpreting Gruen and Ketchum's retail aesthetic—recounting the colors, the crowds, and the designs. They took their readers through stylish new New York restaurants, automats, chain stores, and boutiques. Their articles also had the unintended effect of legitimizing Gruen and Ketchum's new field of retail design and elevated the stores to the level of high New York art. Later, Gruen enthused that an article in *Fortune*, even if too critical, was valuable because it placed his name before "those people whom we want to influence."[96] But in the end shoppers, not architectural critics, were the most important reviewers.

Gruen knew this and had his own theory, based loosely on psychology, of the arcade's popularity. The relationship between window shopper and merchant, he warned in a 1941 article for *Display World*, was a fundamentally antagonistic "psychological contest." A merchant must bewitch a passerby and overcome a natural "resistance," a "phobia of entering a store." The merchant's first goal was to transform a person—often without the slightest intention of buying or even looking"—into a captivated window shopper. A magical storefront—"architectural forms, materials, artificial light, signs, and the interesting arrangement of the displayed merchandise"—accomplished this transformation. Next the designer had to "lead the window shopper, whose resistance is already slightly weakened, unconsciously along the show windows towards the entrance door." The shopper's resistance would be broken by more display windows. In this "psychological battle," the consumer would be entranced by "the best possible view of the merchandise." A "victory," Gruen vowed, would be inevitable. By "setting the dramatic high point of your display near the entrance door," people would unconsciously cross the threshold.[97] For Gruen this was just the start of employing sophisticated and invisible devices to entice customers into shops—tricks that even critics did not notice.

At the same time that Gruen and Ketchum designed their arcade stores, Gruen also began experimenting with a new storefront. In 1939 another former Viennese merchant asked Gruen and his new partner, Elsie Krummeck, to design his Fifth Avenue store. For Gruen, this was the fourth retail commission from fellow Jewish refugees.[98] Gruen and Krummeck had met and fallen in love while working on the World's Fair. Gruen divorced Lizzie in 1940 and married Krummeck the next year; they remained architectural partners for twelve years. Krummeck, from a German Jewish family, had grown up in Brooklyn. She attended Manhattan's Parsons School of Design and then worked as an exhibition designer at the Chicago World's Fair of 1933. As Gruen and his first wife had shared a passion for Viennese theater and Socialism, so Gruen and Krummeck shared a passion for retail design.

The Altman and Kuhne candy shop was the first design of a very fruitful partnership and won the new partners instantaneous praise. On December 3, 1939, readers of the *New York Times* saw the "striking" shop as the front page's lead image. The paper went on to sing the praises of the designers.[99] Days later, the *New York World-Telegram* ran its own article about the candy shop. "Altman and Kuhne, who just opened their swanky candy shop in the Gotham Hotel, scorn the prosaic showcase," the reporter trumpeted. The novel design with "individual revolving tables and wall niches" elevated the candies so that the shopper had "the feeling they're as precious as sapphires and diamonds." The Architectural League of New York continued the praise by awarding the candy shop a place in its year-end exhibition of outstanding modern design.[100]

For the Altman and Kuhne candy shop, just across Fifth Avenue from Lederer's, Gruen and Krummeck devised a new facade that was completely glass. "The Store as Show Window," Gruen proudly proclaimed the design. With a twelve-by-ten-foot piece of plate glass and no partition at the back of the show window, Gruen and Krummeck used the store interior as the main attraction. Magazine articles praised the ingenious design for creating "an open candy box." Unlike the arcade's emphasis on display space, the "open front" eliminated window displays and brought the store to the sidewalk's edge. "The store," one journalist marveled, "is much too inviting for Fifth Avenue traffic to walk right by even in rain or zero weather." Window shoppers gathered at all hours of the day and night to stare at the store's candies. "The sheer glass wall," Morris Lapidus explained, "made the storefront part of the interior and the interior became a part of the front."[101] With this little candy shop, the open front arrived on Fifth Avenue.

The open front dissolved the traditional masonry facade with huge expanses of glass. In arcades, show windows encouraged window shopping and thus entrance to the store. With an open front, designers attempted to blur the distinction between window shopping and browsing the sales racks. Gruen insisted that store interiors needed to amuse potential customers with displays, goods, lighting, salespeople, color, and other customers. "With an open front, the opportunity exists to utilize all the life, color, and activity of the interior sales space as a store front attraction," Morris Ketchum explained.[102] One retail textbook complained that shoppers were reluctant to enter a specialty store. However, with the open front, "the interior of the store has considerable value." When people "see other customers inside the store, they are likely to enter also," the text glowed.[103]

Altman and Kuhne featured a glass staircase in pink and white—very visible from the outside—that led to a semi-private tasting room; the walls were covered with satin, and fluorescent lighting concealed in bronze channels bathed the store in a white light. "The curved stairway, the decorative indirect fluorescent lighting scheme, and the attractively designed displays for candy," marveled one enthusiastic reviewer, "become a window display."[104] Observers even credited glass fronts with policing powers. The open front made "every customer conscious of being visible from the outside" and "has resulted in reducing theft," one retail text boasted.[105] Gruen and Krummeck ensured that the store's spectacle now included salespeople, interior decorations, goods, and even customers.

A decade earlier, another transplanted Viennese architect, Frederick Kiesler, had also imagined doing away with the storefront. In his 1930 *Contemporary Art Applied to the Store and Its Display*, this eccentric architect (he would become famous in the 1960s for his connected architecture based on plants) wanted to dispense with window displays so that people could ogle the appealing interior. "Strangers often hesitate to enter an exclusive shop if they cannot easily see the interior from the street," Kiesler explained. His "see-through front" or "look-through background" would feature a rich vista into the store as an invitation to stop and buy. As he proclaimed, "The metamorphosis is now complete. Show window and interior are one." The ideal shopper, Kiesler exhorted, "should see things that you consider it important for her to see, a certain view of the interior itself or a special display inside."[106] With Gruen and Krummeck's Fifth Avenue open front, Kiesler's predictions seemed to come true. Other architects soon exploited the open front for their modern stores as well. In 1944 architects Pietro Belluschi, Walter Gropius, and Jose Fernandez all proposed versions of an open front store in *Pencil Points*. Gropius celebrated the fact that his design using a flesh-colored glass door, black glass walls, rotating displays, and invisible spotlights would create more spectators for a store. Belluschi, the Seattle modernist, claimed that his design exploited "in a more definite and organic way the idea of the open front." The magazine applauded his effort because the store "lures the casual window shopper and guarantees that customers who enter . . . are reminded of other items they might be persuaded to buy."[107] For Gruen and Krummeck, Altman and Kuhne's successful open front also promised to be a step toward more income.

With these store designs and favorable reviews, Gruen propelled himself into the upper echelon of New York retail design.[108] When Steven Klein—an aspiring storeowner and fellow Jewish émigré—bumped into Gruen on Fifth Avenue, he hired him on the spot to build a swanky candy store, even though Klein had only two hundred dollars of the two thousand dollars that Gruen said he would need. For Barton's Bonbonniere, a kosher candy shop at Eighty-First and Broadway, Gruen and Krummeck created the entire merchandising package in a colorful circus theme of primary colors. The Museum of Modern Art hailed the store as a "gay and attractive modern shop." The designers created a standard identity for Barton's storefronts, interiors, logo, and packaging, and Klein used these designs to open branches throughout New York City when the first store proved enormously successful. Journalists went so far as to credit the amusing designs for the chain store's phenomenal success. (In 1952, Barton's asked Gruen to design its fiftieth store for Sixth Avenue and Thirty-Fifth Street in Manhattan.)[109] As the open front and arcade facades gained Gruen more attention, he publicized his initial successes in another form.

In the same way that Mumford and Hamlin minutely analyzed Gruen's stores, designers also wrote extensive treatises on retail strategies. Gruen's writings gave him a showcase for displaying his retail theories, advertising his own work, and seducing new clients. He aimed his writings directly at merchants, promising that good design would sell more goods. Gruen was nothing if not opinionated. He combined his theories of consumer behavior with practical advice about storefronts, show windows, displays, and lighting, and he eventually landed clients

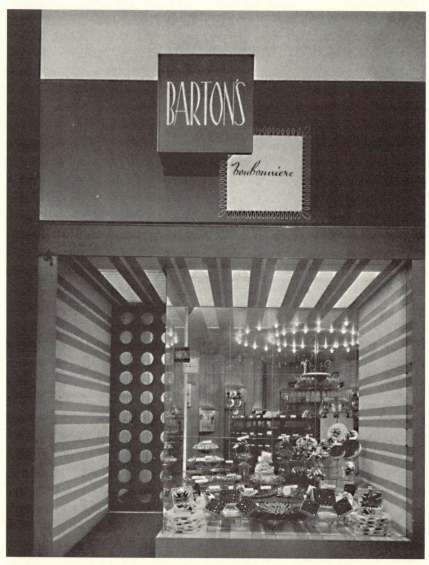

FIGURE 7. Gruen and Krummeck used an open front to display the candies and tempt customers into this New York City candy shop. From "Recent Work of Gruenbaum, Krummeck and Auer," *Architectural Forum* (September 1941), 192.

well beyond New York City. Theories came and went, but throughout the late 1930s and early 1940s designers wholeheartedly believed that they could control a consumer's responses.

"We want to influence emotional rather than rational powers," Gruen reminded merchants. By creating "the right atmosphere" through "very subtle means," Gruen believed he could sway customers. "Shape, light, and color" were the three most important devices for fashioning a store's "individuality or character or atmosphere."[110] Concern with the ability to shape a store's "character" was not unique to Gruen; the concept only affirmed designers' own conviction of their irresistible powers of persuasion. But Gruen's philosophy captured the essence of this new faith in a designer's ability to entice, persuade, and ultimately control the customer's emotions and purchases. Designers' ideas about this subject could best be summed up by the phrase "impulse sales." A modernized store—as a "machine for selling" or "a store that pays"—was based on an emerging consumer theory of "impulse purchases."[111]

In 1940 the *New York Times* ran a lead article about the hypnotic appeal of store designs. Through "special packages and designs" designers were promoting "impulse buying" in shoppers, the paper marveled. Others had noticed, too. In a lengthy exposé on window displays, *Fortune* explained that designers used their tricks to forge "a frightening hypnotism of the public." A successful window display would stir up desire and coax a spectator into a store, *Fortune* told its readers. And Morris Ketchum explained that "the economic success of any store depends on how well it stimulates impulse buying."[112] In their purchases, people were moved more by packaging than by price, more by feeling than by facts, designers claimed. Modern lighting "speeds buying decisions and impulse purchases," one store architect promised. "Impulse sales" was as much the designer's belief as what they promised their clients to deliver. "Sales depend on INSTANT ATTRACTION," *Architectural Record* observed.[113] A study of national retail trends maintained that store display "gives notice to the consumer in motion that the buying impulse awakened in him may be satisfied instantly."[114] Of course, all of Gruen's attention to fostering impulse sales appeared as the Great Depression loomed heavily over retailers.

When sociologists Helen and Robert Lynd returned to survey Muncie, Indiana, in 1935 to follow up on their popular *Middletown*, they found that people shared a prevailing attitude toward the Depression. Common sense held that the country's economic doldrums were a state of mind, a matter of consumer confidence. The Lynds quoted the local newspaper's complaints about under consumption: "This whole depression business is largely mental." The "Loosen Up!" editorial, sounding like a Babbitt booster, explained that only shopping would pull the country out of the Depression. "If tomorrow morning everyone should wake up with a resolve to unwind the red yarn that is bound about his old leather purse, and then would carry his resolve into effect, by August first, at the latest, the whole country could join in singing, 'Happy Days Are Here Again,'" the editorial guaranteed.[115]

In *Middletown in Transition*, the perceptive sociologists suggested that the cycle of production and consumption had effectively stalled because consumers had become anxious about purchases. If only people would spend, then the Depression would end. The Muncie editorialist was not alone in believing that consumption would end the Depression. As President Roosevelt intoned: "We are going to think less about the producer and more about the consumer."[116] Of course, this emphasis on the consumer was not wholly original to 1930s economic theory. Since the turn of the century, the consumer had been gaining a more prominent role in economic theories. "Culture is the result of more satisfying combinations of consumption," economist Simon Patten wrote in 1912.[117] In *Selling Mrs. Consumer* (1929), Christine Frederick, a leading consumer-rights advocate, described how consumption fueled the American economy. "The idea," she claimed, "that workmen and the masses be looked upon not simply as workers or producers, but as consumers" was "the greatest idea that America has to give the world." In 1938 Lewis Mumford characterized the new American economy as one where "consumption and service must take precedence."[118] The rise of the consumer in the nation's economy and mentality had an immediate impact on retailing.

If ending the Great Depression was seen as a matter of boosting consumer confidence, then one of the best ways to combat peoples' blues was to shore up the front line of defense, the retail store. Retailing, after all, counted on the strength of every consumer's faith in the American economy.[119] Just as companies during the Depression hired industrial designers to restyle products like refrigerators, automobiles, toasters, and pens, so designers worked to refashion stores and make them irresistible. Shopworn displays were seen as eyesores that discouraged people from opening their wallets and buying more.[120] "The percentage of impulse sales has been rising steadily and we still have just begun to scratch the surface," one store designer joyfully declared. As the consumer became a powerful force in economic calculations, the notion of tempting the consumer into unintended purchases gained more and more credence. Gruen was one among a chorus of voices recommending store modernization; retailers, economists, architects, government officials, the glass industry, politicians, and city planners all saw potential economic improvement in redesigned stores. Nowhere was this faith in a future of renewed consumer strength more alive than in retail architecture.

Drawing on his theater experience, Gruen employed two familiar metaphors for describing the drama of modern storefronts: the advertisement and the stage. "The functions of the exterior are to serve as advertising poster," Gruen trumpeted. As the most prominent commercial medium, the advertisement provided a compelling example of how visual design might induce consumer desire. The stores should follow "rules similar to those which are met in newspaper advertising," Gruen explained.[121] "After all," Morris Lapidus pointed out, "the storefront is really a billboard, designed on the same principles as a poster."[122] Both promoted a product, either a brand or a store, through a colorful, appealing image to create a personality for the goods. In *Architectural Record*, Lapidus used a Gruen and Krummeck store to illustrate architecture as advertisement. He juxtaposed an arcade storefront with a Swiss Railroad poster; the relationship appeared to be crystal-clear. But achieving the clarity and legibility of a two-dimensional advertisement in a three-dimensional store proved difficult.

Department stores had tried a related strategy by displaying wares in fantastic scenes to conjure up associations with exotic places or significant events. Historian William Leach describes how Wanamaker's of Philadelphia used vignettes of the Orient and the American Revolution to associate goods and the department store with romantic places and patriotic themes.[123] Morris Lapidus called this process the "identity" or "advertising value" of the store and believed it was the most difficult aspect for store designers to perfect. The storefront design should be unusual so as to attract attention, but not too bizarre to diminish the store's appeal. An important element of the storefront design, of course, was the show window.

Morris Ketchum captured the extreme belief in the show window's persuasive powers in a 1941 article. Ketchum moved beyond mere merchandise display or customer temptation and pondered how show windows fundamentally transformed their subjects. Inspired by service stores (barber shops, tailors, cleaners, and service stations), Ketchum wanted to "*place a living product on view—human labor.*" He foresaw an exhibition that would work toward "dramatizing the craftsman, the technician, and his product." "This opportunity to display human activity," Ketchum argued, "can be translated into powerful advertising."[124] Ketchum's proposal was not that far-fetched. Merchants and designers passionately believed that show windows could elevate and alter their subjects. *Fortune* explained that "at their best," show windows transformed merchandise "from its place in a show window to its place in the window gazer's life—or, even better, in his dream life." Leach does not exaggerate when he describes the show window's grip on the public imagination: "Nothing competed with them for selling power, not the advertising cards, not the posters or billboards, not even the early electrical signs." A detailed study of almost seventeen thousand show windows across the country claimed that the show window instilled in people "a desire for a particular commodity."[125]

Novelist John Steinbeck recalled his own enchantment with Manhattan show windows of the 1930s. Steinbeck cast Manhattan as "the Temptation" and himself as St. Anthony, and he equated living in New York to "visits of the Salvation Army to a brothel—necessary and fascinating but distasteful." Steinbeck realized that he had become a true New Yorker while leering into a show window. With "trains grinding over head" and snow "waist-high in the gutters," Steinbeck stopped to gaze into a drugstore's window. He became mesmerized by a "latex cooch dancer [that] undulated by a concealed motor." For Steinbeck, the window's image produced "a kind of light and a kind of feeling blended into an emotion which if it had spoken would have said, 'My God! I belong here. Isn't this wonderful?'" After his epiphany, Steinbeck felt that "everything fell into place." "It was beautiful—but most important I was part of it. I was no longer a stranger. I had become a New Yorker."[126] For designers, Steinbeck's ecstasy was exactly what they attempted to create, a community of contented consumers. Steinbeck, like Gruen, saw the show window as possessing a beguiling power over its audience.

Although show windows were extremely important, in modern stores the focus turned more and more to the goods. The goods became the architecture's shining ornament. As historian Walter Benjamin observed about retailing, "the architectonic function of wares" was crucial.[127] Shoes, candy, clothing, and jewels became the architecture's flourish. "Merchandise can tell a unified story," Lapidus observed.[128] If a storefront functioned as an advertising poster, then the arcade and the open front invited people to step into the poster's promising world.

For Gruen, luring people into the store's illusory world had another precedent as well: the theater. "Ten thousand little glamorous shows put on by the merchants," Gruen wrote about New York City stores. And the storefront was the "stage of these little shows." Gruen loved drama—drama in retail, on the stage, and in his daily life, and he meant the comparison between New York stores and theaters to be taken literally. "The importance of the show window which, as its name implies, presents a show, is obviously to impress the public," Gruen exclaimed. He insisted that arcades' show windows were "little theater displays," and "the exhibit is gratis." [129]

As spotlights highlighted the action on a theater's stage, so too spots in stores animated the stars of its show—the goods. Describing one storefront strategy, Gruen said that he wanted to "transform this space into a regular 'display stage' with all the features which stage technique offers"—though the design should not reveal "backstage display construction and lighting," which would detract from "the main show of the merchandise."[130] With an audience on the sidewalk, the facade as curtain, the sign as marquee, the show windows and showroom as the stage, and stockrooms as the backstage, the store as theater provided an appealing metaphor for commercial spaces. Of course, in this metaphor Gruen cast himself as the all-powerful playwright, director, and stage designer. And, as in a stage production, the director hoped to focus all eyes on the performers.

Gruen wanted to make shopping into a delightful and amusing way for people to while away their hours, temporarily to transcend their own concerns.[131] "The environment should be so attractive that customers will enjoy shopping trips, will stay longer and return more often," Gruen later explained. Purchases were the consumer's ticket off the city's sidewalks and into the store's lush environment.[132] Instant attraction, instant satisfaction, and impulse sales were all predicated on a designer's ability to make the goods appear irresistible. Practical materials would make these emotional appeals; structural glass, fluorescent lighting, incandescent spotlights, and glass storefronts were the best tools to influence the emotions. Colors, lights, and glass, Gruen exclaimed, had a "psychological influence on the customer."[133] His stores filled people's hearts, minds, and eyes with images of glamour and the good life based on the pursuit and enjoyment of material possessions. Retail stores promised a life of never-ending distraction, abundance, amusement, and comfort. One of the most important materials for creating these images, Gruen and other designers believed, was glass.

Gruen was a master with glass. "Glamour in glass," one reviewer enthused about a Gruen and Ketchum arcade. "From Darkness to Delight," another magazine declared. Glass covered his storefronts.[134] In 1939 one national survey estimated that the average show window in America measured six by six feet. The Altman and Kuhne window on Fifth Avenue easily doubled that average, making it "a paradise for window shoppers," according to Mumford.[135] For an architect who later became infamous for his shopping center's blank facades and artificially lit interiors, in his first work Gruen was praised for transparency.

Of course, show windows were not the only element that could be made from glass. Glass "never exhausts its design possibilities," Pittsburgh Plate Glass promised.[136] The company exaggerated only slightly. With glass showcases, ceilings, tiles, mirrors, shelves, doors, windows, walls, and display cases a designer could fashion an entire store out of glass. Gruen's stores literally glittered and gleamed, creating an expanding new landscape of glass.[137] Plate glass show windows served as "A Visual Front" that "lets people see in, and almost without thinking, they walk in."[138] The objects became the principal focus of architects' and consumers' visions; "seeing is selling," the *Glassic* proudly explained. One store designer declared, "Store designing is ninety percent display and ten percent bricks and stones."[139] Since arcades and open fronts depended on tremendous amounts of glass, glass manufacturers like Libbey-Owens-Ford, Pittsburgh Plate Glass, and Kawneer vigorously promoted the designs.

This new interest in glass as a design element came at a critical moment. The Depression had rocked the glass industry, as the production of plate glass plummeted from a high of 150 million square feet in 1929 to a mere 52 million by 1932.[140] In six months the glass giant Libbey-Owens-Ford lost a whopping $420,000 owing to the economic downturn.[141] Much of the industry's losses was attributable to the slowdown in automobile sales. The glass industry responded by expanding into other product lines, especially architectural glass for retailers. Of course, the industry already had close ties to retail through the marketing of plate glass windows, but during the Depression it greatly increased its architectural product line for storefronts. Gruen's glass store designs came as a welcome and much-needed boon. The companies soon offered complete storefronts (windows, trim, tiles, showcases, and doors)—"Machines for Selling," one company boasted.[142]

An earlier product of choice had been cast iron. At the end of the nineteenth century, a few companies had sold complete cast-iron storefronts. To update their stores, merchants could choose from an eclectic mix of storefronts in Italianate, Venetian Gothic, or French Second Empire styles. Tinned sheet-iron fixtures and ceilings were also sold in standardized sizes and configurations for ornamenting the store's interior. Similarly, and on a much broader scale, the glass industry in the 1930s began trying to sell complete store packages. "Modern Store Fronts," Kawneer promised merchants in 1930 were "a means of attracting greater crowds."[143] In 1939 Libbey-Owens-Ford created its own trade journal, the *Glassic*, to promote its architectural glasses. Four years later, the company patented the "Visual Front" system of plate glass and aluminum trim, claiming that "with its big areas of clear glass, [it] puts the whole store on display." "Mirrors," Libbey-Owens-Ford told merchants, "double the amount of goods on display."[144]

The glass companies' expansion into retail design also provided much-needed work for designers and architects. The companies sponsored nationwide competitions for the best-designed modern stores featuring glass products. For instance, in 1935 *Architectural Record* and Libbey-Owens-Ford sponsored a "Modernize Main Street" competition. In response, architects devised stunning commercial designs. The eminent judges—architects Albert Kahn, William Lescaze, and John Root—applauded the winners for creating stores of "simplicity" with "pure colors contrasting light and shadow."[145] Industrial designer Walter Dorwin Teague won a Pittsburgh Plate Glass commission to research and develop architectural uses for glass products. His firm went on to design twenty-eight different glass storefronts, which Pittsburgh Plate used in advertisements and for a traveling exhibition. Morris Ketchum won a Kawneer Company competition in 1942 for a furniture store design and then designed at least thirty-one glass-covered stores for the company.[146] The stores, like a World's Fair exhibition, became displays of both goods and glasses.

Gruen also got in on the new opportunities. The Pittsburgh Plate Glass Company hired Gruen and Krummeck to design a prototype of a men's shop for use in advertisements. Of course, for the fictitious Sire shop the designers relied solely on the glass company's products. Glass products covered the three walls of a generous arcade. To the right and left were floor-to-ceiling show windows. On the rear wall, the Sire store featured a large display case for full-size mannequins.[147] Pittsburgh Plate Glass loved Gruen and Krummeck's extensive use of glass. The company placed the Sire shop in a national advertising campaign promoting its storefronts, offering to send out free blueprints to interested merchants or designers. The National Retail Dry Goods Association published the design in its journal. And the art magazine *Pencil Points* gave both Gruen and Pittsburgh Plate Glass free publicity by placing the design on its cover.[148] Gruen also penned articles promoting modern store design for the plate-glass industry's national journal, the *Glass Digest*.[149] The close relationship between glass companies and architects benefited both parties. Architects found much-needed work and new clients while glass became de rigueur for modern store designs.

A significant part of Gruen and Krummeck's Sire shop was not the windows but what surrounded the windows, a fancy-sounding material called Carrara Structural Glass. In the 1930s, architectural glass tiles received a major facelift—from older white tiles to every color in the rainbow—robin's egg blue, tropical green, jade, black, and violet. The tiles were marketed under many brand names (Carrara Glass, Vitrolite, Sani Onyx, Rox, Vitrolux, Glastone, Thermopane, and Extrudalite), but their function remained the same: to surround show windows with more glass and more color. Throughout the 1940s, Pittsburgh Plate Glass spotlighted Gruen and Ketchum's Lederer shop, with its gray glass walls and green glass ceiling, to advertise its Carrara tiles. The company featured the store in its "Eye Appeal" advertisements for modern store designs long after the store opened on Fifth Avenue. "Give the job to GLASS," the ad proclaimed.[150] The glass tiles pushed retail design beyond the more traditional appearance of materials like brick, stucco, masonry, and wood and became a way to create a conspicuously modern store.[151]

The new retail style was marketed from Boise to Baltimore. Glass stores were now "available in identical quality throughout the country," the Pittsburgh Plate Glass Company advertised.[152] With prefabrication of modular units, the glass industry offered a modern storefront for any site on any street in any American town. In one advertisement the company filled a map of the United States with their warehouses. With thirty-two factories, seventy-eight warehouses, and thousands of dealers, Pittsburgh Plate Glass covered America with its products.[153]

Similarly, Gruen and Krummeck's commercial designs soon received attention in national magazines. Other retailers looked to Fifth Avenue's modernism—arcades, open fronts, and glass—as an inspiration for American Main Streets. The publicity led to new commissions for stores across America, from Los Angeles to Seattle, El Paso, and Oklahoma City.

Gruen had come a long way in a short time. After fleeing from Hitler, he quickly made a name for himself in New York retail circles. Helping produce two Broadway productions, working on World's Fair exhibitions, designing Manhattan stores, and writing articles on modern store design, Gruen had worked in a variety of realms. While commissions gave Gruen a diversity of work experiences, retail design emerged as his most promising opportunity. However, he soon exhausted his Viennese connections. In 1940, President Roosevelt, just reelected, began preparing America for war with Germany. Surprisingly, retail design would get a new push upon America's entry into World War II. The war would pull Gruen and Krummeck's work in new directions—and away from Manhattan. Their retail designs would also have to respond to new circumstances that they never could have imagined while living there.

CHAPTER TWO

How Main Street Stole
Fifth Avenue's Glitter

Stores lead a double life. They are factories with machinery behind the scenes; machinery which must be well-oiled, invisible and inaudible. To the outside they present the gayer side of the double life—they are show places and exhibits with the aim of arousing interest in the displayed merchandise.
—Victor Gruen, 1947

Victor Gruen's prospects looked bright going into the 1940s. His architectural career had taken off. Cyril Magnin, of San Francisco's famous retailing family, awarded Gruen and Krummeck the designs of his Reno (1940) and San Mateo (1942) branches of women's clothing stores. The partners were also hired to design two branches for another California chain of women's apparel stores in 1940. In 1941 *Architectural Forum* ran a fawning seven-page spread, even giving Gruen and Krummeck complete liberty with the text. They composed a passionate explanation of their "underlying principles of store design," touting the virtues of their "sales factory" that could increase sales two to three times. While the secret of outstanding creations was a matter beyond "theoretical considerations," the designers promised that "an imaginative scheme . . . like a musical theme" enhanced a store's "technical and psychological devices" to assure "success."[1] The article gave Gruen the limelight that he craved; now he was writing, designing, and promoting. Calls for more commissions poured in—for a women's clothing store in Oklahoma City, a candy shop in New York City, a women's shop in White Plains, and more.[2]

Gruen's personal life looked bright as well. His spirits were up; "Life could never be grim," he remembered about this time.[3] He was thankful to be far from Vienna's violence and in the United State's relative peace and prosperity. Victor and his wife Lizzie's divorce was so amicable that she even went to work for one of his New York City clients, Barton's Bonbonniere, as a buyer. In May 1941 Victor Gruen and Elsie Krummeck left New York for the sunshine of Los Angeles, and the month after arriving married on Santa Catalina Island. Even though they had "very little money," the newlyweds optimistically gave their rented house in Hollywood a fresh coat of paint and purchased the latest in modern furnishings. Their firm immediately began to grow. Michael Auer, a younger designer who had been trained in Budapest and Zurich, and Rudi Baumfeld, a childhood friend of Gruen's from Vienna, joined the firm in 1941. Most promising was the commission from a new kind of client with deep pockets: a national chain store. This commission would allow Gruen to take the strategies of the "sales factory" from Manhattan to Main Street, and the move onto a national stage would shape and Americanize Gruen and his designs.

The new client was the Grayson-Robinson stores of California.[4] Grayson's sold lower-priced ready-to-wear clothing and accessories for women. In 1938 the company had operated sixteen shops throughout California. By 1945, the chain had grown to forty-three stores (called Grayson's in the West and Robinson's in the East) stretching from Philadelphia to Seattle and El Paso to Los Angeles.[5] By 1950 the company was the seventeenth largest retailer in the country, doing $85 million in sales—a figure equal to Washington, D.C.'s Hecht department store. Through the war years, Grayson's grew at a phenomenal rate; only the Lerner stores of New York outpaced it in sales of women's clothing by 1950.[6] For Gruen and Krummeck, designing for the chain was a dream come true.

Grayson's was owned by a "flamboyant" businessman from California, Walter Kirschner. "He and his henchmen were a bunch of rascals on the brink of gangsterism," Gruen later recalled. Kirschner was famous for his all-white suits, ten-gallon cowboy hat, and white convertibles full of "lovely girls." Not content with one pool at his house, he built two. Even with wartime restrictions on new construction, Kirschner cut deals to erect ostentatious new branches. When no one else was building, the wheeler-dealer had a knack for digging up capital to build his stores. According to one story, Kirschner and Gruen traveled to Portland, Oregon to find property for a new branch. Gruen scouted out what he considered the best location for the new store, which, to nobody's surprise, was the most expensive downtown property available. After looking over the building, Kirschner decided that he had to have it. He sent the owner's wife a bouquet of flowers and then headed to the local bank to apply for a loan. When the banker asked him for collateral, Kirschner said that he had just negotiated to lease Portland's choicest property—which should serve as sufficient collateral. Kirschner got the loan, the lot, and a new store.[7]

Gruen's guardian angel Ruth Yorke had introduced him to Grayson's, setting up a meeting between Gruen and a vice president over a dinner. The vice president asked Gruen to review the layout of a new dressing room. Gruen, not content simply to rearrange mirrors, suggested an entire new store design—facade, show windows, display cases, lighting, and dressing rooms. It was an ostentatious solution to a simple problem, and the gamble paid off. The vice president was impressed and after one meeting hired Gruen to prepare drawings for an entirely new store. Gruen had snagged his first commission for a national chain store. Over the course of his career, Gruen—drawing on his abundant skills as a salesman and his lack of inhibitions—would often create opportunities like this for himself.[8]

During the war years, at a moment when retail construction had fallen even below the Depression's lows, Grayson's grew at a phenomenal rate, making "a killing during and just after the war."[9] While the rest of the architectural profession waited for the war to end, Gruen and Krummeck consistently found work with their chain-store client. From 1940 to 1945 Grayson's accounted for 90 percent of the architectural firm's nearly $700,000 business.[10] Although the architects completed work for other stores, most notably J. Magnin's high-end women's shops in Northern California, Grayson's remained their best client, in more than just monetary ways, until 1948. Grayson's was especially well-versed at financing their nationwide expansion, and Kirschner had a gift for raising money.[11] In 1945 alone, Grayson's opened twelve new stores, purchased a chain of seventeen Midwestern clothing stores, and bought the Manhattan department store S. Klein on Union Square. Kirschner was all financed through the issuance of 50,000 shares of preferred stock.[12] He was also willing to pour capital into architectural statements sure to attract attention. For Gruen and Krummeck, the commissions propelled them from a small regional design team onto the national stage of retail architecture.

Kirschner's desire for publicity and Gruen's desire for recognition dovetailed perfectly. Nevertheless, Gruen still had to create eye-catching stores to fulfill their ambitions. Gruen's first designs pulled out every trick in the book. He combined arcades, open fronts, giant show windows, towering facades, trick lighting, and bright colors. After his initial successes the design budget, and his salary, increased significantly. For the 1941 remodeling of Robinson's in Buffalo, the cost ran to almost $150,000.

Grayson's growth during the war years was not a coincidence. The retailer's success was tied directly to the record numbers of women entering the workplace. As women took jobs in war-related industries previously open only to men, their wages and, more important for retailers, their disposable incomes increased dramatically. Nearly four million new women workers entered the labor force between 1940 and 1944. While women did not receive pay equal to men, overall their wages increased dramatically over their prewar levels. By 1944 more women were working in factories across the country than had been in the entire labor force in 1940. Women in California enjoyed a higher minimum wage than in any other state. In San Francisco, the number of women working outside the home soared from 138,000 to 275,000.[13] To exploit this new female market, Grayson's opened branches in cities growing with the wartime economy, especially in the West. San Diego, the fastest growing city in the United States, saw its civilian population increase 38 percent from 1940 to 1943, Seattle 21 percent, and San Francisco 18 percent.[14] Grayson's opened "Victory Stores" in all these cities.

Not surprisingly, sales of women's apparel and accessories accounted for the largest area of retail growth during the war.[15] While women had long been disparaged as working to earn "pin money," their new wages produced a greater demand for women's clothing. Not only did women have more freedom about how they could spend their hard-earned incomes; they also needed clothing for their new jobs. From 1939 to 1948, five thousand women's apparel stores opened, and the sales for women's chain stores tripled to $966 million (while sales for men's stores, department stores, and supermarkets barely increased).[16] The *Wall Street Journal* summarized the market's phenomenal rise in the face of wartime difficulties: "Despite rationing, restrictive price ceilings, serious merchandise shortages and rising labor costs, store sales and earnings have mounted as national income has increased. In consequence, store growth has continued."[17] As a low-priced store, "Where Smart Women Buy Smart Clothes for Less," Grayson's was perfectly poised to capitalize on these wartime changes.[18] Overnight it became a national presence in retail.

Grayson's coast-to-coast expansion was part of a larger trend, the rise of specialty chain stores. While variety stores had moved into American towns starting in the 1910s, the specialty stores' inroads, especially in the 1940s, forever altered where and how Americans shopped. Up to that time, the majority of retail companies with a nationwide reach were variety stores or grocery stores like F. W. Woolworth, A & P, S. S. Kresge, W. T. Grant, and S. H. Kress; Kresge, for example, operated nearly seven hundred stores by 1945. Smaller specialty stores and department stores, however, were still associated with specific cities.[19] Specialty stores implied quality, as the name was derived from "specialty goods," items infrequently purchased that had an added attraction for the consumer. The stores specialized in one type of attractive merchandise: jewelry, women's clothing, shoes, or candy. And consumers were willing to pay more for goods purchased at a specialty store. During the war, specialty stores began to perfect niche marketing to a smaller group of middle-class consumers, who might be persuaded to spend more on attractive goods sold in a modernized store.

Not everyone saw the spread of chain stores as a positive develop-ment. At least since the Depression, opposition to chain-store growth had been quite vocal.[20] Chain stores, opponents argued, were destroying local, independent merchants. Texas representative Wright Patman introduced legislation in 1935 to impose a federal tax on them. "To pro-tect the independent merchant, the public whom he serves, and the manufacturer from whom he buys, from exploitation by unfair com-petitors," Patman declared in the preamble to his bill. The Robinson-Patman Act would have prohibited "any discrimination in price between purchasers of goods of like grade and quality." Moreover it would have effectively removed any price discounts because of "bigness" or "effi-ciency." Chain stores' "lower-prices in a new trading area are possible only by the fact that the losses thus incurred can be absorbed in the higher prices obtained in established territories," Patman explained. This "cut-price policy" destroyed "local competition."[21] Strong opposition to the bill arose from chains, realtors, and banks, and the bill died in com-mittee, but not until after it had been vigorously debated for two years. Before it died, Patman held hearings in which Congress questioned chain-store executives and independent retailers about the impact of chains on the local economy. *Chain Store Age*, fearful for its con-stituents, followed the hearings closely. The magazine provided monthly updates and printed congressional testimony that extolled the virtues of chain stores. For instance, its May 1940 issue carried the entire testi-mony of one department store president.[22]

Although Patman complained that chain stores destroyed local businesses, their impact was more symbolic than actual. Even after the war, chains were a mere 5 percent of all stores, and only 22 percent of the total retail dollar was spent at chain stores.[23] This was not for lack of interest on the part of customers, for consumers' "increase in buying power over the last decade has actually come faster than additional store space could be built to accommodate it."[24] As a specialty chain expanding nationwide, Grayson's was pioneering this new kind of retail establishment. And, with its success, Grayson's helped legitimize a new consumer experience for Americans striving to be part of the great and growing middle class; one historian, calling on his own childhood memories of a small Midwestern town, remembered that "big business itself came directly to Main Street through the chain store movement."[25]

One of the telltale signs of big business's arrival in middle America was its shockingly new architecture. Being able to spend more money on new stores than independent retailers, chain stores built more grandiose structures. When Kirschner hired Gruen and Krummeck to design his stores, he wanted to stand out from his competitors. During the 1940s, specialty stores showcased the new display strategies that had been promoted since the 1920s on a grand, but dispersed, scale. Without chain stores, store modernization would have begun in fits and starts without the capital or impetus to build anew.[26] Grayson's, like other expanding chains, tried to make an auspicious beginning in a local market for its branches. The *Chain Store Age* editor believed that chains succeeded because they could spend more money on a prominent location and on "high standards" in architecture.[27]

Grayson's was a trendsetter on both accounts. With its ostentatious architecture, put up seemingly overnight in a city's most active commercial district, the store was impossible to ignore; it became the talk of the town. Grayson's never gambled on risky locations; the retailer and Gruen always chose either the heart of downtown or a popular retail strip. The Seattle Grayson's, for example, opened for business on downtown's premier shopping street, Third Avenue between Pine and Pike Streets. It was half a block away from Seattle's best department store, the Bon Marche. Other national chains like Woolworth's (built the same year as Grayson's) and Kress were in the immediate area. The Lerner Shops, the nation's largest women's apparel chain, operated right next door to Grayson's—giving the block strong pulling power for women shoppers. In Philadelphia Gruen modernized an older Woolworth's on Market Street for the Robinson's branch. The store was located on the

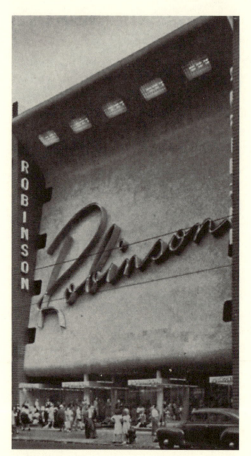

FIGURE 8. Gruen and Krummeck's design for Robinson's on Market Street in Philadelphia, c. 1945. From Louis Parnes, *Planning Stores That Pay* (New York: Architectural Record Book, 1948), 197.

main trolley lines amid the city's largest department stores and national chain stores. The three-story store opened down the street from Philadelphia's premier retailers: John Wanamaker's and Strawbridge and Clothier's. The national chains W. T. Grant, S. S. Kresge, and McCrory's operated nearby.[28] When Grayson's moved onto a city's most competitive retail street, it wanted to make a splash. Gruen's experience with putting on shows in Vienna served Kirschner's company well.

"Better physical appearance" was the second most important reason for chain stores' popularity.[29] Grayson's architectural ambitions translated into Gruen and Krummeck's good fortunes and notoriety. "America's Newest and Most Beautiful Store," the Buffalo Grayson's immodestly called itself. Touting a "streamlined hosiery island, Tomorrow's Modes, spacious lobby, and a magnificent two-story salon,"

Grayson's wanted to peddle clothes to every "debutante" and "dowager."[30] Between 1940 and 1946, Gruen and Krummeck designed eleven stores for Grayson's. With so many stores opening in different cities, the partners quickly developed the essence of the chain's identity: a cursive sign, spacious show windows, high arcades, and bright lighting. They used motifs from their New York store designs, rendered on a much grander and more flamboyant scale. While Ciro's and Lederer's one-story arcades on Fifth Avenue were the talk of the town, for Grayson's the partners used much larger arcades, gigantic signs, glowing neon, and soaring show windows. "Grayson strives to create striking contrasts . . . [through] architecturally dominant building[s]," *Chain Store Age* enthused, using "high fronts," "modern lines," "arcades," "spaciousness," and "lighting."[31] To compete with Hollywood Boulevard's bright lights, Gruen and Krummeck designed a Grayson's store with a projecting arcade ablaze with fifty-eight neon strips. In 1938 Steckler's one-story arcade on Broadway measured eleven by sixteen feet and was considered quite vast and daring; only one year later the arcade for Grayson's Seattle store rose three stories above Third Street. For the Philadelphia Robinson's store on Market Street, the designers created a three-story arcade front with a glass mosaic that one architect likened to a "billboard."[32]

As Grayson's, and chain stores in general, opened up on America's Main Streets, they brought their modern retail style with them—"all the dreams of modern architecture. . .all the sleek products of modern science . . . all the arts of modern lighting and display." Architect Morris Lapidus, who himself worked for the growing chains of Barton's Bonbonniere and Bostonian Shoes, detailed the prominence of this aesthetic in his 1941 "Store Design" article for *Architectural Record*. (Gruen took special notice of this landmark article; he cut it out and pasted it into his scrapbook.) "If the problem of selling the same products to the same people is the same everywhere," Lapidus argued, "here is a chance for truly national architectural expression." He closed his article by visually proving his point—he mixed shoppers and Main Streets from Portland, Maine, and Mobile, Alabama. Gruen heartily agreed with Lapidus, declaring, "If you know one American main street you know them all!"[33] Gruen and Lapidus held that if shoppers were the same across America, then stores could be the same as well. Gruen and Krummeck's wide-ranging commissions were proving this theory. They were designed to fit in anywhere and everywhere in America.

And as Grayson's went national, so did Gruen and Krummeck. "Stores

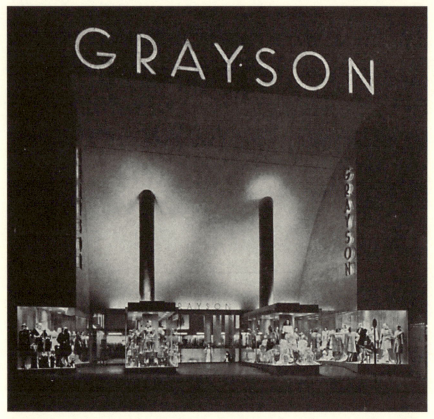

FIGURE 9. Gruen and Krummeck's design for Grayson's in Seattle, c. 1941. From Louis Parnes, *Planning Stores That Pay* (New York: Architectural Record Book, 1948), 192.

all over the country were born on their drafting tables," a trade magazine bragged about Gruen and Krummeck's work. The magazine marveled at their coast-to-coast breadth. "New Stores Bring Metropolitan Beauty to Smaller Communities," was *Chain Store Age*'s portrayal of the partners' work.[34] "No matter how small the city, I made each store as exciting and architecturally dramatic as the stores on Fifth Avenue," Morris Lapidus triumphantly recalled.[35] Of course, the chain stores' rapid modernization compelled other merchants to attempt their own remodeling campaigns. For instance, in 1946 Grayson's opened a brand new store in Salt Lake City. *Chain Store Age* reported that its next-door neighbor planned "to remodel his store to bring it up to the apparel chain's standard."[36] Grayson's, through Gruen and Krummeck, was setting the standards for contemporary retailing.

The coast-to-coast work of Gruen's architectural career stimulated a more personal change as well. In December 1941, right after Pearl Harbor, Victor decided to Americanize his name from "Gruenbaum" to "Gruen." When applying for U.S. naturalization status, he took the opportunity to request a name change to Victor David Gruen. Gruen's change was in no way consistent. For instance, he still used "Gruenbaum" for a few articles published after 1941.[37] In all of his writings, the verbose architect never explained the change.

Gruen's daughter thought that her father adopted "Gruen" out of fear of anti-Jewish sentiment arising in the United States upon the country's entry into World War II. "At the time they were still very fearful of how big the Nazi thing could get . . . if they could ever be in danger," she recalled. Gruen's fear had some justification, as German Jews had been interned in Britain. His son attributed the change to "Gruen" as a career decision—both the architectural profession and the retail chains were dominated by WASPs. Both son and daughter thought the "simplicity" of "Gruen" helped make his American architectural career easier.[38] And the switch coincided perfectly with the expansion of his work beyond New York City and into a wider American realm. Tellingly, the first public reference to "Gruen" appeared in *Chain Store Age*, in an article about his Grayson designs.[39] Although we can only speculate if Gruen was attempting to conceal his Jewish ancestry, taking the name David may have served as a personal compensation, a way to maintain his connections to his Jewish heritage in a less overt way. David's fight with Goliath and his later reign as king of Israel represented the Jewish people's ability to overcome extreme difficulties. Gruen hoped that he, too, would overcome adversity and prosper in America.

On his naturalization application Gruen also expressed his strong desire to become an American citizen "as soon as possible." He declared that Austria had "ceased to exist," and "as a victim of the Nazi system, I am in full agreement with the aims of the United Nations in their fight against Hitlerism and Fascism."[40] He had studied the Constitution and read up on American history. His "future lay in America and [he] settled in to become a part of it," he would later write. When America entered the war in 1941, Gruen, at the age of thirty-eight, tried to join the army. Rejected, he enrolled in classes for airplane design.[41]

Whereas before the war, Gruen's Austrian upbringing and architectural experience were frequently accented in articles about him, during

FIGURE 10. Architect Morris Lapidus cut-and-pasted shoppers from Maine onto a street in Alabama to prove that commercial architecture could provide a national architecture for America. From Morris Lapidus, "Store Design: A Merchandising Problem," *Architectural Record* 89, no. 2 (February, 1941): 132.

the war these aspects were rarely mentioned. Neither in terms of his European design influences nor in terms of his persecution by Hitler's invasion did journalists comment on Gruen's Austrian roots. Perhaps the press, overly fearful of an immigrant's loyalty during the war, did not want to dwell on Gruen's Austrian or Jewish background. Since every immigrant was seen as possibly suspect in terms of patriotic commitment, Gruen's ethnicity was whitewashed. His retail work, however, became in effect part of the war effort.

Wartime employment put extra money in Grayson's customers' pocketbooks, and Gruen and Krummeck employed the war as a decorative theme. Grayson, like other businesses, went to great lengths to connect its stores with the war effort. Prominent show windows became patriotic advertisements displaying "Buy War Bonds" posters.[42] When the Grayson's Inglewood store opened in 1942, the manager promised to extinguish the decorative lights to show that the store was "100-percent behind the United States Army." *Architectural Forum* applauded Gruen and Krummeck for planning "a Victory Store with non-critical materials."[43] Grayson's also extended its evening hours to serve working women. One Seattle defense worker recalled how downtown stores

FIGURE 11. Grayson's advertisement for the opening of its "Victory Store" in San Francisco. From *San Francisco Sunday Examiner*, c. 1944.

remained open into the evenings and changed their stock for female Boeing workers.[44]

Gruen and Krummeck, aware of the possibilities for favorable press and under very real material constraints, designed Grayson's branches as overtly patriotic pronouncements. For a Los Angeles store the partners literally turned the facade into a billboard for the government's war effort; "Buy War Bonds" ran across the top of the facade three times and "Victory Store" was above the two show windows. Gruen and Krummeck used the war to sell goods and goods to sell the war. As the War Production Board reviewed every construction project, Gruen and Krummeck had no choice but to use nonstrategic materials. Since wood, plaster, some fabric, and paint were unrestricted, however, merchants could still undertake remodeling campaigns.[45] On the other hand, constructing new stores during the war was a difficult proposition. If done incorrectly, the new stores might be criticized as unpatriotic and wasteful. Luckily for Grayson's, Gruen's theatrical background proved invaluable. He was "literally building stage sets for selling until the war was over."[46] Gruen and Krummeck, always willing to seize publicity, chose to turn their material constraints into an advertising gimmick. At Grayson's in San Francisco, instead of a metal or neon sign, they fashioned an undulating screen with blue and gold lettering—all in wood. "Wartime note is struck by mammoth nameplate," *Architectural Forum* crowed. A prominent "Victory Store" sign hung below, visually connecting the store and the war. Fireproof fabric on the store's ceiling, wooden umbrella stands, wooden display cases, colored fabrics on the walls, and wooden ashtrays all replaced scarce wartime materials. One article took great pains to explain that Grayson's glass doors were purchased well before Pearl Harbor. [47] Through such designs, Gruen and Krummeck connected Grayson's architecture and the chain's identity with the war effort.

Retailers' promotion of their wartime sacrifices and patriotic commitment was one part of a nationwide trend. Novels (Ernie Pyle's *Here is Your War* and *Brave Men*), radio broadcasts (Arturo Toscanini's ABC concerts on ABC), pop songs (Glenn Miller's dance tunes), pin-up posters (Betty Grable), war bonds, victory gardens, clothing styles (women in clothes like military uniforms), and rationing (sugar and flour) together created a popular culture that advertised and supported America's involvement in the war.[48] For many Americans, commitment to the war became real while they were shopping on the home front. Retail experts directly connected civilian morale with retailing. Columbia University professor Paul Nystrom explained that "attractive and effective window and store displays helped maintain optimistic and patriotic citizens . . . there is nothing so heartening to the average consumer as a shopping trip through a live, active retail store with its goods smartly and brightly displayed, with appeals on every side to life and the enjoyment of living."[49] The new Grayson's stores, as exemplars of Nystrom's bright displays and smart wares, "helped maintain the patriotic and optimistic citizens" of Nystrom's prescription; shopping on the home front helped make patriotism tangible and consumable for Americans. Whether through war bonds, ration cards, military clothing styles for women, "Victory" stores, or bright interiors, shopping was transformed into a patriotic act of national solidarity.

Grayson's consciously sought to create a national image and to connect its stores with urbane styles. Every store carried identical dresses,
skirts, and blouses, direct from New York.[50] "Nowhere in this broad land
. . . even on the smartest metropolitan avenues . . . is there an establishment to compare with it in glamour, beauty and facilities," Grayson's
advertised. "New Stores Bring Metropolitan Beauty to Smaller Communities," *Chain Store Age* declared. Through Grayson's stores and other
chains, people separated by geography began experiencing identical
shopping spaces and identical goods.[51] During the war, twenty-seven
million Americans left their homes either for new jobs or for the armed
forces.[52] For transient Americans, familiar brands or national chains
held special appeal; Grayson's stores catered to this young, mobile market. When people in Seattle, Buffalo, El Paso, and Philadelphia all
bought the exact same New York goods in a Gruen and Krummeck-
designed Grayson's, they began to picture themselves as more united
and alike (though there is no evidence to suggest that Grayson's
intended this overt political consequence).[53]

While Gruen and Krummeck could have reused their New York store
designs, the competitive commercial strip drove the designers to perfect
a new commercial aesthetic geared to the automobile. In New York, their
shops had been located on pedestrian streets, like Fifth Avenue or
Broadway. Downtown stores, Gruen explained, were designed "to attract
Joe Pedestrian's attention to [a] specific store and sell him on the idea
of entering that store." The strip, appealing to "Mr. Parker," forced the
partners to confront what would be the most influential change in postwar American architecture, and perhaps American life—the automobile
and its roads.[54] Designing for the rush of the streets was fundamentally
different than for a parade of pedestrians. Grayson's located all of its
Southern California branches on automobile strips (Inglewood, Los
Angeles, Hollywood, and Santa Monica). For these stores, Gruen and
Krummeck had to reimagine the facades, show windows, artificial lighting, signs, and entries; every aspect had to appeal to mobile Americans.
Of course, on the strip parking the car was the first challenge.

Ample parking for autoists had long been a thorny problem both
downtown and on the strip. Inadequate parking facilities were blamed
for downtown retail's decline. Gruen even warned downtown merchants
that "there must be cooperative effort . . . to provide parking and off-
street unloading [for cars and trucks] . . . that are choking the business
center."[55] Out on the commercial strip—with rows of stores on either side
and traffic whizzing by—the parking lot's location had long been

debated. Should parking be placed behind the store, in front of the store, be split between front and back, or even be on the store's roof? All these solutions had their drawbacks. If cars were parked in front of the store, then the building would have to be pushed back from the road, making it less visible to its ideal patron, the passing motorist. But when parking was placed behind the store, shoppers had to enter through the shabby service doors and next to garbage cans. Gruen and Krummeck often came up with the solution of designing two separate facades—the front for motorists and the back for pedestrians. In their first Southern California commission, the 1940 Santa Monica Grayson's, the partners designed a grand front entrance and an all-glass rear entrance as well; they did the same in Inglewood. One review explained the design's practicality: "Because auto-minded Inglewood shoppers are accustomed to driving to their neighborhood stores, Gruen designed the store's rear with a beauty equal to the fronts of many other establishments. A customer may drive up to the spacious rear parking lot and walk only a few steps to the mobile-oriented location."[56] Designing a store with two facades of equal importance remained a frequent solution to entice auto-minded customers. As cars zipped by pedestrians, Gruen and Krummeck developed ever more ostentatious designs to capture motorists' fleeting glances. The stores also had to compete with the thrill of driving itself. As one observer noted, "Americans live in their cars. . . . Here they enjoy the sensation of motion, of action and progress."[57]

If most Americans feasted on the auto's motion, action, and progress, others with more genteel sensibilities bemoaned the view through the windshield. The commercial strip was blamed for everything from causing the Depression and depreciating property values to making municipal coffers decline and promoting tacky aesthetics. In 1939 another author, appealing to the middle-class audience of *House and Garden*, launched into a diatribe against commercial strips. The author described ugly and unpleasant shopping streets with "architectural grotesqueries" arranged in "a disorganized melee of buildings, streets, and sales appeals that add neither to the wealth nor to the happiness of the nation." This unsightliness, for the author, led directly to residential blight in the surrounding neighborhood.[58] Just as Lewis Mumford had hoped that commercialism could be quieted for Fifth Avenue, these critics wanted trade to be less tawdry. If Gruen was aware of these harsh judgments, he never let on. He continued to design flamboyant Grayson's stores for cities' strips. The blight of these strips—which was often described in language laden with thinly veiled class references—seemed a bountiful blessing to others, including Gruen and Krummeck.

Designing stores for Hollywood and Crenshaw Boulevard, Gruen and Krummeck worked on the most competitive and flamboyant strips in America.[59] Just as Gruen had helped fashion Fifth Avenue, he now helped define the strip's outrageous vocabulary. While Grayson's stores were much too substantial and costly to be confused with other much-denigrated single-story retail buildings, they freely employed the strip's flashy aesthetic. For the speeding driver, Gruen and Krummeck wanted to make Grayson's hard to miss. "Novel Design Proves to Have Customer Pulling Power," *Women's Wear Daily* exclaimed about one Grayson design's visibility. Show windows, arcades, signs, and facades all became grandiose and gigantic. "High fronts," *Chain Store Age* explained about Grayson's, "are considered desirable in attaining dom-

FIGURE 12. Gruen and Krummeck's design for the Hollywood Grayson's, featuring fifty-eight neon tubes covering the top of the arcade. From Morris Ketchum, Jr., *Shops and Stores* (New York: Reinhold, 1948), 168.

FIGURE 13. Gruen and Krummeck's Wynn Furniture store for an automobile strip in Inglewood, California. From Louis Parnes, *Planning Stores That Pay* (New York: Architectural Record Book, 1948), 211.

inance and attracting attention from a distance." For a Hollywood Grayson's, the designers were limited to one story, so they employed row after row of white neon lights to cover the arcade's ceiling. "One of the most brilliantly lit fronts on an already bright street," *Architectural Forum* marveled. A review of the Inglewood Grayson's claimed that neither pedestrians nor motorists could escape the store's "60-foot tower featuring colors of chartreuse and white." Another Gruen and Krummeck Inglewood store, Wynn Furniture, was designed solely to entice motorists. A "roadside display case," one article called the two-story transparent structure sporting three cursive neon signs. With its "angular design," "strong colors," "double neon tubes," and "vertical fin, built solely for its spectacular 'modern' quality," the partners employed every flourish to captivate drivers.[60]

While Grayson's pursued new markets outside Los Angeles' downtown, the company also built downtown, completing stores for the central business districts of Philadelphia, Buffalo, San Francisco, and Seattle. One *Chain Store Age* article on selecting locations presented a downtown Grayson's as an example of national chains resisting retail decentralization. "Central business districts in fast-growing cities will also continue to thrive," the article confidently predicted. The California strip's commercial aesthetic of flashy facades and glittering signs also drove the design of these downtown stores. *Business Week* declared the downtown Philadelphia store a "Facade with a Flourish." The author stared at the "towering façade," made of "818,900 pieces of glass mosaic," "a neon sign with a 32-ft.-high first letter," and "mercury vapor lamps to floodlight its 5,694 sq. ft."[61] Such stores brought the strip's scale, lights, and glitz back downtown and gave the latter's aesthetic a metropolitan legitimacy. As Gruen and Krummeck prepared stores for both locations—moving from downtown to the strip back to downtown—their designs for the two became nearly indistinguishable.

The linchpin of this lush retail aesthetic, on the strip or downtown, was strategic lighting. "Retail Stores Go Heavy on Light," one retail magazine reported about Gruen's work.[62] And Gruen loved to light up his stores. "Well designed lighting will add immeasurably to a festive shopping atmosphere," Gruen fervently advocated.[63] Speaking to architects and lighting engineers, Gruen explained how light—the "real star of the show"—had a "psychological" and "emotional effect" on shoppers; it compelled people to purchase goods. A store's "character" was determined by the type and intensity of lighting. Bad lighting created "discomfort, nervousness, restlessness" in shoppers. On the other hand, proper lighting, Gruen wrote, appealed to "our heart and soul" and could make shoppers feel "warmth," "friendship," "awe-filled admiration," "homey coziness," "cool efficiency," or "sweet romance." He revered artificial lighting and celebrated the arrival of the "windowless building."[64] Gruen and Krummeck were never timid when using light. For a Long Beach toy store, the designers suspended seven hobby horses outlined in fluorescents to beckon the customer. Twice Gruen was credited with designing the first store in America to use fluorescents.[65] For a shoe store's facade in San Francisco, the designers placed five large neon signs in green, white, and yellow, with the logo "more miles to a Gallen-Kamp's." In the *Magazine of Light*, General Electric applauded a brightly lit Grayson's facade as "a giant reflector." [66]

"More light, more customers, more sales," a lighting company promised.[67] In the late 1930s and through the 1940s, store designers sought to make looking and buying more visually appealing. "We use light consciously for its psychological effects," Gruen explained. "Lights influence our emotions—our moods . . . and lighting can produce these pleasant buying moods," a store designer observed.[68] Before store modernization theories had caught on, retailers had relied on incandescent lights hung from the ceiling to illuminate the store and its goods. These single fixtures bathed the store in a yellow and direct light. Gruen's ex-partner Morris Ketchum catalogued incandescents' failings. "There is no emphasis lighting on merchandise," he began. Special displays did not sparkle; customers cast dark shadows on goods; and the lights' globes stole the show from the dim merchandise. Ketchum concluded his list by declaring that incandescents were "monotonous" and did not create "impulse merchandise items."[69] Further, incandescent bulbs could not be used in closed display cases because they generated too much heat—ruining merchandise and starting fires. More subtle and seductive methods of retail lighting sought to overcome these failings. And when fashioned correctly, Ketchum contended, light could be "a powerful factor in promoting impulse buying."[70]

By the late 1930s, store designers, inspired by theater marquees and World's Fair buildings, began to use dazzling lighting as entertainment and excitement. "Brilliant Neon Marquee Lighting," *Chain Store Age* declared about the Hollywood Grayson's. Designers long had stressed the dramatic impact of bright lights. "Light is full of strong emotional potency," Gruen reminded the New York chapter of the American Institute of Architects.[71] From the Great White Way to department store show windows, theater marquees, or World's Fair buildings, brilliant lighting had been used as entertainment and enticement. Within stores lighting would be employed, similarly, to sell shopping. With modern lighting techniques, the merchandise would be the brightest spot in the entire store, glowing before the customer. "The merchandise becomes the luminaire from which light radiates and illumines the entire room," one architect explained.[72] Designers believed that the customer could be seduced, and controlled, by strategic lighting. Store architect Morris Lapidus designed retail lighting based on what he called the "moth complex." Through a couple of simple experiments, Lapidus proved to himself and his clients that bright lights irresistibly drew customers. By shining an extra-bright light on a showcase, Lapidus observed that "twice as many people . . . examine the merchandise." For an extremely narrow and deep store, Lapidus designed a "brilliantly illuminated, meaningless rear wall" to draw customers through the entire store.[73] Another retail textbook described a test conducted in Chicago that scientifically proved bright light would increase sales by 20 percent.[74] But designers were not only after bright lights. The trick of spotlighting wares without darkening (or brightening) the whole store was nearly impossible. The solution was found in fluorescent lighting.

Fluorescent lights premiered at the 1939 New York World's Fair, and their impressive illumination, cheap cost, and pure white light caused the director of the Department of Science at the World's Fair to predict that fluorescents would "effect a complete revolution in lighting."[75] He was correct. Two years later the fluorescent light business had picked up to $250,000 a year, much of that due to the retail trade. Promoters promised that the quality of light was like daylight and advertised it as the most natural artificial light yet invented. "Daylight fluorescents give a reasonably true outdoor effect," one store designer maintained.[76] Fluorescents—especially when compared to the yellow light of incandescents—produced a whiter light because the bulb electrically charged gas rather than heating wires, which also resulted in lower electricity costs.[77] Fluorescents had "overwhelmingly captured the public's lighting fancy," Charles Amick, author of the first treatise on fluorescent lighting, observed. In his book Amick paid special attention to retail lighting. He divided the country up according to its lighting levels; small-town stores' show windows used a mere fifty foot-candles of lighting, while big-city displays were ablaze with ten times as much light. Amick, singing the same tune as Gruen, claimed that fluorescent lighting produced "greater sales and profit" by "increasing visibility [and] attention." For Amick, retail stores designed with fluorescents would prove more profitable and urbane than their dim country cousins.[78] Fluorescent lighting re-created daylight so that people never had to stop shopping. Nighttime and dark were banished from the bright, fluorescent store.

Fluorescent lighting quickly became the rage with store designers, and Gruen installed them freely in his stores. In the 1939 Altman and Kuhne store on Fifth Avenue, Gruen and Krummeck liberally placed fluorescents in bronze channels, wall niches, and shadow boxes. The fluorescents at their Broadway Steckler store of 1939 were "nothing short of magnificent—the result a lighting achievement which makes the store a World's Fair marvel at night."[79] Gruen also expounded on his theory of lighting to other architects. Once again he turned to his old passion for the theater to explain retailing. "We should act according to the same rules which a dramatic writer employs when he reserves some punch lines for the end of an act," Gruen explained. "If we throw all our lighting over the entire surface, we have nothing left with which to create punch lines."[80] In retail, combining fluorescents with incandescents was seen as the perfect mix. Fluorescents did not create a brighter store, but a store that was evenly lit. Since fluorescents produced a diffuse light, stores became bright enough to see by and dim enough for spotlighting of individual objects. "Remember that accent lighting or highlighting with clear and tinted spotlights directs the customer's eye to specific articles in the display," Amick advised designers. One author, using a scientific formula based on peripheral vision and lighting, insisted that stores should be lit with twenty foot-candles of fluorescent light, while feature displays should receive ten times as much light.[81] The strategy was to darken the interior with a dim white fluorescent light that would be interrupted by intensely bright, often colored, spotlights.

As fluorescents were meant to be invisible, incandescent lights were used to make goods more visible, to make the wares the "punch lines." The increased emphasis on spotlights to create drama within the store also took a page from theater productions. As movies and plays focused the audience's attention through light, so stores would focus attention on the wares. "Something directly off a Hollywood set," one reviewer applauded a Gruen and Krummeck design.[82] "A store should be designed like a stage set," one industrial designer argued, with lighting treated as "overhead stage lighting." For a few Bay Area stores, Gruen and Krummeck even hired a former theater designer to install the stores' lighting system.[83] Of course, all this theatrical lighting worked to make the goods more enticing to customers.

The mix of fluorescents and incandescents, for Gruen, also required a redesign of the store's interior. Ideally, the lighting would be invisible, offstage. "Concealed lights are excellent," one retailing textbook told merchants.[84] The best way to hide lights and not distract the customer, Gruen claimed, was to install a new "flexible ceiling." Gruen tirelessly promoted the merits of the "flexible ceiling," writing articles promoting the design and using it widely in his stores. By replacing a plaster ceiling with a grid of acoustic panels and lights, the new ceiling would be flat, smooth, white, and invisible. Other mechanical equipment like sprinklers, air-conditioning ducts, and electric lines could also be hidden behind the smooth, flat ceiling. The prefabricated, standardized components could be assembled to cover over any existing ceiling.[85] During the war, Gruen and Krummeck even deployed fireproof fabric for one Grayson's ceiling.[86] Together fluorescent lighting and a false ceiling created a more uniform and standardized retail environment. And with invisible, dramatic lighting and spotlighted merchandise, the entire store was now a gigantic show window.

Just as glass companies promoted store modernization to sell glass products, so lighting companies marketed the new retail strategies to sell more lighting. Sylvania, which aggressively marketed its fluorescent lights, was described by a jealous rival company as giving away free lights and "installing sockets . . . on main streets throughout the United

States."[87] "Many progressive merchants," Sylvania claimed, "enjoy the distinction and publicity certain to be received from being among the first to use this new lightsource."[88] Following a familiar pattern, Gruen and Krummeck received loads of free publicity for their innovative use of artificial lighting. In 1946 the *Magazine of Light*, published by General Electric's Lamp Department, used four Gruen and Krummeck designs to promote ideal retail lighting. "Street traffic," the magazine declared, "is compelled to respond to bold design embodying so much eye appeal."[89] General Electric also featured Gruen's lighting in an instructional film for merchants entitled "Seeing Is the Biggest Thing in Selling." "The particular stores we selected," the director explained, "were considered perfect examples of lighting practices which General Electric seeks to foster."[90]

This interior of fluorescents, spotlights, and false ceilings, like the glass companies' storefronts, created a standardized setting for stores across the country. The popularity of store modernization suggests a growing willingness on the part of customers to discard a posture of restraint toward consumption, even in the midst of war. According to designers and merchants, shopping could now be as much about entertainment as about purchases. Gruen hoped that an entertaining and enticing store would persuade people to linger, shop, and buy goods. By the end of the war, Gruen and Krummeck's work for Grayson's had helped institutionalize this new commercial aesthetic.

In the 1940s this new attitude became increasingly evident at retail trade shows. At the landmark Store Modernization Show of 1947 held in New York City, the designers asserted that the retail battle could be won by entrancing shoppers; the game had become about entertaining the customer to create more sales. In fact, speakers connected the two concepts over and over again. "To the outside they [stores] present the gayer side of the double life—they are show palaces," Gruen explained to merchants. If a merchant spent a day or two shopping for ideas at the Store Modernization Show, the organizers promised that the visit would be the difference between "being the merchant with the smartest shop on your street (and crowds of customers) or just another Retailer."[91] Newspapers evinced an acceptance of retailing as entertainment; Grayson's openings were covered as if they were Broadway openings. A number of articles even went so far as to acknowledge that perhaps shopping in the new environments was even more fun than seeing a show. Indeed, shopping was coming to resemble a form of public performance in which not only the objects but the people themselves were on display. Designers wanted frivolity to win out over sobriety; there would be no penny-pinching in a Gruen and Krummeck store.[92]

After eight productive years, Grayson's and its designers had a major disagreement over a proposed store design. The chain then fired Gruen and Krummeck. Gruen, ever the showman, turned the apparent failure into further publicity. He wrote a lengthy letter to *Architectural Forum*, in which he lambasted Grayson's for the store's bad taste and poor planning.[93] The extent to which designing stores for auto-minded shoppers had influenced Gruen and Krummeck was evident in this quarrel. Planning a store for Crenshaw Boulevard in LA, Gruen and Krummeck designed a two-facade store—a bold front facade "to catch the attention of the automotive public" and a rear facade facing the parking lot. Ignoring the designers' advice, Grayson's insisted on a front facade with more show windows and two entrances, which Gruen belittled as causing "confusion for drivers." The fracas led to the severing of ties between them. Gruen, in his letter, and perhaps in his own mind, acted as if *he* had fired Grayson's.

Gruen began his letter by claiming that his designs had propelled Grayson's to the top of its field. He overlooked the fact that Grayson's had been responsible for his own meteoric rise within the store design field. The chain store had kept Gruen and Krummeck in the black through the 1940s, and commissions placed their name in front of the public during the war years. Local newspapers ran opening-day articles, Grayson's took out extensive advertisements, glass and lighting companies used the stores in national ads, the architectural press followed the new stores, and Gruen used the designs as illustrations for his own articles and speeches. Gruen and Krummeck could not hope for any more publicity than the Grayson's account had given them.

Yet something was missing for the two designers. With all the recognition, they still did not have status. Gruen craved legitimacy. Perhaps Gruen's readiness to sever ties with Grayson's so dramatically may have sprung from his interest in a much larger and much more profitable kind of retail project. He was still working as a designer, not an architect, and longed to turn his ambitions beyond one store design. While working for Grayson's, Gruen had become captivated by shopping centers as the ultimate achievement in retailing. As innovative, large-scale planning projects, shopping centers could not be segregated in the "Trade" section of *Architectural Forum*. More than a mere store or solitary building, shopping centers were sold as a powerful city planning tool. A planned shopping center, promoters believed, could stop the hodge-podge development of the commercial strip. At least that was the reformers' opinion. For department stores, shopping centers represented another way to generate more sales; the large buildings with plenty of parking promised to give retailers more "pulling power" with the public. With great difficulty, Gruen would attempt to balance those two impulses—reform and retail, beauty and business—in his future shopping center projects for postwar Americans.

CHAPTER THREE

Wartime Planning for Postwar Prosperity

Shopping centers have the further advantage in that they can be built without government money and in that they serve the dual purpose of being useful in case of a war emergency, as well as for our peace economy.

— Victor Gruen, 1943

Planning for the end of World War II became a popular obsession in wartime America. "We can plan for peace as well as for war," the vice-president of the National Resources Planning Board informed city planners. Chain stores hopped on the bandwagon. *Chain Store Age* published a three-part series telling merchants the importance of "Planning Today for the Store of Tomorrow."[1] Not one to joke, *Architectural Forum* proposed an ambitious plan to redesign the entire American city. From factories and city halls to gas stations and motels, the magazine wanted to reorder every facet of American life. To demonstrate the project's practicality, the editors chose the real city of Syracuse, New York, for its experiment in city planning. In its size, demographics, income, problems, and potential, Syracuse, the editors explained, represented a perfectly average American city. Seemingly so typical, the remade Syracuse would serve as an extraordinary example that other American cities could follow. The magazine declared its goal to be "complete redevelopment of the city after the war."[2]

Architectural Forum designed the improved city as a reward for Americans' wartime sacrifices. The magazine's editors stressed the social contract of World War II: serve the country and be served by the country, sacrifice for the good of the country and be rewarded with goods. The Syracuse issue of *Architectural Forum* followed on the heels of the immensely popular and inventive 194X Housing issue (the X standing for the unknown year that World War II would end). For the postwar house, architects had experimented with construction techniques, pre-fabrication, and materials. "What design might look like if freed from the restrictions of everyday practice," the editors had cheered. Architects made fanciful houses out of fabric, pressure-molded plastic, precision concrete, and light metal. One architect even offered a portable house-boat as the perfect fit for America's increasingly mobile population.[3] For the Syracuse issue, *Architectural Forum* struck a much more cautious note. The 194X buildings would use practical technology and familiar materials to erect striking, modern architecture. The editors instructed the architects not to experiment with construction methods or the build-ings' functions. Instead, they should concentrate on design and style. The magazine touted this practicality to its advertisers. The buildings, they wrote, would "be realizable in the immediate postwar period": "They are not prophecies."[4] By emphasizing practicality over fantasy, the magazine's conception of a well-ordered city with modern buildings would seem attainable by any and all of America's cities.

To create a tempting vision of the postwar city, the magazine turned to architectural luminaries, relying on young modernists to fashion avant garde buildings for the model postwar city. William Lescaze, the Swiss modernist famous for his Philadelphia PSFS skyscraper, turned his attention to the prosaic gas station. He created a futuristic design with a glass-enclosed restaurant overlooking a new superhighway. Oscar Stonorov, an earlier Viennese refugee, and his disciple Louis Kahn designed the city's hotel. Mies van der Rohe, billed as "one of the world-famous founders of modern architecture," designed the art museum. Charles Eames, the Los Angeles modernist, redesigned the city hall as a series of overlapping bridges to symbolize "a truly democratic type of community." The editors turned to commercial designers Gruen and Krummeck to prepare a place for the people of the redesigned postwar city to do their shopping.[5]

Undoubtedly, *Architectural Forum* picked Gruen and Krummeck because of the partners' past retail achievements. (The magazine's seven-page spread featuring the firm's retail work for Grayson's and Barton's Bonbonniere had run just twenty months earlier.)[6] Although the partners believed that good design contributed to a retail store's suc-cess, they had never expressed interest in city planning or addressed the larger context of their designs. While they took external factors into account (traffic patterns, parking, and competition), the partners had never spoken about how a store might blend into its surroundings.

Indeed, the one criticism leveled at Gruen's Fifth Avenue store designs was that their stores' style and color clashed with the existing buildings.[7] *Architectural Forum*'s invitation to design a prototype of the postwar shopping center would force Gruen and Krummeck to broaden their vision of retail design beyond one store and to acknowledge the relation between retailing and the city. The exercise would propel the partners in wholly new and unanticipated directions.

Though concerned with individual buildings, the editors of *Architectural Forum* strongly believed that the main purpose of the Syracuse project was to build a better community. The Master Plan would ensure that buildings would benefit the entire city, not just their owners. By applying theories of urban planning promoted since the 1920s, *Architectural Forum* hoped to dictate the postwar city's appearance and functions. Since the famous New York City zoning laws of 1919, politicians and planners had used zoning in an attempt to improve their cities. First and foremost, the zoning laws sought to separate a city's different functions. Factories were forbidden to locate near houses. Wholesalers were moved out of downtown. Likewise, stores were separated from housing. Much to planners' frustration, however, cities still had plenty of mixed-use neighborhoods. Stores, houses, apartment buildings, and factories were still freely mixed in most American cities. *Architectural Forum* sought to correct the situation in the reordered Syracuse; they did not want to "build the wrong things in the wrong places." The Master Plan's primary goal was to impose order—"livability and human efficiency."

The Master Plan directed how highways, a city center, public facilities, and stores could be laid onto an existing city. The magazine's plan divided the city into three zones: commercial, residential, and industrial. Commercial and municipal functions would be downtown. The only new residences were apartment "super blocks," which would insulate single-family homes from traffic, manufacturing, and offices. Single-family houses, separated by parks, would ring downtown, and five small industrial areas would be relocated along new highways. The Master Plan would tidy up the existing city's disorder. It also would guarantee that the architects' modern buildings served the community.[8]

While building on popular urban planning theories, the *Forum* did create one innovation—it decided to completely remake Syracuse's downtown. Reacting to downtown congestion and spreading commercial strips, *Architectural Forum* banished cars from downtown to create a pedestrian paradise. Syracuse's Main Street, or the Mall, as the editors renamed it, consisted of eleven blocks that were completely closed to

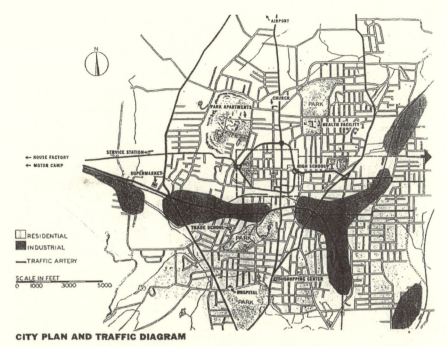

CITY PLAN AND TRAFFIC DIAGRAM

FIGURE 14. Plan for the city of Syracuse showing strict division between residential, industrial, and commercial facilities. Gruen and Krummeck's shopping center is located toward the bottom of the map at the intersection of two highways. From "New Buildings for 194X," *Architectural Forum* (May 1943): 70.

traffic. Ten new buildings would grace this reorganized downtown. The Mall, strengthened by the dual attractions of city hall at one end and a theater at the other, would be Syracuse's centerpiece. The editors envisioned the Mall as "a large plaza which might well become the town's social and cultural center." They did not undertake these bold moves lightly. With falling values and declining taxes, downtown was in serious trouble. "Downtown merchants," they explained, "are becoming concerned with the loss of trade to new shopping areas where parking is less of a problem." By closing Main Street, the editors hoped to compete with the new auto-oriented shopping strips—like the ones that had helped Grayson's do so well—and save downtown. [9]

Paradoxically, the editors also planned a new commercial center at the shopping center, imagining that such a move would help, not hurt, downtown prospects. As downtown was transformed into a pedestrian

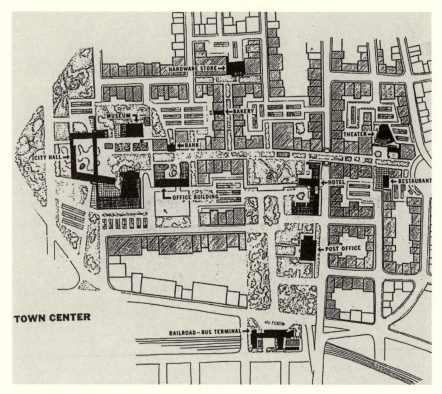

FIGURE 15. Proposed redesign of the town center for Syracuse with its new pedestrian "mall" and new architect-designed modern buildings. From "New Buildings for 194X," *Architectural Forum* (May 1943): 71.

oasis, the shopping center would provide city residents with another pedestrian paradise. This strategy, the magazine believed, would relieve some of the parking pressures on downtown and allow it to specialize in high-end retailing. By creating a new shopping center for an existing city, the editors also hit on a novel idea. Nearly all previous American shopping centers had been constructed as parts of housing developments. (The Country Club Plaza, built as one part of the Country Club housing development outside Kansas City, was the most successful example of this strategy.)[10] But the Master Plan would separate the shopping center from housing, so as not to cause blight or lower the values of houses.

For twenty years, city planners had seen shopping centers as a potential way of stopping both suburban sprawl and rampant real estate speculation. *Architectural Forum*'s editors believed the same thing and imposed one condition for Syracuse's new architecture: every building had to be a "stable, long-term investment."[11] This stipulation sought to avoid the construction of what were contemptuously called "taxpayers." "Taxpayers" were retail buildings that allowed developers to collect enough rent from the tenants to pay the city taxes on the property.[12] Investors built taxpayers, like billboards at the time, to gamble on a lot's anticipated appreciation.[13] Row after row of one-story "taxpayers" on cities' fringes, usually beyond the reach of zoning laws, were the biggest symbol of the 1920s frenzy in real estate speculation. For city planners, these taxpaying placeholders represented the bane of ordered urban growth plans.

As early as 1926, the Kansas City developer J. C. Nichols condemned commercial strips of taxpayers as "the ugliest, most . . . disorderly of places." Nichols blamed these retail developments for "bringing about an unattractiveness that threatens to mar the beauty . . . of the residential regions of American cities." Like other planners and developers, he blamed this aesthetic mess on "too much land zoned for business purposes, permitting a very wide scattering of business property throughout residential areas."[14] As Nichols fussed about the strip's appearance in the 1920s, with the economic downturn of the Depression the complaints against taxpayers became louder and more extreme.

Taxpayers, according to their critics, not only created a horrible eyesore—they also led to economic ruin. The "over-zoning" of lots for commercial usage "stimulated speculation" beyond reason, explained city planner Harland Bartholomew. This greedy mistake led to the exact opposite of the investors' goals. Instead of increasing the wealth of the investor or the city, liberal zoning policies led to "depressed values."[15] The solution seemed simple: limit the supply of commercial land and speculation would cease. The retail innovation of the shopping center—because it would unite all commercial buildings and halt speculation—seemed like the perfect weapon in the war against commercial blight.

"The economic success of a neighborhood community and the well-being of its inhabitants depend to a great extent on the planning of the neighborhood shopping center," claimed two of the strongest and most unlikely proponents of the shopping center. Liberal urban planners Catherine Bauer and Clarence Stein, although better remembered as advocates for public housing and regional planning, enthusiastically promoted shopping centers as the best way to fight strips. In 1934 they authored a landmark argument for shopping centers in *Architectural Record*. Writing during the Depression-era retail jitters, the authors

underscored the need to calculate scientifically a town's retail requirements. Bauer and Stein declared that half the stores in America were
economically obsolete and should be eliminated. For instance, for the
ten thousand residents of Radburn, New Jersey, Bauer and Stein calculated that sixty-three stores would perfectly meet the community's
needs. Taking their cues from chain-store sales, they determined that the
stores would conduct $4.6 million in yearly sales. The shopping center
would eliminate the waste caused by duplication inherent in the free
market; it would be the local expression of a more systematically controlled national economy. The shopping center, used along with stringent zoning, would put chaotic and unsightly strip developments out of
business, making stores "an attractive feature instead of a monotonous
eyesore." Shopping centers would also put an end to the uncontrolled
"speculative" market, which led to horribly "inflated speculative expec-
tation-value." By bringing retail establishments together and controlling
future development through strict zoning, the shopping center would
eliminate the city's commercial strip and sanitize its retail environment,
Bauer and Stein promised.[16]

At first glance, Gruen and Krummeck—successful commercial architects of chain stores—seem an odd choice to lead the fight against the
growth of commercial strips. Their previous work had promoted the very
aesthetic that *Architectural Forum* was now fighting. The partners' best
projects for Grayson's could easily be seen as glorified "taxpayers,"
complete with neon signs, colored lights, and giant windows—the very
type of architecture that appalled the *Architectural Forum* editors. The
Forum editors, however, understood that for the shopping center to succeed, it too needed to be attractive, to both merchants and planners.
Therefore, the magazine turned to Gruen and Krummeck because, as one
of the nation's most prolific commercial architects, they knew retailing's
methods and could hopefully rein in its excesses. In this way, the *Forum*
hoped that the new shopping center would find a broad base of support
among both retailers and reformers.

Architectural Forum never provided the partners with an exact location for their Syracuse shopping center. And Gruen and Krummeck
never asked. The magazine's editors vaguely said that the shopping center was to be located in a "neighborhood." With no specific site in mind
the partners conveniently situated the shopping center on two major
streets within a perfect grid. The site's local details remained unex-
plained and unexplored. The mutual understanding between the partners and the magazine was that the shopping center's design, like a

modern storefront, would be generic enough to work in any city. Of course, making it a tasteful part of a neighborhood and not an aesthetic menace depended on the shopping center's appearance. Gruen and Krummeck prepared three different designs for the 194X project.[17] They had only two months to come up with final plans, and they worked hard to combine practicality with originality. The magazine's editors and the architects wrote letters back and forth, attempting to hammer out the definition, appearance, and parameters of the postwar shopping center. This process, hitting on many contemporary questions about the city and its relationship to retailing, served as a quick education for Gruen and Krummeck in the state of American shopping center design.

The magazine first informed the partners that their design should be for a "small neighborhood shopping center rather than a suburban center." The building would include small shops, a service station, a small movie theater, and a corner drugstore. Six days later, Gruen and Krummeck responded. The partners wondered about the wisdom of building only one small neighborhood shopping center for a town of seventy thousand. It would have to be "quite a large center."[18] Part of this question was undoubtedly a confusion over what the term shopping center meant. Since the 1920s, the term had referred to any dense trade area, whether located in a downtown, a city neighborhood, or a suburb. For instance, in one advertisement for the 194X issue, the editors referred to the project quite narrowly as a "Neighborhood Center Drug Store." In correspondence, the partners and the magazine freely used the terms "shopping center," "neighborhood center drug store," "center," and "neighborhood shopping center."[19] In their first proposal, the partners chose to ignore the magazine's advice and designed a large retail facility for the entire city.

Wanting to avoid the strip's problems with cars and congestion, Gruen and Krummeck attempted to fashion a peaceful place for shopping. Instead of lining both sides of a street with stores, the partners grouped the stores together and placed them "between highways." They faced the stores "towards a plaza" graced by a "garden restaurant, milk-bars, music stand, and other recreational facilities." The plaza, according to Gruen and Krummeck, would be the shopping center's main attraction, a place for Americans to do more than shop.[20]

Working in his Hollywood studio, Gruen sat down and attempted to calculate all possible functions for the future shopping center. He divided the shopping center into both "Stores" and "Communal" functions, then outlined a proposal for twenty-eight stores and thirteen public facilities. Two markets, eight clothing shops, two drugstores, a cafeteria, a bar, a department store, a movie theater, and a service station would satisfy the shoppers. On the communal side, brainstorming Gruen let his imagination run. He included a nursery school, a post office, a library, stables for ponies, a gameroom, a theater, a clubhouse, an auditorium, an exhibition hall, an information booth, restrooms, and announcement boards.[21] While stores outweighed communal areas in pure numbers, the partners saw communal functions as crucial to the shopping center's role within the postwar city. By mixing retail and nonretail establishments, profitable and subsidized functions, the partners predicted that the shopping center would serve as "the center of cultural activities and recreation." It would become "the one important meeting place of the community," like "the market place or main square of the older cities." Gruen and Krummeck realized that their dream of providing public facilities would be costly. In all their previous retail projects, they had never fantasized about pony rides, libraries, or theaters; commerce would have to underwrite the communal parts of the shopping center. Gruen and Krummeck explained that the development "should not be for too small a community, lest it should not pay to erect the communal facilities." While calculating what to include in the postwar shopping center, the partners forgot to address its architecture. The center's style, color, materials, and design were never mentioned. For architects who had built their reputations on their commercial confections, the 194X project propelled them beyond a store's style and forced them to contemplate the building's larger social functions.[22]

Architectural Forum also held definite ideas about the shopping center's role in the perfect postwar Syracuse. In a letter to all 194X participants that crossed in the mail with the partners' first proposal, the magazine's publisher, Howard Meyers, outlined his dreams. Meyers wanted practical buildings that could be built immediately after the war's end, not some "stratospheric approach to planning, construction and equipment." Meyers insisted that each building provide adequate off-street parking, and he wanted the shopping center to be a neighborhood facility for fifteen hundred families. It should be accessible "by pedestrians, since the homes are all within walking distance."[23] In no way did *Architectural Forum*'s publisher address Gruen and Krummeck's burning question over what sort of facilities—public or private—were to be located at the shopping center. Meyers, like most Americans, presumably believed that the shopping center would be devoted primarily to retailing.

Gruen and Krummeck responded ten days later, acknowledging the publisher's wishes and submitting a revised proposal. Not content to confine himself to the small-scale project Meyers envisioned, Gruen instead wrote a long letter to George Nelson, the *Forum*'s associate editor, in which he further contemplated a city's retail needs and how a shopping center could solve them. First, he envisioned two different types of shopping centers: one for a neighborhood and one for the entire city. Ever ambitious, Gruen's conception of the neighborhood was much larger than *Architectural Forum*'s. He proposed that the neighborhood shopping center could serve twenty to twenty-five thousand people, while a larger "office center" or "business center" could cater to the whole city. According to Gruen, the immense "office center" would be the perfect place for civic organizations, municipal authorities, an auditorium, a first-run movie house, an exhibition hall, specialty stores, and a high-class department store. Gruen then turned his attention to the neighborhood center.[24]

Gruen and Krummeck proposed "a circular building" surrounded by a landscaped walk and parking lot and located at a highway intersection. Like a dartboard, the shopping center was made of concentric circles, from highway, parking lot, and landscaped walk to the stores on the interior. Gruen pictured an all-glass building about 140 feet in diameter. Nonstructural glass walls would separate the shop interiors, while "archways and aisles" would link all the stores together. These sliding glass walls, Gruen and Krummeck explained, would literally make the storefronts disappear. "The shopper may proceed from store to store without leaving the actual building."[25] Thus, Gruen and Krummeck took a large step toward creating an open interior retail space of connected stores, predecessor of the now ubiquitous mall. With this radical design, their plan moved away from architects' prevailing ideas about shopping centers, which often featured a landscaped courtyard. Gruen and Krummeck's wholly enclosed interior design more directly referenced earlier American department stores and European arcades than village greens. But Gruen would have to wait fourteen years before he could successfully design and build an enclosed shopping center.

One other architect also imagined bringing separate stores under one roof. In the October 1940 issue of *Architectural Forum*, Morris Ketchum, Gruen's former New York partner, proposed an ingenious scheme for uniting retail stores. Two years after Gruen and Ketchum's collaboration on Fifth Avenue, Ketchum also had turned to theoretical projects. He drew up a retail innovation that he called the "store block." Ketchum proposed covering an entire downtown block with a one-story retail structure. Patrons would park their cars on the store's roof. On the rear of the parking lot Ketchum placed a slim, seven-story glass office building. The retail building, vaguely resembling a department store, contained twenty-six different stores, all under one roof. Wide aisles between the stores gave people ample space to stroll, so that, as Ketchum explained "each store becomes an island, with window shoppers on all sides." This would be the ideal retail environment, where the shopper would be surrounded by the show windows' tempting goods. Recalling Ketchum and Gruen's earlier Fifth Avenue designs, the retail building opened up to the sidewalk with a prominent cantilevered cornice. Ketchum, like *Architectural Forum*, thought of his design as a way to revitalize America's Main Streets. While mixing retail and office buildings on such a large scale was in itself novel, Ketchum pushed the concept even farther. He dreamed of constructing adjacent "store blocks" to create a pedestrian paradise on Main Street. Momentarily ignoring cars, Ketchum painted an idyllic picture of his remade downtown. "Main Street's paving can be torn up, gardens planted, and the citizens can enjoy open air lounging and dining with their window shopping, with no traffic light to bother them," Ketchum imagined. While Ketchum's emphasis on an enclosed interior space foreshadowed Gruen and Krummeck's circular design by three years, because of the war the innovative idea was soon lost.[26]

For their 194X proposal Gruen and Krummeck also drew inspiration from their new hometown of Los Angeles. Looking at Southern California's proliferating highways, automobiles, and retail facilities, Gruen thought that the spreading metropolis could serve as a model for postwar America. In his letter to *Architectural Forum*, Gruen described how Los Angeles could be the exemplar for "an automotive-rich postwar America." Prophetically, Gruen saw in the sprawling city's new "shopping habits and sales organizations" a model for America's future retail practices. By attracting business away from what Gruen quickly dismissed as the "overcrowded downtown sections," Los Angeles shopping centers had become "the really important everyday meeting places."[27] In his first two proposals for *Architectural Forum*, Gruen imagined that a shopping center could create more opportunities for people to come together, enjoy themselves, and shop.

George Nelson wasted no time in responding to Gruen and Krummeck's second proposal. He hated it. The editor especially disliked the concept of an enclosed circular building. The shopping center would lose its best quality, a courtyard, Nelson complained—so what would pedestrians do without a bucolic courtyard where they could linger and lounge? He then turned to the location. Why, he asked, had Gruen and Krummeck placed the center at a highway intersection, which could only lead to severe traffic tie-ups? Nelson closed his letter by reminding the partners that a landscaped "plaza idea might be less expensive and much more agreeable than the present scheme."[28]

Gruen and Krummeck took Nelson's comments to heart. In the final version the circular store disappeared and the central court returned. The novel design of many stores under one roof completely vanished. The partners settled on a rather conventional proposal of two buildings forming a U around a plaza. A covered walkway connected all the stores and provided shelter for window shoppers. The shopping center stretched over an entire block, with parking at either end. While their final design seemed much more modest, the partners did imagine eventually expanding the shopping center. They proposed that after the shopping center's initial success two more buildings could be added to create a rectangle that would surround the courtyard.

. Gruen and Krummeck accompanied their final design with a three-page memorandum explaining their shopping center, much of which was printed in the magazine alongside the design. At its best, the shopping center "harmonizes with the character of its residential neighborhood," the architects explained. The front, decidedly unlike the strip's typical stores, would be "modest," with "no commercial advertising," more like the "quiet" retail architecture that Mumford had applauded on Fifth Avenue."[29] Gone were the three-story facades, sweeping arcades, neon signs, giant show windows, and glowing fluorescents.

The partners, who had often been praised for using innovative materials, continued the practice in their shopping center. On the stores, Gruen and Krummeck used glass facades that slid entirely away to open up the sales floors to interested shoppers. For the building's street facade, the designers suggested using a new kind of plywood with a hardwood veneer that had been developed for the war. Transparent plastic, taken from the turrets of B-17 bombers, projected out of this facade as miniature showcases. Opaque plastic brightened up the covered walkway's cement columns and the drugstore's wavy storefront. Luminescent paint made the ceiling of the walkway shimmer at night.[30] As in the partners' store designs, their experiments with materials would bring eye-popping lights and colors to the shopping center.

Following Nelson's advice, the project's jewel would be an outside

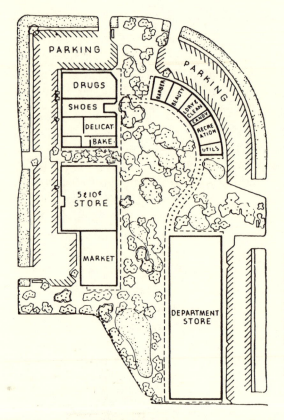

FIGURE 16. Plan of the Linda Vista shopping center in the government's bomber town outside San Diego. From Morris Ketchum, Jr., *Shops and Stores* (New York: Reinhold, 1948), 270.

plaza. But Gruen and Krummeck went in the opposite direction from Nelson's pastoral park. Their courtyard contained plenty of distractions, including a lily pond and an enclosed play area off a shoppers' lounge. The area would be "landscaped as a park," with "a garden restaurant, milk-bars, music shells, and other recreational facilities," they explained. In the evocative drawings of the shopping center, however, the court was barely depicted, as if the architects could not yet imagine how to render a non-retail space. Gruen and Krummeck continued to tout the communal functions of the shopping center by including a library, a post office, and a community room. They also included a lounge for tired shoppers "equipped with fireplace, arm chairs, and tables, open to all shoppers for rest, recreation, and club activities." This room would also contain "a pingpong table, games, and so forth." These facilities, the partners hoped, would transform a retail facility into "the center of cultural activities and recreation" for the neighborhood.[31] In

FIGURE 17. Gruen and Krummeck's published drawing of their 194X shopping center design—looking at the corner restaurant and across the courtyard. From "New Buildings for 194X," *Architectural Forum* (May 1943): 101.

this way, Gruen held onto the belief that the shopping center would satisfy Americans' social needs.

By 1943 the idea that a shopping center might serve as both a retail facility and a social center was very popular. Four years earlier, an architect writing in *House and Garden* had first recommended bringing theaters, playgrounds, schools, and other attractions into the shopping center as a crucial piece of a larger civic improvement process.[32] But public amenities were not added simply out of civic-mindedness. Many experts viewed them as a way to make the shopping center more profitable. "Amenities can help to create atmosphere," two shopping center proponents explained. As Gruen told chain-store managers five years later, the challenge was to make "the project a cultural and community-minded center and thus inducing the shopper to spend more time there than in the ordinary shopping areas." By inviting "people to prolong their stay at the center," the stores would become even more profitable, he claimed.[33] This strategy had been greatly emphasized in big city department stores for at least forty years.[34] In the 1950s, Gruen would not mince words, promising that "more people—for more hours—mean cash registers ringing more often and for longer periods."[35] Further, the communal functions would work to allay community fears about commerce creeping into a residential neighborhood.[36]

The partners' lofty social goals for their commercial project had echoes in other architects' 194X buildings. For instance, Charles Eames designed a city hall with an auditorium, exhibition space, and outside restaurant. The hardware store included a gallery "to house exhibits and displays on technical advancement" and to show movies. Pietro Belluschi, the Seattle modernist, envisioned an office building with squash courts, massage parlors, a coffee shop, and a clubroom.[37] In fact, across the board the 194X architects insisted on placing many functions in one building, combining work, entertainment, and merchandising. Paradoxically, as *Architectural Forum* attempted to divide the city strictly into functional zones through the Master Plan, the architects undermined this concept by bringing several functions under one roof.

While architects theorized about shopping centers, World War II provided a practical application for those dreams. With thousands of people migrating to work in new defense plants, new housing was urgently needed. The federal government designed, financed, and built entire towns to house defense workers. Willow Run, Michigan; Linda Vista, California; McLoughlin Heights, Washington; Westchester, California; Los Alamos, New Mexico; Aluminum City Terrace, Pennsylvania; and Channel Heights, outside Los Angeles, head the impressive list of bomber towns constructed by the government. With new housing came new needs for retail centers. The federal government conceived of shopping centers as a necessity for their wartime developments. The center would provide basic retailing and much-needed public space. "America needs peace not only in the wide world but on Main Street too," *Better Homes and Gardens* explained to Americans. The popular magazine saw great virtues in the government's shopping centers; they would achieve "peace, order, and stable values."[38]

These wartime shopping centers also freely mixed retail, recreational, and civic functions. In the government-built community of Linda Vista outside San Diego, federal designers located the shopping center directly next to the town's theater and community building. The shopping center included a recreation room and an auditorium for the town's residents. Two architects stressed how the shopping center performed a "community service like the churches, schools, fire house, and meeting hall."[39] At the two-thousand-family Aero Acres in Middle River, Maryland, the shopping center boasted a supermarket, a movie theater, a recreation hall, six stores, restaurants, and offices. Morris Lapidus applauded the fact that the shopping center was "built to serve [the] war workers' community."[40] While all the defense towns featured some kind of retail facilities, the size and design varied widely, from a few minimal stores to an entire shopping center and community complex. More often than not, an architect proposed grand plans, only to have the designs scaled back due to lack of money or materials. Since Washington had a limited budget, many of the shopping centers went unbuilt or were greatly reduced. Lapidus lamented that the shopping centers remained "blank spots on the site plan." "Haste, waste, and confusion usually thwarted their full realization," Morris Ketchum explained.[41] Still, the government-built shopping centers provided a tangible example of the feasibility of the shopping center. It no longer seemed the pipe dream of a few reformers.

In a well-publicized proposal, architect Eero Saarinen designed a multibuilding shopping center for the giant bomber town of Willow Run, Michigan. Saarinen situated the commercial, educational, and civic activities of the town at one central location. Everything that an American could want would be found at the community center: the city hall, a post office, a movie theater, a hotel, a grocery store, and shops. Morris Ketchum saw Saarinen's arrangement as "a model for post-war planning."[42] But government administrators scrapped all Saarinen's ideas. Other towns fared better. In Los Alamos, New Mexico, the U.S. Atomic Energy Commission freely combined retail and nonretail facilities in the town's shopping center. A post office, town hall, radio station, bowling alley, theater, luncheonette, recreation hall, and offices were all built in the central shopping center. "For this is more than just a shopping center, it is the center of all community life," two retail architects observed.[43] Other developers, beyond the federal government, also saw value in expanding beyond retail functions. For one Chevy Chase, Maryland, shopping center the developer included recreational facilities to generate more traffic. The six-store center featured a top-floor ice skating rink, a basement bowling alley, a shooting gallery, and rooms for table tennis and archery.[44] The government's wartime shopping centers, publicized and analyzed in architectural magazines, paved the way for more ambitious postwar retail facilities; this building boom provided a much-needed object lesson in successful shopping centers for the future. Looking back at the wartime centers, two commercial architects applauded the government for having "strongly influenced the design of more recent, privately promoted centers."[45] With the 194X proposal, Gruen and Krummeck did not go as far as Washington's shopping centers for bomber towns, but they did propose that the retail facility enrich both cultural and commercial life for Americans.

While a shopping center design represented a new scale for Gruen and Krummeck, their ongoing store commissions informed their new retail facility. The problem of the shopping center called upon their expertise in designing for both pedestrians and automobiles. Whereas individual stores were either on a pedestrian street like Fifth Avenue or on an auto-oriented Miracle Mile, the shopping center united the two places and tried to appeal to both experiences. Moreover, the shopping center combined the two speeds more clearly than any of their past commissions. Gruen and Krummeck's designs for the street-front and courtyard facades best reflected this split. They designed the street facade to capture drivers' eyes; the inside storefronts had to entice pedestrians. The trick, of course, had now changed from luring people into the store to drawing them into the shopping center. In this respect Gruen and Krummeck's 194X shopping center had to balance retail strategies and urban planning ideals. The design combined retail theories of seducing consumers and reformist ideals about placing stores within a residential neighborhood.

But the partners could only sacrifice so many bright lights for staid respectability. On the facade, two entrance pylons of translucent plastic glowed from hidden lights to advertise the shopping center's presence to passing motorists. A large blinking sign ("SHOPS") declared the building's purpose. The exterior favored blank, colorful architecture and a large sign; long, flat walls of plywood were hard to miss even from a speeding car. Inside the center, the designers used miniature display windows to attract passing pedestrians' attention. Shoppers entered through a large archway that led to a covered walkway connecting all stores. With only one way to enter or exit, the shopping center worked like a giant retail store. The colonnaded walkway was essentially a projecting arcade for every store. The colonnades also cut down the sun's glare, so that shoppers could more easily ogle a merchant's wares.[46] On Fifth Avenue, the arcade seduced people into the store; in the shopping center, people would always be walking within the arcade. As the arcade had been designed as a psychological trap to win the retail battle between merchant and customer, so the shopping center greatly improved the merchant's advantage. As the arcades had provided a place of repose from the city sidewalk's hustle and bustle, so the courtyard offered sanctuary from the noise and distractions of the commercial strip. This arrangement would create a "quiet shopping atmosphere," the partners claimed. At Gruen and Krummeck's shopping center, however, one could never quite escape the show window's appeals.[47]

Gruen and Krummeck's postwar shopping center did not revolutionize retailing, and no commissions resulted from their 194X design. In fact, their retail work continued in the same direction. Chain-store designs for commercial strips remained their bread-and butter projects. Yet planning the postwar shopping center pushed Gruen and Krummeck to think more broadly about retailing's future direction and its relation to the horizontally expanding metropolis. The project also compelled the partners to think more clearly about their own architectural interests for the approaching postwar era. Would they continue to design individual stores or turn to larger retail facilities? Would they continue arranging show windows or could they rearrange all of retailing with a shopping center?

The partners concluded their description of the 194X project by confidently suggesting that "larger shopping centeres [sic] could be built on the same principle." Eight years later Gruen began planning a 109-store shopping center for Houston. The Houston center, while only partially realized, would draw heavily on the 194X shopping center proposal. Once again Gruen turned to an enclosed courtyard with stores opening onto an interior space. A decade after the 194X project, when Gruen planned an incredibly expensive and ambitious shopping center for J. L. Hudson's of Detroit, many of the same concepts served as his inspiration. These larger centers would cover four blocks, with roads passing underneath the buildings. Gruen and Krummeck predicted that these centers could support stores, day care centers, and movie houses; the diversified shopping center would create "a place for a new kind of community life."[48] When Gruen first described "larger centers" in 1943, the idea seemed fantastic and futuristic; yet the proposal may have been the one realistic prediction of the entire 194X city issue. Indeed, the American metropolis's form and feeling would be more profoundly shaped by the construction of giant shopping centers than by all of *Architectural Forum*'s other 194X proposals combined.

At the same time that Gruen and Krummeck were working on the

194X shopping center proposal, Gruen also began to envision more compelling reasons to build immense retail facilities. With America deeply involved in World War II, Gruen proposed an elaborate civilian defense measure. Looking at the German blitz of London, Gruen worried about the concentration of American cities. He insisted that the American population should be spread out to prevent decimation by enemy bombing. "Decentralization," he insisted, "cannot be haphazard or unplanned." Instead, he proposed building "nuclei, crystallization centers which, in case of an emergency, can be used as relocation, evacuation, and welfare service centers." Further, the government would not have to put money into these centers but simply encourage the private sector to build them through tax cuts. "Regional shopping centers," Gruen explained, with their "merchandising storage, shelter areas and large, paved parking areas" would serve as the perfect bomb shelters for Americans, useful "in case of a war emergency, as well as for our peace economy."[49] The shopping-center-as-bomb-shelter idea never caught on, but in the postwar era retail facilities would take off in many unforeseen directions that forever changed the ways Americans shopped and lived in cities and suburbs.

CHAPTER FOUR

Seducing the Suburban Autoist

We are convinced that the real shopping center will be the most profitable type of chain store location yet developed, for the simple reason that it will include features to induce people to drive considerable distances to enjoy its advantages.
—Victor Gruen, 1948

The years immediately after World War II were a difficult time for Gruen and Krummeck. After the very public break with Grayson's, their business stalled. And the *Architectural Forum*'s 194X project had not resulted in any shopping center commissions. Retail construction all but disappeared in the immediate postwar period. Consumers may have been spending their hard-earned money on new houses, cars, and appliances, but investment in retail projects slowed to a trickle. A major part of the problem was the question of what retailing would look like in postwar America. Would it be located downtown or in the promised suburbs? And if retailing moved to the new suburbs, would it be along the 1920s model of commercial strips or in the largely untested shopping centers? Such questions would only be partially answered in the architectural projects of the late 1940s.

Without the constant work for Grayson's, Gruen and Krummeck had to find new clients. Reduced to creating designs for individual stores, the partners relied heavily on work for their one consistent client, J. Magnin's shops of San Francisco.[1] They also had two small children to raise and support. Their marriage, however, was on the rocks. Once inseparable, Gruen and Krummeck had begun to drift apart, both professionally and personally. Gruen later remembered these days quite bitterly by saying that Elsie was content only when taking care of a baby.[2] As generating new business grew more difficult, Gruen escaped into more grandiose schemes and occupied himself with dreams of even larger retail projects. These ambitions carried him away from his day-to-day concerns.

In a 1949 article for *Women's Wear Daily*, Gruen lamented that Americans no longer enjoyed their lives. Personal difficulties giving an edge to his words, Gruen described how Americans squandered their days trapped in automobiles, driving from store to store. He reasoned that World War II had been fought for peace, democracy, and the American Way of Life, but peacetime seemed to bring only more frustrations. People were living in ugly houses in even uglier cities and shopping in ugly stores. Because of "poor planning and lack of coordination," Gruen claimed, "the postwar dream cost too much money." He spoke of planning as a healing force, as rejuvenating, as an economic stimulus. Of course, as a commercial architect his thoughts soon turned to the state of American retailing, which on the whole, presented "a very unenjoyable picture."

Gruen was unambivalent in his disdain. When describing retailing's failures, the forty-six-year-old architect was unrelenting. Even the retail developments that appeared to be planned—suburban shopping centers—were impostors. "They are using the old formula of arranging . . . stores along one side or two sides of a busy highway, like pearls of a necklace," Gruen explained. "And the only progress," he continued, "is that more space for parking has been allowed than was the case before the war." He saw these new shopping centers as nothing more than glorified Miracle Miles, just as tacky and tawdry as the old strips. These commercial developments degraded daily life—with "the shopping public bothered by gas fumes and by noise." The visually "impressive store fronts" formed an "empty façade."

After dismissing all retail developments as a blight on America, Gruen then suggested a remedy. Rather than advocating a turn away from retailing or strips, Gruen simply offered to clean them up and improve them. For a solution, Gruen looked to his own work. "Specialty stores," Gruen crowed, "have made great strides": "They are offering their customers surroundings which, by making the shopper feel comfortable and 'at home,' create an excellent shopping atmosphere." He then suggested that better-designed retail businesses could become a beneficial part of any community. "A suburban store," Gruen optimistically opined, "wants to become part of the community." Gruen turned to retailers as the only viable way to uplift the national mood. Successful specialty stores, Gruen asserted, provided a model for remaking all of America. People loved to shop and, for Gruen, this enjoyment could be translated into other areas of American life. In turn, improving shopping conditions would also improve the outlook of all Americans. The entire argument seemed a stretch. But Gruen hoped that his criticisms would generate more clients and that he could then improve the appearance of American retailing.

Specifically, Gruen recommended building larger and larger retail facilities that would simultaneously improve the American metropolis and uplift Americans. He offered bold prescriptions backed by a blind faith in the beneficial aspects of larger and larger retail developments.[3] "It [the shopping center] should fit into the community by its architectural treatment, just as well as by its neighborly merchandising methods," Gruen advised. It was an odd and tenuous proposition, but in making it, he set himself up as the only one with the ability and vision to solve America's architectural problems. As always, Gruen was stirring and inspiring, but the only concrete answer he could offer was larger stores.

A few months before his *Women's Wear Daily* article appeared, Gruen had attended the opening of Milliron's, his first department store for the booming suburbs of Los Angeles. Drawing on his specialty store designs for this his largest commission to date, Gruen enacted the ideas in his article. He also returned to the insights from his 194X proposal for shopping centers. In 1947, four years after the 194X shopping center proposal, Gruen and Krummeck finally won a commission that might let them test their theoretical concerns from the 194X proposal.

For Gruen and Krummeck, Milliron's was a major triumph—their first full-fledged department store. It promised to be the partners' largest and most challenging commission to date; it was also their first major Los Angeles commission, and in some respects their first suburban shopping center.[4] Here they could put into practice their ideas to merge retailing and automobiles, commerce and community. Most importantly, the partners could test their rhetorical flourishes about public amenities in a real building, in a real location (the wartime suburb of Westchester), for a real client. Gruen hoped to bridge the gap between splashy commercialism and 194X idealism, to marry the profits of the specialty store with the planning of shopping centers. It would be a difficult marriage, but it was in the combination of these two concerns that Gruen would discover his own voice.

In the 1940s the wartime suburb emerged as one of the most distinctive Southern California landscapes. From Fontana and San Bernardino to Richmond and the San Fernando Valley, developers quickly built suburban developments of single-family houses around the new defense plants. By spreading L.A. thin and giving it a more dispersed definition, these suburbs redefined the entire region.[5] None epitomized this wartime growth more than Westchester. Located in southwest Los Angeles, Westchester had been built to house the aircraft industries' workers and their families. It had thirty-two hundred single-family houses and ten thousand residents. The commercial heart of the new suburb would be the Westchester Business District on Sepulveda Boulevard, which cut through the middle of the three-thousand-acre residential tract.

The developers, Frank Ayers and Sons, laid out the business district to meet every possible consumer need. Large plots zoned solely for commercial development, stretched over five blocks from Ninety-Second Street to Manchester Boulevard, facing onto Sepulveda Boulevard's eight lanes. Behind the commercial lots, developers placed parking lots that could accommodate up to 3,300 cars. Rather than undertake the development of the facilities themselves, the developers sold the plots to individual parties. Unfortunately for the new residents, rather than taking a lesson from the government's bomber towns or looking to earlier residential developments, both of which included retailing, these individual businessmen met the market demand haphazardly and slowly. In 1947, when Gruen and Krummeck began their commission, much of the commercial district remained vacant. Rising from this retail desert, the new Milliron's would have to respond to its location on two major boulevards (Sepulveda and La Tijera) in every detail.

The Westchester store was Milliron's first branch, and the company wanted its first foray into the suburbs to be completely unique. As Westchester and other Los Angeles wartime suburbs drew people away, downtown's prospects grew bleaker and bleaker. Two analysts estimated that in 1929 Los Angeles residents had completed one-third of all their retail transactions downtown; by 1949 the level had dropped to 12 percent.[6] Yet, even with the opening of the Westchester branch, Milliron's did not abandon downtown. Indeed, Gruen and Krummeck first worked for the department store on a "Modernized, Redecorated, [and] Redesigned" interior for the downtown store's six floors.[7] When Milliron's and Gruen turned to the suburbs, they entered a world that placed completely new demands on both retail and store design.

Milliron's and Gruen's most pressing concern centered on the branch store's suburban location along two busy boulevards. "We are in complete agreement with you that the treatment of this suburban location should be one of complete suburbanity," J. W. Milliron wrote to Gruen

early on in their relationship.[8] Milliron declared that he was not interested in building a typical downtown department store for the suburbs;
he wanted a revolutionary new form, a store that expressed urbanity in
the suburbs. Gruen and Krummeck also had "suburban" notions. When
Milliron's opened for business in March 1949, architects and journalists
saw premonitions of the postwar future, where patrons could drive to a
one-stop retail space.

"A car," two shopping center architects observed about Los Angeles in
1951, "has become as essential there as a pair of shoes, with significant
results upon business." The Viennese Gruen and the New Yorker Krummeck saw the spreading city of highways, strips, suburban housing
developments, and suburban retailing as the American city's future writ
large. "The development of Southern California seems so interesting to
us because the cities and towns here have mostly been developed since
the automobile," Gruen had enthused in correspondence about their
1943 shopping center design. He felt that "shopping habits and sales
organizations as they have developed" in Los Angeles could serve as
models for "an automobile-rich postwar America."[9] Later, Gruen
described 1940s Los Angeles as a metropolis with "stringlike tentacles of
freeways and highways [that] stretch farther and farther, until they meet
with tentacles from other cities."[10] Gruen, who had been in Southern
California only eight years when Milliron's opened, was still absorbing
the city's novelty and soaking in its car culture.

A flood of attention greeted the new store's opening. The local and
national press loved it. Journalists saw Milliron's as a bellwether for
postwar retailing. Parking, display, and location all seemed altered by
Milliron's opening. "Something New in Stores," *Architectural Forum*
proclaimed. *Interiors* magazine ran an eight-page spread hailing Milliron's as the "Department Store of Tomorrow." The article predicted that
all future department stores would be designed following the Milliron's
model: one-story stores built on inexpensive suburban land catering
only to motorists. The magazine perceived Milliron's as a symbol of
"urban decentralization," an entirely new way of American life in which
both necessities and luxuries would be available without downtown's
hassles. "The citizen of suburbia is finding it less and less necessary to
travel to town . . . [with] the accompanying inconveniences of snail's-
pace traffic and inadequate parking," the article concluded on an upbeat
note.[11]

"Milliron's is designed for customers who get around on four wheels
rather than on two legs," one journalist observed. Gruen fashioned the

building for people cruising down the eight lanes of Sepulveda in a car. Like the partners' 194X shopping center, the store was located at the intersection of two busy commercial streets. Unlike the 194X project, however, the store had to compete with neighboring stores and the thrill of driving for Westchester's customers. Gruen and Krummeck responded by employing the tricks of the strip. "Red brick, green fins, and white concrete overhang unite in a facade no prospective customer can miss; not even from a speeding car," one magazine exclaimed. The first thing people noticed about Milliron's was its street facade. Instead of traditional show windows, the architects placed four glass boxes on the Sepulveda Boulevard sidewalk. Measuring twenty by ten feet, the "free-standing buildings" were set at thirty-degree angles "to catch the eyes of passing motorists."[12] The building was a show-stopper in a busy, competitive retail district (and could never have been located in a residential setting as was the 194X project).

Because of the need to accommodate great numbers of cars and people, the Milliron's design posed a giant logistical challenge. While Gruen and Krummeck had designed several Grayson's stores for commercial strips, Milliron's presented a problem on a wholly different scale. Unless handled skillfully, the numbers of cars and people moving in and out of the department store promised to create more traffic headaches than customers. Downtown stores had long placed a premium on parking. In fact, by the 1950s observers had begun to blame difficult parking for downtown's decline.[13] As Gruen liked to explain, Americans had built their cities in the nineteenth century for the horse and buggy. With twentieth-century population growth and the popularity of cars, American cities had become obsolete. On the strip, merchants and their architects debated parking solutions endlessly. And they sought to avoid downtown's failures. One department store's management emphatically declared, "We should not build any new stores unless we have adequate parking facilities immediately adjacent to these new stores." Being on "the right corner of the right street" now mattered much less than providing ample parking. Gruen also reflected on the suburban parking mess. At the typical store on a strip, Gruen explained "People enter the store from the parking lot through the rear entrance, which mostly is blocked by delivery trucks and garbage cans."[14] His use of a rooftop lot at Milliron's (for 220 cars) solved two persistent problems; the cars would neither block the driver's view of the store's signs nor bring patrons around to the rear of the store. The rooftop lot also solved Gruen's bigger headache of designing two different facades.

FIGURE 18. Rooftop parking lot for Milliron's. From Geoffrey Baker and Bruno Funaro, *Parking* (New York: Reinhold, 1958), 134.

While rooftop parking was certainly in the air by 1947, with Milliron's Gruen once again rendered a novel idea in a sensational manner. Rather than concealing automobiles, he turned the mundane practice of parking into a thrilling performance.[15] The entrance and exit ramps theatrically stretched across the entire back of the building to form a gigantic curving X. The futuristic ramps reminded one observer of the 1939 World's Fair buildings; they were "a private elevated highway. . .worthy of Robert Moses' larger viaducts." Others applauded the way the entrance ramps were designed to "look spacious and easy."[16] Gruen did not stop there; he placed an all-glass restaurant, a daycare center, and an auditorium on the roof. The restaurant's plate-glass windows provided diners with an inspiring vista—one journalist called the view "refreshing"—of automobiles both in the parking lot and on the Boulevard. In Gruen's hands, the parking process had become a dramatic show.

The department store's slight stature shocked many observers. In downtown department stores, verticality had always been highly valued, both out of necessity and for prestige—height equaled status. In the less densely built suburbs, stores could purchase cheap land and build hori-

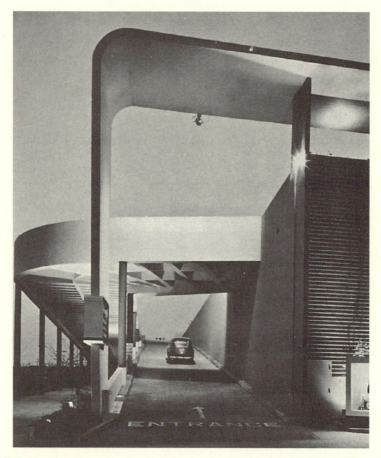

FIGURE 19. The dramatic ramp to the rooftop parking lot that was likened to a World's Fair building. From Geoffrey Baker and Bruno Funaro, *Parking* (New York: Reinhold, 1958), 121.

zontally. J. W. Milliron had originally envisioned the branch as a three-story structure, but Gruen and Krummeck convinced him that a one-story building would cost thirty to fifty percent less because of lower construction costs, no investment in elevators, and more usable space. Milliron was wary, however; a one-story store would present a less than auspicious image. It might even resemble a large "taxpayer." Gruen overcame this image problem by turning to theatrical design. He worked hard to create the illusion of a more spacious and sensational store. Most customers entered the store by taking an escalator down from the rooftop; during their "grand entrance through the roof," they were

FIGURE 20. Main facade of Milliron's with show windows on the sidewalk. From "Something New In Stores," *Architectural Forum* 90, no. 6 (June 1949): 107.

treated to a view of the 90,000–square-foot interior. One article exaggerated that Milliron's was "the equivalent of a five-story building" on one floor. For the main facades along the boulevards, Gruen created what appeared to be a soaring structure. With bright green vertical fins of concrete and a prominent white cornice, these bold fronts rose thirty feet above the street. "Thus, from all important angles, Milliron's appears to be a two-story building," *Architectural Forum* marveled over Gruen's sleight of hand.[17]

The Milliron's design was horizontal architecture for the newly horizontal suburb. The facades, Gruen explained, expressed "the size and importance of the store to the people living in the community and to those driving past."[18] While contemporary observers worried that at only one story Milliron's was spread too thin, the building would later be criticized for being too dense. In 1971 architectural critic Reynar Banham grumbled that Milliron's "with its roof-top parking and crossed Futurist ramps leading up to it, imposed an over-all compact pattern that might have made better sense somewhere more short of space."[19] Ironically, the rooftop parking that Banham disdained was the one feature that contemporary observers praised unabashedly. Milliron's symbolized new suburban retail practices in more than its illusory height and exciting parking.

Milliron's was technically a department store, but many journalists and architects saw it as much more. *Architectural Record* gave the store top billing in a survey of postwar shopping centers. Gruen and the developer, however, envisioned Milliron's as only the first part of a seventy-two-acre Westchester Shopping Center. They planned to add a row of stores along Sepulveda Avenue. (Some authors worried that these additions would make the parking wholly inadequate.)[20]

Although primarily for "autoists," Milliron's also included a bit of pedestrian space—but carving out that space along heavily traveled streets proved difficult. Gruen and Krummeck steered clear of the landscaped courtyard that had been the jewel of their 194X design. Instead, they set the main facade back from Sepulveda Boulevard twenty-five feet, thus creating space for a wide sidewalk, a sidewalk planting area, benches, the four show window boxes, and additional decorative plantings between the windows. In a nod to nature, the surface parking lot contained boomerang-shaped planting areas. "Landscaping for pedestrians and cars also," two observers cheered.[21]

If the idea of a shopping center oriented around a green courtyard was difficult to accomplish in a suburban department store, including public amenities—so crucial to the 194X proposal—would seem nearly impossible. Gruen did attempt to bring other functions into Milliron's, however. Since the turn of the century, downtown department store-owners had seen an economic benefit in providing services for shoppers. Wanamaker's, in Philadelphia, provided an auditorium, art displays, a church organ, a restaurant, and lounges for weary shoppers' entertainment. Retailers hoped these extras would attract more customers who would feel good about the department store and shop longer.[22] Postwar department stores continued the tradition. "On the roof, are departments the shopper may want to visit before, after, or even without buying anything downstairs: restaurant, beauty parlor, auditorium, [and] nursery where mama can check Junior before venturing into the foray," one article explained about Milliron's extra facilities.[23]

In addition to luring more customers to the department store, these services also generated favorable publicity. Often suburban residents greeted the arrival of shopping centers with consternation. "An application for a large or medium-sized shopping center will arouse unfriendly reactions in residents of surrounding areas arising from various fears and anxieties," Gruen admitted.[24] To avoid the common criticism that commercial structures fomented aesthetic and economic blight, department stores had to do something to win over their suburban neighbors' good will. In these residential areas, the store's extra services compensated for suburbia's lack of public spaces and services. Whereas department stores once offered perks for individual shoppers, now they provided services for the entire community. Suburbia was the key difference. If earlier in the century department stores had operated in a commercially oriented downtown, in the postwar era the branches opened on commercially zoned strips surrounded by suburban houses. When Milliron's announced its plans to include an auditorium, the local paper declared, "Civic Leaders Hail Announcement of Milliron's Store Auditorium." The auditorium would be "available for local civic and club groups," and a local choir director declared that the "establishment of an auditorium is our biggest need, in Westchester as almost everywhere else in Los Angeles." Thus, suburbia's commercial life would underwrite its cultural life; as one observer confidently predicted, the auditorium would be "offering a valuable public service."[25] According to this arrangement, a commercially viable business would provide new suburbanites with their communal spaces and cultural activities. Whether or not this arrangement would work well remained to be seen.

Milliron's momentarily set the quickly changing standard for postwar department store branches.[26] In 1949 the Milliron's design seemed strikingly innovative; a mere five years later the building would look very small and theoretically simple. In those five years suburban retail facilities would move in a new direction and toward a scale that would completely transform the way Americans shopped. Whereas Milliron's attempted to attract the automobile by facing the strip and appealing boldly to that mobile population, future retail schemes would shun the strip and attempt to create their own separate worlds.[27] Those who declared Milliron's a harbinger for postwar retailing were only partially right. Retail decentralization on less expensive land did continue apace after Milliron's. Department stores did flock to the suburbs. And architects did try to create forms to satisfy the demands of both cars and pedestrians. But department stores built as solitary branches would soon be the exception rather than the rule. "The isolated branch store in the suburbs is headed for trouble," *Architectural Forum* proclaimed the year after Milliron's opened. The article singled out the Westchester development, "where almost everybody travels by automobile," and declared it in serious trouble. The arrival of the "integrated shopping center" seemed to sound a death knell for places like Milliron's.[28]

Gruen learned quite a lot designing Milliron's. As was becoming his standard practice, he translated his newfound knowledge into a series of articles. While the futuristic styling of the building attracted the press, Gruen touted his work's more practical aspects. Architects' opinions of his work held little interest for Gruen; he focused instead on the more pressing issue of generating new clients. As he explained in 1949, "The aim of good public relations with clients is to a—get them, and b—keep them." To that end, in his articles, he used detailed examples to brag about how he had saved Milliron's money through his ingenious design. In *Chain Store Age* Gruen explained that a department store was first and foremost a "business enterprise" that had to be "run on a profitable basis." He argued that "only as economy is achieved in the construction of the building can returns of sufficient size be expected." Milliron's was a "Triple Target for Economy"—"economy in cost, economy in space, and economy in operation." From the removal of dust-catching displays to devoting an unprecedented two-thirds of the total building to sales areas, Gruen expounded on the smart economics that shaped his design. He even went so far as to explain that the plantings around the building saved painting costs by keeping pedestrians away. Even in its most dramatic aspect—the rooftop parking—Gruen promised there would be substantial savings. The extra cost of reinforcing the building for the parking would be made up by the less expensive one-story construction costs. Maximizing efficiency was not easy. The architect, Gruen suggested and wished, had to be given complete control over "all phases and parts of the store." Only through one architect's "overall planning" would "the merchandising functions of the store" be integrated into "the design of the building construction."[29] And, of course, Gruen always pointed out that he was the best architect to create a profitable department store.

Gruen's articles promoted his services to merchants in language they understood—dollars and cents. A few years later, Gruen took his case directly to the money brokers. He spoke to an American Bankers Association conference on the "Basic Planning Concepts of Correlated Shopping Center[s] Expounded to Bankers."[30] But it is clear from his writings and speeches that he still believed that architecture held a higher purpose as well. In a *Chain Store Age* article of July 1948, before Milliron's had even opened, Gruen hinted at his ambitious goals for the department store branch. With the peace economy just warming up, Gruen envisioned a larger public good being satisfied by commercial facilities— "market places that are also centers of community and cultural activity." Making his case to retail executives, Gruen emphasized that shopping centers could prove highly profitable for chain stores. "The real shopping center," as opposed to an unplanned string of stores, he promised, "will be the most profitable type of chain store location yet developed." Gruen predicted that the postwar shopping center would "include features to induce people to drive considerable distances to enjoy its advantages."[31] Drawing on his theories of environmental engineering in retail, Gruen insisted that higher profits would result from luring people into the shopping center for extended stays. With art, fountains, community spaces, landscaping, giant department stores, leading chain stores, and plenty of parking, the regional shopping center, according to Gruen, would provide suburbanites with a place to commune, shop, and lose themselves. Milliron's put some of those promises into practice.

It would not be accurate to say that Gruen's reputation was built solely on Milliron's fame; he had already designed a number of well-publicized stores. But because it was a department store, Milliron's catapulted him onto the national stage. Gruen later characterized the commission as being his "first great break."[32] Before Milliron's had even opened, Gruen began to set his sights on larger, more profitable retail projects. He wanted to complete more department stores and even larger retail commissions. By 1950 Gruen, working without his wife's help, had completed four ambitious shopping center designs for Los Angeles, Detroit, and Houston. He let his ideas run wild. No one tempered his ambitions, and without these constraints, Gruen's proposals became even more grandiose, ambitious, and impractical. In the four designs, no one brought Gruen's flights of fancy back to earth.

Gruen started with Los Angeles and proposed at least two different versions of a shopping center for his new hometown. The first proposal, which he detailed in his July 1948 *Chain Store Age* article, called for fifteen buildings strung together in a Greek cross. The whole design was a far-fetched idea. At the cross's center, Gruen placed a seven-story warehouse tower to create a "monumental landmark." Between the buildings, Gruen placed a pedestrian mall with "rest benches, flower beds, drinking fountains, tree groups . . . and announcement boards." He promised that separating automobiles and shoppers would "relieve the intense nervous strain under which we all live" and create "psychological comfort" for the shopper. The shopping center, Gruen claimed, would have the "character of a large park surrounded by shopping facilities."

The center's retail outlets included a movie theater, department stores, smaller department stores, a farmer's market, a variety of stores, and a supermarket. Gruen also recommended including an outdoor bandshell, an exhibit hall, a nursery, a small civic hall, a wading pool, and a first-aid station. He also envisioned dining rooms, lunch counters, and kiosks with milk bars, juice stands, and cafes. Gruen was very clear about the purpose of the numerous attractions: they would generate a profit by inviting people "to prolong their stay at the center" and would "impress the center's facilities deeply into the minds of the people living in a wide surrounding area." Shopping would become linked in the new suburbanites' minds with "cultural enrichment and relaxation." Of course, "enrichment" would come to both the merchant and the suburbanite. In Gruen's thinking, little separated public benefit from private profit.[33]

By September 1950 Gruen had substantially revised his design for the L.A. shopping center and unveiled it in the *Los Angeles Times*. The now-named Olympic Shopping Circle was a circle of buildings. At its center, instead of a peaceful pedestrian court, Gruen placed parking for one thousand cars. Lots providing for an additional two thousand spaces surrounded the buildings. The *Times* ungraciously described the design as "a large doughnut with space for 1000 cars in the 'hole' and 2000 around the outside."[34] The only pedestrian area would be a broad colonnade connecting the stores.[35] Even in its more modest version, the shopping center remained unbuilt. Gruen received a small fee for his work on the preliminary drawings and turned his attention to other, more promising shopping center projects.[36]

As Gruen re-created himself as a shopping center architect—a specialization that really did not exist in the 1940s—he also began criticizing his earlier store designs. Gruen's change of heart was a pragmatic move, since the shopping center's archenemy was the strip's retailing. His earlier Grayson's designs—with their gaudy signs, giant facades, and thousands of lights—epitomized what he now denigrated. "What has happened up to now [in store design] is nothing but the creation of future commercial slums!" Gruen lamented in 1949.[37] His change of heart led to more than a few contradictory moments. In 1949, while railing at the Miracle Mile's store designs, he also won the Store Modernization Show's prize for best store design of the year.[38] His store was prominently located on a strip.

Two years earlier, while giving a talk at the first Store Modernization Show, Gruen argued against merchants' pursuit of a modernized storefront. He began his talk in his typically humorous and contentious style. "I was asked to speak today about modernizing store fronts," he proclaimed. "Well, to begin with, let me say I am against it." He, who had been promoting and designing modernized stores for the last decade, now declared that all the hoopla was misguided. Going in the exact opposite direction, Gruen made a functional argument that facades should reflect the purpose of the interior; "contemporary architecture has realized that the exterior of a building is only the reflection of the interior." He argued that modernizing was so much architectural frippery—wasteful and dishonest. He dissociated himself from the store modernization theories he once so vigorously promoted. In an awkward moment one architect at the show sang Gruen's praises for inventing the open front while Gruen questioned the open front's validity. Gruen reversed his earlier opinions by insisting that stores should not "expose their insides to everybody." He explained that stores were like people—"introverts and extroverts"—and that for "high-class" or "exclusive" stores, open fronts made no sense.[39]

Of all the speakers, Gruen distinguished himself with his witty repartee. The *New York Times* ran a front-page story about the Store Modernization Show, quoting profusely from Gruen's entertaining speech.[40] Since Gruen understood retailers' merchandising methods all too well, having perfected many of them, his searing critiques rang true. By speaking against ostentatious design and sly trickery, Gruen set himself up as a judge of retail's proper look, as possessing higher standards of taste than other, more crass, commercial architects. With this strategy, Gruen simultaneously critiqued the strip's flashy architecture, embraced shopping centers, and generated more publicity for himself. It seemed a winning, if at times hypocritical, hand. Gruen's arguments paid off. Indeed, he generated his next shopping center project largely by critiquing contemporary retailing and promising the client a radical solution.

While Gruen completed drawings for the Olympic Circle, he also finished a plan for a new Detroit shopping center. Again, he worked on this project without Krummeck. Employed by the J. L. Hudson department store, Gruen announced his design to the public on June 4, 1950. Years later, he fondly recounted how he came to convince Hudson's to undertake the project. In 1948, a snowstorm had canceled all flights out of Detroit, and Gruen was stranded.[41] Like any good commercial architect, he headed straight to the largest department store in town, J. L. Hudson's. (Only Manhattan's Macy's topped Hudson's in sales or size.) Gruen took a tour of the downtown store with its architect, who stressed to Gruen that Hudson's was dead set against branch stores. While Hudson's deeply impressed Gruen, especially in its size, selection, and displays, he found Detroit's downtown shabby and wanting. As he later recalled, it "was showing all the signs of deterioration which had started to appear in all American cities." For the next part of his tour, Gruen left downtown and drove out to look over the new suburbs. As in other American cities, he found "sprawling suburbs" with "miles of retail strip development." It was a scene Gruen knew all too well and found appalling. Low-priced department stores clogged the major intersections; lower-end stores lined the roadside; and automobiles, not surprising in Detroit, dominated. The strip, unappealing as it was aesthetically to Gruen, obviously worked economically; it was stealing downtown's customers. There, in Detroit's seemingly endless commercial strips, Gruen saw Hudson's nemesis and savior. The nemesis was suburban retailing; the savior was suburban residents.

When Gruen returned to New York City, he quickly jotted down his impressions and sent off a ten-page letter to Hudson's president. Gruen told Hudson's that if downtown deteriorated, so would their business. Drawing on his recent Milliron's success, he recommended that the department store consider opening "superior" branch stores to fight off suburbia's "strangling ring of competitive stores."[42] Though Gruen's theory was not earth-shattering, it did convince Hudson's to take action by hiring him as a real estate consultant. Gruen was asked to scout out a suitable shopping center for a Hudson's branch. He readily agreed.

As in so many instances, Gruen seized on this small opportunity and transformed it into a much grander possibility. After spending days driving around and surveying Detroit, he informed Hudson's that the city held no sites worthy of the venerable department store. Poorly planned layouts or proximity to downtown rendered all available shopping centers ineligible. According to Gruen, Hudson's would do itself more harm than good by opening a branch in one of these shopping centers, so he offered another plan of action, one that was quite self-serving. "We found only one way out of the dilemma," Gruen recalled.

"The J. L. Hudson Company had to build its own shopping centers in such locations as were sufficiently distant from the core area." The Hudson-owned centers (as designed by Gruen, of course) would be "of such design quality that the image of the downtown store would be properly reflected not only in the branch store but in the entire arrangement of the center."[43] Moreover by controlling the development of its own shopping center, Hudson's could detail its exact location, appearance, and tone. Gruen, ever the bold optimist, recommended that Hudson's build not one but four shopping centers, which would ensure that the department store dominated the new suburban marketplace around Detroit. Gruen advised Hudson's to act quickly and buy the sites immediately. Oscar Webber, the president of Hudson's, reacted perfectly.

Gruen, a cagey salesman, had played to Webber's ego. The president also thought that Detroit's existing shopping centers did not approach Hudson's standards. Webber detested "the sordid shopping strips . . . [and] refused steadfastly to have the proud Hudson company be any part of them."[44] With its own shopping center, the retailer could compete in the suburbs and expand its market share. It could also transform itself from a large retailer into a real estate speculator, developer, and landlord. The whole concept lit Webber's imagination. He hired Gruen to prepare a twenty-year development plan.

Although he flattered Webber with his initial concept, at first Gruen found it difficult to work for Webber. The architect remembered the Hudson's executive as being an "authoritarian" and a "conservative." He ran his business "like a Prussian general." Webber insisted that Gruen brief him every morning at 9 A.M. sharp. If he was a minute late, Webber exploded. Gruen also remembered Webber as a fiercely anti-Semitic man who was "harboring more prejudices against Jews[,] Germans and non Republicans."[45] He later claimed that Webber became more tolerant toward Jews, eventually even hiring them at Hudson's, because of his and Webber's close working relationship. At the start of their association, however, Gruen felt under the gun to produce plans for this demanding man.

Under great secrecy, Gruen and a newly hired junior partner, Karl Van Leuven, began to plan from a Hudson's boardroom. They made surreptitious trips out into Detroit's suburbs to examine possible sites. A mere three weeks later, they emerged with a plan calling for four regional shopping centers: Northland, Eastland, Westland, and Southland. They proposed that Hudson's locate its shopping centers "along the fringe of the now existing built up residential area" to guarantee "further decen-

tralization beyond that area." Gruen maintained that the farthest fringes
of Detroit were appealing for three reasons. First, land farther from the
city would be cheaper, and branches located there would not cannibalize Hudson's downtown sales. Second, Gruen imagined that the residential suburbs would eventually expand beyond the shopping center,
creating a larger potential market. Third, by building on the fringes,
Hudson's would be able to guard against any unwanted developments.[46]

Gruen wanted all future Hudson's development to "be planfully developed in harmony with the centers." He recommended purchasing at least
100 acres of land (and up to 300 acres) to guard against "future disturbing development."[47] This prescription—that owning acres of land
would stave off other development—was crucial to shopping center promoters' arguments. Prohibiting other retail developments, especially
pirate stores that could steal Hudson's business, was key to Gruen's
shopping center strategy. He had already picked out prime acreage for
the first two shopping centers on Eight Mile Road—ten miles from the
downtown store.

In his decentralization proposal Gruen was at his most confident and
grandiloquent. He had been dreaming of a large shopping center since
his *Architectural Forum* project of 1943. But the architect who proposed
shopping centers for Hudson's in 1950 was not the same architect as in
1943. In the intervening years, while working for Grayson's, Gruen had
become quite adept in the tricks of commercial architecture. The work
also gave him more confidence in his abilities to design for a variety of
settings, and he had managed to visit many American cities. He had also
become passionate about shopping centers. He promoted them tirelessly.
The concept, he believed, could give him the power to shape larger
swaths of the American metropolis, hundreds and hundreds of acres.
When Hudson's purchased 460 acres of land for Northland, for instance,
the company gave Gruen a free hand to lay out the entire tract. Using
Hudson's capital, Gruen could reshape and reform gigantic pieces of
property.

After Gruen and Van Leuven outlined their plan, Hudson's went to
work. In addition to the 460 acres for Northland, the department store
purchased 116 acres for Eastland.[48] The architects hoped to start with
Northland, which had a larger potential market, but a zoning snafu
forced them to begin with Eastland. Eastland was not the ideal starting
place. Its audience was small and wealthy, and because of the site's
proximity to the Detroit River and Lake St. Claire, the stores could not
pull clientele from all sides. Upper-class neighborhoods (like Grosse

Pointe) meant a lower population density, and Gruen worried that the wealthy would always prefer shopping downtown.[49] Despite his worries, for the most part the statistics were in Gruen's favor. In one report, Gruen explained that Eastland would succeed because of the recent suburban boom around Detroit. The city of Detroit had grown by 13 percent, while the suburbs had expanded by 25 percent. The suburbs near Eastland's site, Gruen continued, had exploded: Gratiot 952 percent, Grosse Pointe Village 271 percent, and East Detroit City 149 percent.[50] He situated Eastland to cater to and capture that growing suburban population of working and middle-class residents.

In an article analyzing Eastland, *Architectural Forum* counted people as well, using the term "pulling power" to encapsulate the advantage a shopping center had over a branch store. The ability to comparison shop in a densely developed area had made downtown popular. People would brave traffic jams and parking problems in order to compare prices. But suburban department stores were often too isolated for this advantage, the magazine complained. Suburban shopping centers, on the other hand, would usurp downtown's "pulling power" through their own density of stores. Shopping centers that were "big enough to hold all the stores required for a family's buying needs-from high-priced apparel to a toothbrush, from furniture to shoe repair shops"—would create "planned competition." "When this cumulative pull is transferred to the suburbs," *Architectural Forum* predicted, "downtown can expect to lose some business."[51] Gruen hoped that the magazine's glowing predictions were at least partially right.

When the architects completed their preliminary drawings for Eastland, Hudson's was thrilled. With great fanfare, the store announced the plan on June 4, 1950; the drawings of the space-age shopping center appeared on the front page of the *Detroit Free Press*. Inside, the paper featured more illustrations showing a circular Hudson store, colonnaded sidewalks, and a central parking plaza.

Gruen envisioned Eastland as a gigantic ellipse of nine buildings. Covered sidewalks connected the boxy two and three-story buildings. Gruen placed a circular Hudson's, looking like it had been borrowed from the 1939 World's Fair, at one end of the shopping center.[52] The central part of Eastland's ellipse would serve as a giant parking lot with some trees and plantings.[53] A thin pedestrian bridge, three hundred feet long, cut across the sea of parking. Slicing diagonally across the center parking lot would be a sunken four-lane highway for patrons and deliveries.

The design attempted to meld large amounts of automobile infrastructure with a great amount of retail. His plan threw buildings, bridges, throughways, and parking structures together in an incongruous manner. However, Eastland would be an automobile lover's dream. Six thousand cars could easily park there (compared to 15,000 downtown, where an estimated 100,000 autos entered daily).[54] The *Architectural Forum* article on Eastland observed that "widespread automobile ownership" had "liberated the customer." Since people could travel anywhere in their cars, the most important feature to offer them at a shopping center was "a place to park the car." Gruen did that, and his design, like a cabaret performance, used a little bit of everything. Surprisingly, he left out what most other architects at the time employed as their centerpiece: a central courtyard.

By 1950, a principal pedestrian area had become standard in shopping center designs. As early as 1934, Clarence Stein and Catherine Bauer had called for a green space at the center of their shopping center design. The shopping center should "face toward green open spaces and turn its back to the road," they advised. They also planned for the retail development to connect to parkland, imagining that the park would act as a buffer-thus protecting residential property values and providing an appealing leisurely route for people to stroll to the shopping center.[55]

Other architects brought the park into retail's orbit. Of all the government-built shopping centers of World War II, Linda Vista outside of San Diego received the most publicity. The shopping center also contained a generous landscaped court at its center. Its architect, Whitney Smith, boasted that "there are no cars on Main Street in Linda Vista." Comparing Linda Vista's charms with commercial strips' failures, Smith observed that "instead of hot pavement and trolley tracks there are benches to sit on, shrubbery, flowers, trees. Instead of garish store fronts and a raucous discord of signs there are the order and peace of an early village green." Not blind to the commercial potential of the landscaped courtyard, Smith explained that "facing all stores to the court gives all merchants an equal chance to attract customers." [56] Gruen was well aware of the perceived value of placing retail in a pastoral space.

In their 194X proposal, Gruen and Krummeck also had placed a courtyard, completely separated from the parking lots, at the shopping center's heart. In 1948 Gruen praised the idea of placing a "Mall" between store buildings. He insisted that malls formed a necessary part of "shoppers' convenience" because they provided "a quiet, restful atmosphere."

"Shopping areas," he elaborated, "would be spacious, park-like, free from automobile traffic."[57] But whatever Gruen may have been convinced of in 1943 or advocated in 1948, he forgot for his Detroit design. Instead, he designed Eastland for the auto alone. Eastland contained not a green oasis but a giant parking lot dotted with trees. This shopping center was an improvement on, not a replacement for, downtown—so Gruen gave it the allure of downtown's density and commercialism without its parking problems. He wanted to use downtown's lights, color, sidewalks, even crowds to re-create a hustle and bustle for business.

For all the grand designs and good press, Eastland was mothballed by April 1951. In a press release, Oscar Webber blamed the material shortages due to the Korean War for halting the plan. Webber went on to explain that, "the government has taken steps to curtail commercial buildings of all types through curbs on means and methods of financing, as well as controls on materials used in construction." Undaunted, he declared that he still believed in the goal of Hudson's building shopping centers around Detroit. And he promised to "push the program to completion as soon as conditions permit." The forced delay of Eastland turned out to be a blessing in disguise. "We almost laid an egg," Gruen later remembered.[58] Although never mentioned in the press swirling about the project, the shopping center's design was an odd mixture of many competing elements. With parking on both sides, parking in the courtyard, and a road dividing it in half, the shopping center became a large traffic hub with no unifying motif.

Once again, Gruen saw a road leading toward a shopping center turn into a dead end, although the amount of publicity generated by the Eastland proposal must have partly consoled him. *Architectural Forum* had used Gruen's design for its shopping center issue, and Gruen also made use of the commission to sharpen his ideas. Around the same time, he was further refining his ideas on yet another shopping center design, this time in Houston.

In 1950 Houston developer Russel Nix hired Gruen to prepare drawings for what was billed as the largest shopping center in the world. Gruen worked on the project with Houston architect Irving Klein and real estate consultant Larry Smith. Since Gruen was not licensed as an architect in Texas (he had only recently received his license in California), Klein acted as the associate architect. As originally proposed, the Montclair Shopping Center contained two department stores, a super-

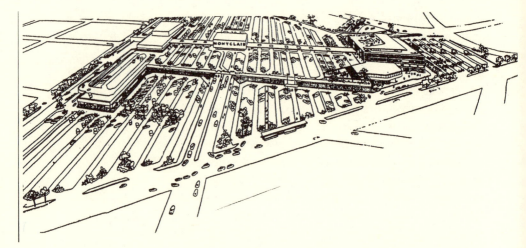

FIGURE 21. Gruen's drawing of the proposed Montclair Shopping center for Houston. From Victor Gruen and Larry Smith, "Shopping Centers: The New Building Type," *Progressive Architecture* 33, no. 6 (June 1952): 90.

market, 109 other stores, rooftop parking for three thousand cars, and an enclosed mall area. The team's proposal was audacious. It touched on city growth, retail potential, and demographic figures.

Gruen (who wrote the proposal) put forth a convincing argument for the need for a large-scale shopping center, basing much of it on detailed market analysis. He observed that Houston was the second-fastest-growing city in America, behind Los Angeles; Houston's population had soared from 384,514 to 594,417 in the 1940s. The population in the suburbs had doubled in the same time, to 802,102. "Houston now ranks first among the nation's metropolitan centers in rate of growth of retail trade in the fringe area outside the city limits," Gruen observed.[59] He marshaled all these population growth figures to argue that a large regional shopping center would reap tremendous profits.

Gruen went on to explain how shopping centers would be extremely profitable. After criticizing the Miracle Mile, which forced people to drive from place to place and required "a miracle shopper to use the facilities fully," Gruen proposed a solution: the modern shopping center. The Montclair shopping center, according to Gruen, would offer "relief from traffic tension" and render all other shopping facilities—"another center or downtown stores"—completely obsolete. With his own ambitions fully in mind, Gruen maintained that only with a gigantic shopping center could an architect design an improved shopping facility. A "conventional street pattern and crazy-quilt ownership pattern of downtown property" limited an architect's ability to create a peaceful shopping experience, Gruen complained. With a large blank slate, however, an architect could exert control over all the building's factors of transportation, building design, and parking. This total control, especially in Gruen's hands, would lead to the creation of a paradise for the public.

In the design for Montclair, Gruen continued the dream.[60] The proposed shopping center was not particularly graceful, but it included an amazing number of features. It had parking on the roof, an avenue rerouted below the shopping center (a major, and expensive, innovation), two department stores (one five stories high), generous pedestrian spaces, and, most ambitious, an enclosed mall. Gruen also pictured a rooftop restaurant and curved parking ramps. While the Eastland proposal was devoted to the car, in the wildly fantastic Montclair Gruen provided the pedestrian with generous spaces.

For Montclair, Gruen also turned back to his original idea for the 194X project: an enclosed shopping space. He proposed bringing all stores inside and creating a covered street; it was an audacious proposal. The mall (air-conditioned because of Houston's humidity) stretched for three football fields, with stores on either side. Gigantic, the mall spanned the width of a typical Main Street (seventy feet wide) and provided people with a comfortable space to stroll and window-shop. It ran from one department store to the other and represented the most original and daring part of Gruen's Montclair proposal. Gruen calculated that the mall would increase "pedestrian traffic" for the merchants. Further, the design would expose "that traffic to the greatest number of stores without the necessity for crossing streets." Surrounded by stores, displays, and goods, visitors would be tempted by two sets of beckoning show windows, the great novelty of which had obvious economic advantages for both the developer and merchants.[61]

An indoor shopping street—journalists loved it. *Women's Wear Daily* predicted that the invention of the mall would be perfect for leisurely shopping: "a traffic free, air-conditioned shopping atmosphere for the customer." The "pedestrian mall," the magazine exclaimed, would be "free from traffic, street noises and the general clamor of a typical downtown shopping area." The *Houston Post* also trumpeted the innovation of the "long arcade, or mall." "Flanked by shops" and other "smaller arcades," the main mall "will be air conditioned, providing the equivalent of a 10-block air conditioned shopping center," the paper informed its readers.[62] As journalists attempted to describe this new indoor shopping invention, the developer tried to figure out how to afford it.

By 1952 a large chain of Houston grocery stores, Weingarten's, had opened a branch in Montclair. The developer Russel Nix declared the grocery store to be only the beginning. *Chain Store Age* applauded the "Texas Beauty" as the center's first store.[63] Nix claimed to have leases signed on over half the commercial properties, two large financial institutions ready to lend capital for the whole project, and a department store lined up. According to one newspaper article, a major insurance company was fronting the necessary funds.[64] In actuality, Nix was desperately searching for more financing. After failing to interest investors, the project stalled. While Nix promised a 1952 opening, Montclair remained on the drawing boards. The major problem with the center turned out to be Gruen's design; it was much too bold and too expensive. The estimated twelve-million-dollar price tag seemed exorbitant, especially considering that Nix did not actually have signed leases from tenants. Further, without the secure commitment of a large department store, Nix could never obtain funding. Remarkably, while Gruen detailed the economic rationale for the retail aspects of the shopping center, he never addressed potential lending institutions or projected costs. Rather he proposed his designs in a vacuum, imagining that the developer would arrange the necessary funding. With Montclair, Gruen's extreme design directly undermined the developer's ability to find capital for the project. To add insult to injury, when Nix was waiting for financing, someone beat him to the punch. Allied Department Stores opened Houston's first large shopping center, Gulfgate in 1956. One of Gruen's competitors, John Graham of Seattle, was the architect.[65]

Perhaps Gruen's Montclair was too good to be true—an indoor, air-conditioned shopping street. A shopping center was eventually built on the site, but it was unremarkable.[66] Indeed, Gruen's earlier ambitious designs of an enclosed shopping mall were nowhere to be seen. Having been fired after his original proposal proved too expensive and impractical, Gruen nevertheless was proud of his Montclair design. In June 1952 he chose a perspective drawing—highlighting the large department stores, sunken avenue, and generous parking lots—as an illustration for a *Progressive Architecture* article, to show how a regional shopping center could look.[67]

While the Montclair project did not pan out, through it Gruen met an invaluable colleague—the real estate analyst Larry Smith. Better than any other architectural partner, Gruen found in Smith someone whose ideas perfectly rounded out his own. Smith gave Gruen the economic credentials and details that he had been missing. They also shared a strong belief in the power—economic and social—of the shopping center. With Smith's market analysis and Gruen's architectural plans, the duo could provide clients with the data upon which to build the dream of a new shopping center. In their Montclair proposal, Gruen and Smith began to develop a strategy of calculating and defining the market for their clients.[68]

After Montclair, Smith and Gruen would work together on literally hundreds of projects. Smith's emphasis on market analysis pushed Gruen toward a new way of conceiving his architectural visions. Later Gruen would explain shopping center architecture in purely economic terms: "Loans for buildings which are to be leased are based not on the structural soundness of the building but on the financial soundness of the tenants; not on the thoroughness of design detail but on the thoroughness of lease writing; not on the aesthetics of the structure but on the beauty of the financial statement."[69] Thanks to Smith, Gruen's emphasis on the "beauty of the financial statement" would remain his paramount concern throughout his American career.

Gruen and Smith continually emphasized how design and economics went hand in hand. In their first article together in 1952, the partners promised that building a shopping center would be profitable. "Civic" attractions, they argued, would create "magnetic powers to attract more people and hold them for a longer time."[70] Working together on a project for the Philadelphia department store of Strawbridge and Clothier, Gruen told the client that he had just sent off exploratory plans to Smith. "As soon as we can get together with him and arrive at a plan acceptable from an economic as well as architectural point of view, we would then be ready to start preliminary work," Gruen informed the client.[71] Above all else, Gruen and Smith emphasized the basic fact that a shopping center should be designed to produce a profit. Standing amid the wreckage of their Montclair proposal, all Gruen and Smith had to do was convince someone to fund their persistent dream.

By the end of 1950 Gruen had designed four regional shopping centers, none of which were built. In these plans, he began to take his theories of controlling and tempting customers to a larger scale; he wanted his shopping centers to be retail machines. The parking lots and roads promised to move massive amounts of customers and goods in and out quickly; the enclosed mall was guaranteed to produce a new level of temptation for customers; the public amenities sought to keep customers entertained and excited. Just as his first American designs for Fifth Avenue stores worked, in Lewis Mumford's words, as a "mousetrap," so these shopping centers sought to capture the customer for longer and longer periods of time. Yet reformist ideas always crept into Gruen's proposals. While not as prevalent as the concepts had been in his 194X proposal, reformist notions appeared in all four of these unbuilt shopping centers. Gruen saw public and civic functions as integral to a regional shopping center's purpose. In these designs, Gruen suggested, commercial and cultural pursuits were not wholly incompatible—in fact, they could enrich one another.

To call these unrealized shopping center designs "failures" is to slight their importance. The designs cemented Gruen's reputation as an architect who specialized in shopping centers. In 1952 he authored, with Larry Smith, a study for the respected *Progressive Architecture* that purported to answer all the pressing questions about designing, building, and operating a regional shopping center. In this particular architectural form, Gruen had discovered monumental architecture that held the potential to remake the American city. Gruen liked that sense of gravity and significance—the sheer size of the shopping center. He often bragged that the American shopping center was the single genuinely new form of architecture of the twentieth century (equal to Gothic cathedrals or Parisian boulevards in importance). Further, his designs for these four shopping centers, although unbuilt, pushed the limits of Gruen's imagination. He had to contemplate traffic, pedestrians, stores, services, deliveries, entertainment, signage, and size. The projects also tested Gruen's ability to design and market his shopping center concepts. In these four cases he failed in his marketing ability; he could generate enthusiasm but no funds. The failures taught Gruen what would become the most significant aspect of postwar shopping centers: capital.

Through this facility in large-scale design, Gruen unintentionally created for himself a unique niche encompassing two worlds: retailing and city planning. It was a niche that Gruen would long occupy and in which, perhaps, he was not always content. As he once complained, an architect harbored a dozen souls in his chest. He had to be an artist, a builder, an engineer, a businessman, a lawyer, a psychologist, a promoter, a public speaker, and a manufacturer. All of which turned him into a "nervous wreck."[72] Part of Gruen's difficulties was of his own making. The shopping center designs, because of their very size, scared investors off. Designing and building a department store like Milliron's with parking on the roof, curving ramps, and a bold facade was one thing. But dreaming about shopping centers with interior malls, thousands of parking spaces, more than a hundred stores, and two department stores was quite another. The plans may have appealed to shoppers and architectural critics, but investors perceived the designs as much too futuristic and impractical. Gruen's fanciful notions would have to be contained in order to be created, he did not let go of the shopping center's promise. After these setbacks, Gruen redoubled his efforts to see a shopping center built as he had imagined it.

CHAPTER FIVE

A "Shoppers' Paradise" for Suburbia

> He [the architect] decides to give the client not what he wants
> but what he ought to want . . . pedestrian areas of attractive
> appearance with sun protection and landscaping and, yes,
> even art, because they will attract more shoppers, thus
> increasing the business of the lessors . . . in other words, that
> he ought to want good design because it spells good business.
> —Victor Gruen, 1956

At the beginning of 1952—five years after the fanfare for the opening of Milliron's department store—Gruen still had not built a shopping center, but not for lack of trying. Without capital, all his grand schemes had fallen apart. His visions of bringing pedestrian lawns, parking lots, community theaters, and spacious stores to suburbia's new residents remained on the drawing board. That year, however, a team of Chicago developers became interested in Gruen's retail dreams. Landau and Heyman, who had made their money in Chicago apartment buildings, turned to Gruen for a small shopping center for Chicago's booming outskirts. The next year, they broke ground for a very small one in the blue-collar town of Hammond, Indiana, next door to Gary's giant steel mills. The three-million-dollar Woodmar Shopping Center was less than revolutionary. Gruen designed a small V with the department store Carson, Pirie, Scott facing the center. In between the V of stores and the square Carson's, he carved out a small open-air mall with a fountain and a few benches. On three sides, parking for 1,160 cars wrapped around the shopping center. Woodmar looked more like a specialty store on a commercial strip than a new departure for postwar retailing—like a recycled Grayson's design. It was a bad omen for Gruen's grandiose shopping center dreams.[1]

Gruen's other main project that year was equally far removed from those dreams. Mayer and Schmidt was a small women's store on a strip in Tyler, Texas. *Architectural Forum* applauded it as "the store that cars built." There was a free-standing building devoted to show windows on the sidewalk to appeal to motorists. Gruen then set the two-story store back from the strip, so as to create what the *Forum* praised as "a de luxe parking lot." The design actually looked like it had been inspired by Gruen's use of a pedestrian courtyard for his 194X project. This time, however, the court was devoted to spaces for forty cars—a far cry from the greenspace, public amenities, covered court, and retail innovations of Gruen's lofty shopping center theories.[2]

This lackluster beginning, however, did nothing to dampen Gruen's ambitions. As Gruen waited for his next big chance, he turned to a medium where he could be as bold and fanciful as he wanted to be. He wrote. In his articles he did not have to worry about unreliable finances or troublesome clients. And the bolder his writings, the more attention he gained for himself and his ideas. With Larry Smith, Gruen surveyed the history and future of shopping for *Progressive Architecture*. The partners stressed the historical precedents for the suburban shopping center—the Greek agora, the colonial town square, and the European plaza. They maintained that the suburban shopping center brought proven laws of retail's past to the new suburbs. The shopping center, they wrote, was not an innovation so much as a culmination of everything that had come before. It was the perfection of what architects, financiers, chain stores, and department stores already knew about retailing.

The forty-two-page treatise provided extensive advice about this relatively untried retail form. Since neither author had yet built a shopping center, researching and writing their article served as their own education in planning as well. They addressed everything from banal details (parking spaces should be at least ten feet wide) to abstract concepts. They attempted to anticipate everything a developer or an architect would want to know. They provided definitions of shopping center terms, a history of retailing, development phases, financial advice, siting information, and store layout. Numerous illustrations showed construction details, building arrangements, and storefronts. They included charts of parking situations, traffic patterns, retail expenditures, and demographic data. They illustrated what they considered the best in landscaping, store design, parking configurations, and pedestrian malls. Their illustrations pictured the shopping centers as vibrant places alive with families shopping surrounded by green lawns, plate-glass window displays, and colorful art. Of course, much of the article sought to convince readers that shopping centers weren't expensive, hare-brained schemes, but economically viable investments.

In a strange twist for an article supposedly about suburban retailing, Gruen and Smith first turned downtown. Long the nation's most glamorous shopping districts, downtowns had been declining precipitously. Though automobiles had made the downtown functionally obsolete, all was not lost. With a combination of slum clearance and suburban shopping centers, downtown could regain its prominence, with regional shopping centers serving as "satellite downtown areas." The latter then would accommodate "the hordes of automobiles" with "restfulness, safety, and esthetic values." More forcefully than ever before, Gruen and Smith pushed for regional shopping centers as both economic and cultural necessities. They claimed that as whites fled from cities to suburbs, "social and cultural activity" had been stifled. A "price tag that spells exhaustion, loss of time, high transportation and parking costs" had destroyed suburbanites' enjoyment of postwar life, they lamented. Gruen and Smith proposed the shopping center as suburbanites' salvation from this social isolation.[3]

Gruen made a similar argument in a different medium—an art exhibition sponsored by the American Federation of Arts (AFA) and paid for by Gruen's largest department store clients (Hudson's, Dayton's, and Macy's). *Shopping Centers of Tomorrow* traveled across the continent, from the Detroit Institute of Arts to the Walker Art Center, the Wichita Art Museum, and the National Gallery of Canada. *Progressive Architecture* applauded Gruen for having created "public relations activity of unusual proportions."[4] Gruen got a plug from the modernist Richard Neutra, a fellow Viennese architect living in Los Angeles. "This Exhibition," Neutra ventured, "seems an educational and civic contribution toward a less troublesome life, and there is a great deal of truly splendid effort invested in it by Victor Gruen."[5] The director of the AFA, Burton Cumming, proclaimed that the exhibition illustrated "a remarkable combination of community planning and architecture for commerce." Cumming saw the shopping center as "a solution that will profit everyone." He wondered if history had ever seen "a secular building [that] has offered a chance to express so much of the life of the community and so many aspects of community life." Gruen had obviously convinced the AFA director of his noble intentions for the shopping center; he hoped the art exhibition would convince the general public of its potential as well.

Gruen began the exhibition with a quick history lesson. "From the time bartering was done under a tree the market has been a meeting place," he explained. "People afoot could mingle leisurely, discuss business, exchange gossip." From stalls around medieval churches to Italian piazzas, these historic marketplaces shared one key concept—they were constructed on a "HUMAN SCALE." This perfect scene was destroyed by the industrial revolution. With towering buildings and idling cars, the human scale had been lost. "Danger, disorder, disintegration are appalling features of our commercial slums," Gruen lamented.

Gruen then listed the failures of modern America. Suburbs were "communities without hearts." Traffic, parking, pollution, and chaos all imperiled Americans. As the United State became "a nation on wheels" and "distant sprawling suburbs," shopping centers became indispensable. Gruen saw America at a crossroads. Either Americans would live with "poor, anarchistically-growing, unplanned suburban shopping centers" or with "well-planned, integrated shopping centers." Of course, the history of retailing as presented by Gruen led inexorably to his shopping center designs. In fact, only shopping centers could clean up America's messes. With colonnades, wind screens, and perhaps someday "covered malls and courts," the shopper could even conquer the weather and shop in "eternal spring." But design, Gruen pointed out, must go beyond pretty buildings. "It is concerned with PEOPLE, their needs, their wants, their happiness," he proclaimed. It was an astounding sentiment. Gruen was sincerely proposing that commercial architecture could bring Americans happiness.

Gruen then provided four case studies to illustrate the benefits of the shopping center of tomorrow. Of course, his firm had designed all four. Minneapolis' Southdale, Oakland's Bay-Fair, Detroit's Northland, and Indianapolis' Woodlawn exemplified Gruen's promise that shopping centers could fulfill larger social goals. However, at this point, as in the past, all four proposals existed only on Gruen's drawing boards.

Gruen concluded his Shopping Center of Tomorrow exhibition with a threat and a promise. He threatened Americans with commercial strips and promised them shopping centers. "YOUR PROPERTY IS NO BETTER THAN ITS ENVIRONMENT," Gruen warned. If Americans did not take action, then their new suburban paradise would devolve into a hellish slum. "Only you as a farsighted citizen," Gruen earnestly intoned, "can see to it that the formless growth of the uncontrolled commercial slum is replaced by integration of the shopping center."[6]

In this exhibition and in other forums, Gruen continued to make a two-pronged argument for shopping centers. He stressed different benefits for different audiences. For businessmen, he trotted out the argument that the shopping center would generate unprecedented profits. For the general public, he claimed that the shopping center would beautify their environment, uplift their spirits, and enrich their lives. One could always find something to agree with in Gruen's arguments. He made his far-fetched ideas seem tangible by providing massive amounts of data and examples. And, as always, underlying all of Gruen's arguments was his own self-interest. He wanted Americans to want shopping centers so that he could design and build these giant buildings.

While Gruen promised his clients vast financial rewards, many businessmen saw shopping centers as unsound endeavors. Even though whites were leaving the cities for the new suburbs, shopping centers were never a sure thing. Their land requirements, size, and construction costs made them incredibly expensive developments. Additionally, the uncertain postwar consumer market made retailing a dicey investment. Developers had an especially rough time finding funding.

In this context, postwar pundits predicted shopping centers' imminent failure. *Business Week* wondered, did America already have "Too Many Shopping Centers?"[7] "Shopping Center Boom Poses Problems," one pessimistic banker declared in the *Journal of Commerce and Commercial.* "From such gaudy planning it is hard to refute the boom in suburbia," he admitted. "But as in most booms, quite a number of people lose money simply because of the tendency to overcapitalize future potentials." He warned that shopping center construction could not continue at its breakneck speed. Shopping centers would either be "killed off by competition from other centers and downtown, or grow ponderous and, like the dinosaur, pass away," he predicted. And a realtor ominously warned, "If the trend continues throughout the country, it [the shopping center] will destroy the value of many millions of dollars of real estate and may completely demoralize many business areas."[8] Reality justified the experts' concerns.

The first major postwar shopping centers failed to inspire investor confidence. When Shopper's World opened in 1951 outside Boston, it was greeted with much fanfare. "An enormous, spreading monument to democratic free enterprise," enthused a *Boston Globe* reporter. The seventy-acre site in Framingham, Massachusetts, had forty-four stores, a 250,000–square-foot Jordan Marsh department store, and parking for 6,000. It was designed by Gruen's old partner Morris Ketchum as a large U-shaped group of nine two-story buildings that surrounded a gigantic open-air courtyard—a colonial New England green for suburbia. But for all of Ketchum's clever designs, Shopper's World failed miserably. The developers, Suburban Centers Trust of Boston, could not entice a second large department store. The second floor of retail space proved very difficult to rent. Within two years, the developer filed for Chapter 11 bankruptcy protection. The colossal failure exacerbated developers' worries about investing in shopping centers.[9]

Even the optimistic Gruen had to admit that shopping centers were risky endeavors. Appearing at a Merchandise Mart press conference in Chicago in 1954, he warned that shopping center developments could lead to the ruin of retailers and lending agencies. With "improper planning," failures would continue. For Gruen, this was a rare admission.[10] Gruen realized that financiers were essential to his dreams. Only the moneybrokers could help him build the large shopping centers he wanted to bring to America's suburbs. And when he took his case for shopping centers directly to businessmen (retailers, bankers, lending agencies, and chain stores), he finally achieved success. Just as he had hailed Milliron's economic rather than aesthetic benefits, Gruen now repeated the strategy for shopping centers. Developers should "want good design because it spells good business." He did not hesitate to warn that the "investor would do well to hold back any desire to economize." "Here, as in other enterprises, the cheapest is rarely the best."[11]

Gruen paid close attention to the capital that provided the foundation for his buildings. "Loans for buildings," he explained, "are based not on the structural soundness of the building but on the financial soundness of the tenants." Money was not given "on the thoroughness of design detail but on the thoroughness of lease writing; not on the aesthetics of the structure but on the beauty of the financial statement." Of course, he always emphasized that his good designs produced those beautiful bottom lines. Shopping centers would return their substantial investment for retailers in sales and for developers in rents.[12]

Gruen soon realized that if the retailer and developer could be combined, the profits would be even greater. The one client who was large enough and desperate enough to contemplate a risky suburban expansion was the department store. Since department stores traditionally had been cities' largest and most important retailers, they worried about the loss of their middle-class clientele to suburbia. But finding the cash to fund an expansion was difficult. Retailing was seasonal, and department stores were often reduced to borrowing huge amounts of money to meet operating expenses during the lean summer months.[13] Further, planning shopping centers required a large capital outlay. The preliminary demographic, market, real estate, and traffic studies and preparation of architectural and site plans added to the development costs.[14] As department stores attempted to figure out how to follow their clientele to the suburbs, other retail experts saw suburban expansion as too risky. Many felt that suburban retailing would never compare to the quality and volume of downtown stores.[15]

Even Larry Smith, the leading economic analyst for shopping center deals, held a gloomy opinion of them. "It is a well-known fact that insurance companies at the present time are going through a period of uncertainty as to the soundness of shopping center investments, especially when the investment necessitates a single mortgage of $6,000,000 to $7,000,000 or more," Smith explained. He suggested that the way to overcome this problem was "segregated financing," where "several companies may finance independently different sections of the shopping center."[16] Some department stores soon picked up on (and modified) Smith's ideas about segregated financing. Perhaps, they reasoned, they could trade on their reputations and turn a profit by enticing other stores to their shopping center developments.

Though the Eastland project in Detroit had been abandoned, Gruen was still employed by Hudson's department store, and he immediately began pushing for the construction of a different shopping center modeled along these lines. Ten miles from Hudson's downtown flagship store, the company broke ground for what it promised would be America's largest shopping center, with the largest department store branch in the world. Gruen devised a plan for Northland that took American shopping center design in a new direction, using outdoor malls, fountains, sculpture, benches, and colonnades to create a dense shopping environment, a pleasurable space for pedestrians.

Northland proved to be a gigantic undertaking. Capitalized to the tune of $25 million, with nearly a hundred stores, a giant Hudson's branch, and its own road system, Northland greatly stretched Gruen's new firm, Victor Gruen Associates. After the protracted dissolution of Gruen and Krummeck's marriage and business, he and his five new partners had founded the new firm in 1951. The partners had an equal share of the firm and received equal salaries, with two exceptions. First, the firm would bear Gruen's name. And, second, Victor Gruen Associates would pay Gruen's alimony and child support. It was a time of many new beginnings for Gruen, for he also married a New York fashion editor for *Retailing Daily*, Lazette Van Houten. The couple had met at a party at the Manhattan apartment of a curator for the Museum of Modern Art.[17]

For Northland, Larry Smith undertook an extensive research project on other shopping centers' parking arrangements, flying to Seattle and studying architect John Graham's traffic plan for Northgate. Victor Gruen Associates also opened a Detroit office, in addition to its Beverly Hills headquarters. "Planning, architecture, transportation engineering, mechanical engineering on a large scale, electrical engineering, interior work, landscape architecture, graphic design" were all a part of Northland, Gruen remembered later. One of Gruen's partners, Karl Van Leuven, recalled visiting Northland's construction site. "There were all those monstrous earth moving machines pushing and shoving and changing the face of some 200 acres," he recalled. After watching this impressive effort, Gruen turned to Van Leuven and softly said, "My God but we've got a lot of nerve."[18]

Northland had not one but five openings. In March 1954, Hudson's arranged previews for employees, journalists, politicians, the neighborhood, and finally the general public. Northland's executives plotted to "spread the opening, from the standpoint of curiosity value, over a nineday period." Hudson's kept its advertising to a minimum, banking on the Detroit newspapers' coverage to generate excitement and keep the shopping center's opening before the public eye. Management promised to ensure that "the newspaper, radio and television publicity . . . will be extremely heavy for a period of several days prior to and following the opening." The newspapers had their own interest in Northland's success—retailers were the papers' largest advertisers. Small type at the bottom of the department store's regular ads (two a day) announced that Hudson's wares were available both downtown and at Northland. Northland's management even urged its tenants not to promote the public opening. They feared that extra promotion would only lead to confusion, traffic jams, unsatisfied crowds, and eventual bad publicity.[19]

Hudson's tried to anticipate everything to guarantee that Northland's opening would be a tremendous success. Municipal policemen directed traffic into the shopping center. Dignitaries had reserved parking spaces in Lot A. Parking lots were equipped with a key machine for shoppers who had lost their car keys. Northland gave a free gallon of gasoline to any shopper who was running low. Six private policemen patrolled the center to maintain order and pass out directories. Management opened an office for lost children staffed by a nurse. In the department store

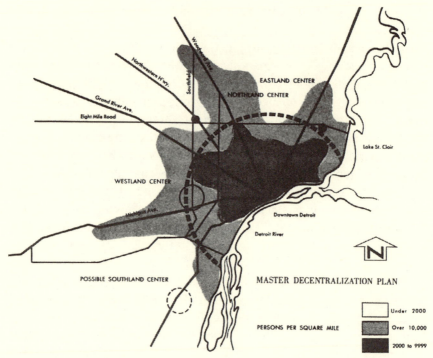

FIGURE 22. Decentralization plan for Hudson's department store showing the proposed construction of four suburban shopping centers. From Victor Gruen and Larry Smith, *Shopping Towns U.S.A.* (New York: Reinhold, 1960), 36.

alone, twelve detectives—six plainclothes and six uniformed—made the rounds. Hudson's expertly handled the press, preparing a fifty-four-page press kit that included biographies of the architects and developers, photos available for publication, and descriptions of every Northland merchant and contractor. Press releases were sent to over three hundred prominent newspapers, news magazines, and fashion publications across the country, attracting the attention of the *Wall Street Journal*, the Associated Press, the United Press, *Time, Look, Life, Newsweek, Business Week*, and *U.S. News and World Report*, which all sent reporters. *Vogue, Progressive Architecture, Ladies Home Journal*, and *Good Housekeeping* also covered the opening, which remained newsworthy for a solid week in Detroit.[20]

Northland was an instant success. "Attendance is averaging 40,000 to 50,000 a day," *Architectural Forum* cheerfully reported, and in April

1959 alone, nearly 330,000 people visited. This "supershopping center," Dorothy Thompson informed readers of *Ladies Home Journal*, "is the most ambitious of such mercantile centers in America or the world." "When the passenger has left the parking lot, he is in a shoppers' paradise." Thompson praised Gruen's design for being "extremely practical" and "perfectly beautiful." Further, the shopping center represented "a model of enlightened planning and social co-operation." In an enthusiastic first-person testimonial, Thompson related how she shopped for six hours straight "without feeling more than a momentary fatigue when I sat on a bench in the bright spring sunshine." With auditoriums, infirmary, post office, bank, and restaurant, "Northland is far more than a shopping center."[21] Another author, writing for *Harper's Magazine*, grappled with "The Big Change in Suburbia." With hundreds of regional shopping centers on the drawing boards, he became exhausted trying to list them all. Instead, he focused on what he considered the country's most significant example. He chose Northland. "Here, surely is a revolutionary step," he wrote, "toward that 'urban decentralization' which regional plan experts have been hopefully talking about for a generation."[22] As this author realized, Northland's success depended on Detroit's decentralization.

When Northland opened, Detroit was the fifth largest city in America and the fastest growing city in the East or Midwest. Its entire metropolitan region grew by 25 percent between 1940 and 1950.[23] And Gruen had located Northland in the fastest growing part of Detroit, its northern suburbs. Located just across the city line in Oakland County, Northland was only ten miles from the city center, but a world apart. *Architectural Forum* reported that Northland shoppers' most frequent comment was "You wouldn't know you were in Detroit."[24] There were 550,000 people within a twenty-minute drive of the shopping center. From 1951 to 1954, while Northland was being planned, 100,000 new residents moved into Oakland County. While parts of Oakland County, especially the town of Royal Oak, grew before World War II, the major expansion occurred after 1945. Single-family residences made up nearly all of this growth. One scholar estimated that the area around Northland had grown over 200 percent from 1940 to 1950.[25] "The fastest-growing, wealthiest suburban region of the Detroit metropolis," was one newspaper's description of Northland's surrounding suburbs.[26] Indeed, the shopping center's next-door-neighbors lived in Magnolia Gardens, an all-white neighborhood with over two hundred houses costing forty thousand dollars each, five times the price of an average suburban house.[27] Northland would be dependent on these new white suburbanites for their sales.

Gruen had spent four long years trying to build a shopping center with Hudson's, so he was thrilled with Northland's completion. He flew to Detroit from Los Angeles to oversee the final touches and celebrate his accomplishment. Ever attuned to the value of free publicity, Gruen made sure to appear at the press preview. He delivered a rousing speech and took the press on a walking tour of his creation.[28]

Gruen began with a grandiose statement. "This is not just the opening of a Shopping Center," he solemnly stated, "but an important milestone for city planners, architects, economists, merchandisers, and the American public at large." America would forever be changed with the arrival of his "Shopping Center of Tomorrow." He told reporters to ignore Northland's impressive size. Never mind that it was the world's largest shopping center with the largest department store branch on the largest site with the greatest number of stores in the world. Rather Gruen claimed "the newness of its concept" held more significance than its over one million square feet of retail stores. At Northland, he explained, the latest concepts in city planning were applied to retailing. By using "scientific design" at Northland, Gruen claimed that he had stamped out commercialism's "ugly rash on the body of our cities." "Countless smoke stacks, telephone poles, power poles, dangling wire, air-conditioning ducts, and myriads of ugly signs" were eliminated at his shopping center. Of course, the shopping center was a direct result of suburbanization—the "powerful wave of migration from the city to the suburbs," which were disconnected from "the mother city," and only made possible by automobiles. When designed correctly, with ample parking, the shopping center could solve every suburbanite's "cultural, civic, and social" needs.

While other American architects employed a simple mall plan that planted grass on Main Street, in Northland Gruen went much farther. The secret was what he referred to as a "cluster scheme." Rather than placing two rows of stores parallel to each other across a grassy mall, he arranged Northland's buildings to form "a number of park-like areas of various shapes, sizes, and treatments." "The space between the buildings" proved Northland's single most important "town-planning element," Gruen informed the press. Depending on their size, he gave the open spaces different names: courts, terraces, malls, or lanes, explaining how he had borrowed the idea from Europe's centuries-old cities.[29] In

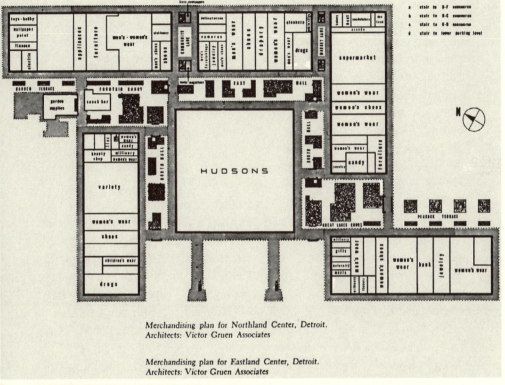

Merchandising plan for Northland Center, Detroit.
Architects: Victor Gruen Associates

Merchandising plan for Eastland Center, Detroit.
Architects: Victor Gruen Associates

FIGURE 23. Plan of Northland shopping center showing the pedestrian malls surrounding Hudson's department store. From Victor Gruen and Larry Smith, *Shopping Towns USA* (New York: Reinhold, 1960), 133.

Northland's colonnaded walks, whimsical sculptures, generous courts, bubbling fountains, and pedestrian-friendly malls, Gruen boasted that he had reinvented a time-tested classic for American suburbia. "Northland is a city within a city," Hudson's advertised. With its own power plant, water tower, police force, and parkland, the shopping center appeared to be a self-contained, private municipality.

If Northland felt like a city within a city, its success depended on a Motor City invention—cars. However, Gruen worried that cars also threatened to destroy the suburban good life. "The millions of gasoline-driven 'spirits' get into each others' way and choke the highways, roads, and parking lots."[30] With 8,344 parking spaces and color-coded parking lots, Gruen wanted to make parking as efficient and painless as possible. After much study, Gruen used forty-five-degree parking spaces, extra-wide eight-foot-eight-inch stalls, double lines between spaces, and bright lights over the parking lots. "A complete, integrated, one-stop shopping center tuned to the Motor Age," the Automobile Manufacturers Association enthused. Gruen wanted to make the transition from driver to customer as easy as possible. "Customers," *Architectural Forum* noted about another Gruen retail design, "feel they're halfway in the store by the time they've parked the car."[31] Unlike his Milliron's design, Gruen located Northland not at an intersection but between two main roads. This strategy gave him extra space to build an interior road system completely separate from the public roads. Drivers arriving at Northland exited the main road on long ramps that dropped them onto a circular road surrounding Northland's parking lots. Shoppers then chose from ten different entrances to the parking lots. This strategy—of bringing traffic quickly into the loop road and then dispersing it—prevented congestion on the public roads (one of the chief complaints about Morris Ketchum's Shoppers World). He planned as much for the pedestrian's enjoyment as the parker's ease. "Within the spaces freed from vehicular movement, open-air civic meetings and concerts should be encouraged in the warm summer months," Gruen rhapsodized.[32] Cars and people would have their own separate systems of circulation.

Northland's cluster scheme radically broke with other shopping center arrangements. By the 1940s it was a commonplace for architects to design shopping centers with a grassy courtyard; Gruen had done just that for his 194X proposal. *Architectural Forum* dubbed the trend "Grass on Main Street."[33] Both Northgate and Shopper's World had done the same, bringing a park into the heart of a commercial center.[34] Gruen, by contrast, belittled the pastoral concept. He frequently explained that he had one goal for his shopping centers: he wanted to create a downtown, not a new commercial park. "The slogan 'Grass on Main Street '. . . betrays a defeatist attitude suggesting the injection of suburban values into an essentially urban environment," Gruen passionately contended. "There should be more pavement than planting." He wanted the shopping center to provide urban density for a suburban community. "A mall is a public space . . . committed to intensive urban activity," one of Gruen's partners explained about their shopping center designs. As Gruen later said, Northland was neither a "machine for selling" nor a "nostalgic reminiscence of the village green" but "an essentially urban environment."[35] With density, diversity, and limited views, a Northland shopper, Gruen explained, would have "new experiences, new surprises, a change of pace, and a change of atmosphere."

FIGURE 24. Photograph of the newly completed Northland shopping center, 1954. Courtesy Time Life/Getty Pictures.

As Gruen sought to create an urban-like experience for suburbanites, his inspiration was informed by the city he knew best, the city of his youth. "Something of the Vienna waltz pervades Northland," reporter Dorothy Thompson wisely observed in *Ladies Home Journal.* Thompson was not alone in picking up on Gruen's Old World roots and inspirations.[36] Another journalist compared a Gruen shopping center to the best of Europe's past: St. Mark's in Venice, Copenhagen's old red brick, "antiquated areas remindful of an Old Roman Road," and the glassed-in splendor of Victor Emmanuel Galleria of Milan, Italy. Readers were informed that Gruen designed his shopping centers following an old European tradition where the architect had complete control over the building, its furniture, art, and all its fixtures. "Victor Gruen designed Southdale from memories of Europe," an *Architectural Forum* review concluded about a later shopping center.[37]

Of course, if Gruen referenced a European city in his American shopping center, it would be Vienna—the only city that truly mattered to him. Gruen's feelings about Vienna were uncomplicated. "He loved Vienna," his daughter Peggy Gruen recalled.[38] Personally and aesthetically, Vienna held Gruen's imagination and shaped his personality. As former partner Cesar Pelli explained, "Victor was much more of a Viennese than a Jew or a Socialist."[39] To Gruen, Vienna was at the pinnacle of urbanity and urban design.

Gruen tenaciously hung on to the memories of the golden days of his Viennese youth. He remembered 1920s Vienna as Europe's "center of intellectual and cultural life." It was the "shining example of social progress as exemplified by large public housing programs and important achievements in public health and welfare." Of course, for Gruen to celebrate Vienna, he also had to forget his own difficult days in the city. He especially had to block out his persecution at the hands of Nazis and his flight from his beloved city. In Beverly Hills, Gruen entertained his friends with stories about 1920s Vienna because, according to his daughter, the city symbolized "a great time for him." She remembered him "singing these old Viennese songs" to amuse his dinner guests.[40] Nostalgia for Vienna's good old days inspired Gruen's ideas about a well-designed, urbane city.

After World War II, Gruen returned to his beloved city for a ten-day trip, to inquire about family property that he had hurriedly left when the Nazis took over Austria in 1938.[41] Gruen always noted this Viennese trip as a milestone of his career; by the mid-1950s he was vacationing there regularly during August, often accompanied by his children. He escaped to Europe to be inspired; he enjoyed lounging in the cafes, sitting in the squares, and looking at the architecture. On one of his many Viennese vacations, he made a purchase to connect himself with the city's artistic heyday. He bought a Gustav Klimt painting, *Schloß Kammer am Attersee*. He also purchased three drawings by Klimt and Egon Schiele, a turn-of-the-century Viennese modernist. Upon his return to California, Gruen proudly displayed this artwork, in a later advertising film that he made for Austrian Airlines, the camera lingered on the Klimt painting, as if to authenticate his Austrian roots. By the early 1960s Gruen, through his firm, had purchased a flat in Vienna's Central District, around the corner from his childhood home. His daughter remembered that "his apartment in Vienna was probably the most expressive of his own ideas," because he never fully enjoyed living in Beverly Hills.[42] By the mid-1960s Gruen had bought a country house outside Vienna in the Prein, which he lovingly restored. To this house he brought one reminder of his California life—a swimming pool. As Gruen traveled—psychologically and physically—back and forth between Los Angeles and Vienna, he also sought to blend the two in his architecture.

While Gruen attempted to solve the formal and financial challenges of his American shopping centers, he also rebuilt his memory of 1920s Vienna, and of Europe in general. In *Shopping Towns USA*, he juxtaposed photographs of people dancing in one of his shopping centers and in the streets of Paris.[43] Frequently in speeches he paired slides of European cities with American shopping centers—Venice's Piazza San Marco and Northland for example. Through such juxtapositions Gruen suggested the possibilities for urban activities in the shopping center and lent his commercial architecture an air of respectability. "I took this picture of a fountain figure in a Swiss town," he once said. "I asked myself, 'Why can't we have that in our American cities—peace, serenity, the integration of the arts and architecture?'" He fantasized about "a Europeanization of America" through his shopping centers.[44]

Gruen often lamented how Americans flew to Paris, Rome, Florence, or Vienna simply so they might stroll through the city. He wondered, "What is it—what makes Europe the aim of millions of American tourists every year?" His response: "It is the unity between human and habitation and nature which are married happily to landscape," along with Europe's "rich public social life." American tourists—"who at home are usually not willing to walk from the garage to the house"—loved walking in Europe's picturesque cities.[45] Gruen wanted the shopping center to be a mini-European vacation for all Americans.

In one speech, Gruen denigrated American cities as "seventeen suburbs in search of a city." "In contrast to the hearts of American cities, the core areas or inner cities of European towns . . . are still filled, morning and evening, day and night, weekdays and Sundays, with urban dynamism," Gruen wrote. On another occasion, he compared Los Angeles' Ventura Boulevard with Le Gran Boulevard in Paris. Paris' streets possessed "the character of real cities, urban qualities and urban functions." Ventura had nothing to recommend it. It had no "life," "vitality," or "human functions." "I haven't seen people sit at sidewalk tables on Ventura Boulevard because there is nothing to look at," Gruen complained. "I haven't seen the kind of life and vitality and intermingling of very many human functions and urban functions." Americans, he lamented, gave up community and chose to live "detached lives in detached houses."[46] Their ugly environment debased their lives. Through his shopping center designs, Gruen hoped to offer a corrective to this grim and soulless American environment.

Not surprisingly, for Gruen, the European city symbolized more than a physical plan to be copied. The cities represented the greatest accomplishments: democracy, high culture, and community thrived in Europe's dense urban environment. To take his readers on a tour through the perfect European city, Gruen rhapsodized about Vienna. "The city is the countless cafes and sidewalk cafes of Vienna," where rich and poor alike could gather and discuss their world.[47] He romantically described his own Viennese life. He walked out of his flat and meandered through the streets. Stopping in cafes, bakeries, and stores, he enjoyed the city's architecture and atmosphere. "From my residence there I can reach, within a few minutes' walk, places of the most diversified character: the opera, the famous concert hall of the Musikverein; the Konzerthaus and two theaters; shops and stores of every description; elegant restaurants . . . both elegant and modest cafes," Gruen wrote. This arrangement brought together "a potpourri of all economic and cultural groups, from modest workmen to millionaires." Gruen believed that, in America, people would come together at the shopping center, which would "fill the vacuum created by the absence of social, cultural, and civic crystallization points in our vast suburban areas."[48] He envisioned his shopping centers having "a community center, an auditorium, a children's play area, a large number of public eating places and, in the courts and malls, opportunities for relaxation, exhibits and public events."[49] This nearly utopian socialist dream, however, would be built by American capitalists.

Gruen believed that special events were one of the best ways to attract people to the shopping center. Baltimore developer James Rouse concurred. "Special events," Rouse said, "are designed to establish and continually strengthen the shopping center's position as a real community center." "The cumulative effect of bringing people to the center," he promised, "is to establish close identification by the public with the center, and thus serve to increase traffic and business."[50] In 1961 the Urban Land Institute heralded "Kiddylands," "Children's Nurseries," "Community Halls," "Cooking schools, homemakers shows," directories for "public notices," bowling alleys, movie theaters, and ice-skating rinks for "their importance to good public relations."[51] Shopping center management staged everything from circuses to celebrity appearances, car shows, and orchestra concerts. Gruen wanted shopping centers to recreate a public culture full of entertainment, events, density, and crowds. Consumerism, in Gruen's vision, would become a way to express social connections and to reconstitute a social community through consumerism. Not unlike other European modern architects, Gruen dreamed of creating a total environment in order to reform people's daily lives and saw no irony in using capitalism to build "a new world, a world belonging all to you." Rather than simply being a prophet for greater profits, Gruen sincerely hoped to use consumerism to create environments that would reform what he saw as, the "unsightly, costly, and frenzied" commercial culture of suburbia.[52] A well-planned shopping center would clean up the strip's neon, turn a tidy profit, and forge a community, Gruen promised.

To remedy suburbia's lack of culture Gruen turned to high art. He convinced Hudson's to spend $200,000 on whimsical sculptures to decorate the courts and malls. "The developer," Gruen remarked, "is given the function of a supporter and encourager of arts." "In every court or mall a delightful piece of modern sculpture attracts the eye," one journalist told her readers about Northland. "Fountains spray water into the air; everywhere there are solid and handsome oak benches where one can sit and gossip or smoke." With "fanciful scenes" created by a giraffe sculpture and a fish mobile, *Life* enthused, "shoppers may just sit and enjoy Northland's architecture, art, flowers and music, that play all the time." [53]

Gruen also persuaded Hudson's to take the landscaping of Northland seriously. The company bought 1,500 trees, 625 flowering trees, 1,900 evergreens, 18,000 shrubs, and 23,000 flowers. He convinced Hudson's to invest heavily in fashioning a park-like atmosphere, even designing special heaters to keep the fountains running through Detroit's cold winters. All this outlay on art and landscaping was not simply in the service of a developer's "civic responsibility." It was not a superfluous expense. The pragmatic president of Hudson's department store emphasized that Northland's "greatest advertising value . . . is its beauty." The art and landscaping "will contribute to the attracting power of the center" and "to the business volume"—in other words, to the bottom line.[54]

Shopping centers such as Northland began to symbolize America's abundance in the suburbs. In the breadth of the shopping center's consumer options, in the variety of its wares, in the very opulence of its spaces, the shopping center became part of the American myth of a consistently abundant economy. The dizzying profusion of shopping centers—"popping up every minute"—also gave rise to strident attacks against consumerism. Journalist Dorothy Thompson, writing in *Ladies Home Journal*, was ambivalent. On one hand, she blamed all manner of ills on Americans' infatuation with getting and spending. "The struggle

FIGURE 25. Giraffe sculptures at Northland that Gruen claimed could work as well as a show window to entice shoppers. Image appeared in "20th-Century Bazaar," *Life* 37, no. 30 (August 1954): 119. Courtesy Time Life/Getty Pictures.

FIGURE 26. Workers tending the extensive landscaping at Northland. From J. L. Hudson's Department Store Archives, Northland Shopping Center.

FIGURE 27. Crowd at one of the many Northland events, c. 1956. From J. L. Hudson's Department Store Archives, Northland Shopping Center.

FIGURE 28. Circus elephant performing at J. L. Hudson's Eastland Shopping Center, c. 1959. From J. L. Hudson's Department Store Archives, Northland Shopping Center.

to attract the public eye," Thompson observed, was responsible "for land speculation, the inflation of real estate values, and the creation of commercial and residential slums." The "commercial spirit" has been described as "the antithesis of the aesthetic, defacing beautiful landscapes with screaming billboards, and blotting out the sky with lurid neon lights." On the other hand, all these accusations may be true, Thompson admitted. But with Gruen's Northland, commercialism wore "a new look." With "music in the air, faint, sweet and gay," Northland created "a sense of leisure, fun, and . . . time." Thompson saw these improvements ushering in a much-welcomed era where, "the much-berated shopkeeper gilds the columns of his emporium with the lily-work of art." Before the arrival of one of Gruen's shopping centers, a local art critic complained that "a store is a store is a store." With the new shopping center's arrival, however, the whole tone and level of retailing was elevated.[55]

While Gruen earned his living by tempting consumers and promoting shopping, his own relationship to commercialism was more ambivalent. Both his children believed that Gruen strongly disliked shopping. "I can't really picture him shopping. I think that was something he left for his wives," his daughter explained. "In the shopping center of tomorrow there are many other things to do besides shopping," Gruen once claimed.[56] Gruen wanted to use commercial projects to link consumerism to an entire range of human expressions—political, social, and cultural, as well as material. But he didn't want to do it himself.

For Gruen and many other recent émigrés who had come of age in the economic downturns of Europe in the 1920s and 1930s, America seemed a dreamland of never-ending abundance. No one could truly appreciate the world of American consumerism, Gruen would write, who has not lived in a world of scarcity (as he had lived in a small flat with his mother, his new wife, and his studio). The colorful, vast, and ever-expanding vista of American consumerism seemed to offer a welcome antidote to frugality and scrimping. But influenced by Socialism, Gruen refused to see consumerism as an end in itself; he wanted to use consumerism's popularity to advance other cultural and social reforms. Indeed, though consumerism seemed to dominate the American dream, it was only part of that dream, Gruen insisted. People may have desired more and more material goods, but they also wanted to gather and gossip with their neighbors. "Whether we understand it or not, we enjoy living together—we enjoy the feeling of being part of the herd," Gruen explained to one Los Angeles reporter. Humans were "social animals" who wanted to take part in "city functions such as the opera and theater." And if that social feeling was lost, Gruen worried, "we feel less and less a part of the social herd and the courage that we draw from being part of everything is diminished."[57] He insisted that a contemporary architect's task was to bring out "the best features of a free democratic society with creativeness and imagination." In retail facilities, Gruen saw democracy's edifice, and throughout his career he saw an underlying moral element in his environments: improved spaces created better, happier people and a better democracy. He stressed that planning environments did not symbolize totalitarianism but instead the application of "democratic" principles of "law and order" to "the physical environment." It would all lead to "life . . . liberty . . . and the pursuit of happiness," Gruen claimed.[58]

By emphasizing the high-minded potential of commercialism, Gruen edged perilously close to a rejection of all retailing, belittling nearly all American retail developments that he had not designed. "The suburban store strip shows commercialism at its worst," Gruen once complained.[59] He characterized the developments, especially commercial strips, as horrible aesthetic blights on the environment. Of course, since Gruen had been relying on store design to earn a living for the last twenty years, he did not turn his critical lens on himself. Rather, he portrayed his own shopping center projects as major experiments in city planning. He continually stressed that his shopping centers would clean up, not debase, the city.

Gruen's critique of the United States extended well beyond crass commercialism. His attempts to reform the environment, or create European cities for American suburbanites, started from a bitter critique of Americans' present ways of living. His most acidic comments surfaced when he, as he often did, compared America to Europe. In one speech, which he delivered on many occasions over the course of at least eight years, Gruen described a lovely summer day when he sat at a Venetian cafe in the beautiful, even holy, Piazza San Marco. As he sipped his espresso and contemplated Venice's transcendent beauty, he was struck by a nightmare and began imagining what Americans would do to the glorious Piazza.[60] "A nightmarish transformation of the Piazza San Marco took hold." American cars, traffic, billboards, noise, and signs suddenly destroyed the peaceful Italian square. He emotionally recounted his dream for his American audiences: "Around the Campanile grew lean-to structures—a gas station, and hamburger stand, and telephone booths. Wires were strung along in web-like fashion overhead. Fluorescent lighting flared up, drowning the moonlight. The large clock on the tower carried neon lights saying, 'THE PAUSE THAT REFRESHES.' The four bronze horses on the Duomo suddenly glowed red and announced a brand of gasoline."[61] From highways to downtowns, advertising, stores, and suburbs, Gruen saw nothing good in America's appearance. He dismissed the American "suburbscape" as "plush settlements of mock historic mansions." He hated "the packed grounds of anonymous mass housing where dingbats are lined up for inspection." Because of the automobile, American cities were an "unfit, unlivable environment, inefficient and ugly."[62]

The country's gross appearance would lead to personal and political failings as well. With widespread suburbanization, "people would live in detached houses and would detach themselves from common experiences." "This detachment," Gruen explained, "would diminish our interest in public and cultural affairs." "Our minds [will] become as canned as the products we buy."[63] He envisioned reforming all of America through his architectural creations; he would change entire regions and entire mindsets. Not surprisingly, Gruen's solution to these major problems was more and bolder planning.

Through shopping centers, Gruen had invented a means to attract capital to advance his large-scale ambitions—changing consumerism, reordering cities, and profoundly influencing American culture in the process. His firm perfected the essentials of a successful shopping center. The scale changed, the city changed, the site changed, locations and clients presented different problems, but Gruen prospered. He had the design of shopping centers down to a science and often offered a similar solution for very different sites. And he continued to set his sights on ever-larger projects. Indeed, for his next major shopping center commission, Gruen tackled the largest environment he had worked with to date. The work would prove to be Gruen's greatest success and largest failure.

CHAPTER SIX

Planning the New "Suburbscape"

Shoppers are, in a sense, a captive audience in the clustered mall.

—*Women's Wear Daily*, 1956

In 1954 Gruen was beginning to enjoy national success. Northland was one of the most popular and profitable shopping centers in the country, and newspapers and magazines unabashedly celebrated his achievement. Indeed, it was at this time in his career that Gruen seemed to hit his stride. And it was then that he came up with his single greatest contribution to American retailing, and perhaps to American consumer culture: the enclosed shopping mall. While he had first proposed the idea in 1950 for Montclair shopping center in Houston, he still had not realized the concept of bringing many different stores and entertainment under one roof.

The ambitious shopping center proposal was made for Dayton's department store of Minneapolis. It was a plan born of hubris, a dear memory, and a future dream. Dayton's first announced its Southdale project in June 1952.[1] After nine months of market analysis undertaken by Larry Smith, the department store acquired 463 acres southwest of Minneapolis, seven miles from the loop, paying approximately $1.5 million for the land, or nearly $3,000 an acre. Dayton's immediately petitioned the town of Edina for a zoning change from residential to commercial. The department store cum developer also mailed a flyer to Edina residents announcing a public hearing where Dayton's would explain Southdale's "importance to modern suburban living" and "the question of zoning." The small town acted quickly and gave Dayton's the zoning change by July. "An almost unanimous show of hands by an estimated 250 to 300 Edina citizens resulted in the Edina Village voting necessary zoning changes," one retailing magazine reported.[2] Dayton's

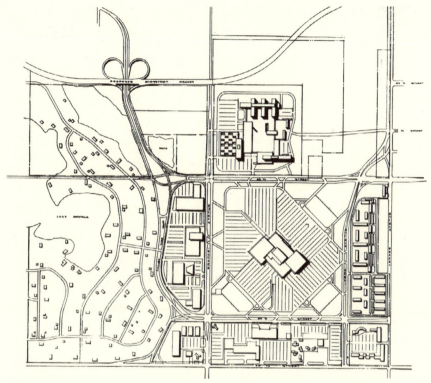

FIGURE 29. Gruen's proposed master plan for the area around Southdale Shopping Center in Edina, Minnesota, conceived to limit the amount of suburban sprawl; the plan was not implemented. From Victor Gruen and Larry Smith, *Shopping Towns USA* (New York: Reinhold, 1960), 108.

set aside eighty-four acres for Gruen's shopping center, which would serve an intended audience of 210,000. This was no ordinary shopping center; the department store promised to build an entire new community. It would transform the sleepy town of 15,000 into the Minneapolis suburb of Edina. The remaining four hundred acres of the tract would be developed following a Master Plan that included houses, apartment buildings, a park, a medical center, a lake, highways, and schools. The department store would plan, finance, and build the entire suburban community.

For his Minneapolis commission, Gruen closely followed Northland's successes. He sought to bring commerce, entertainment, and art to the Minneapolis suburbs. In two respects, however, Gruen broke new

FIGURE 30. Aerial view of the completed Southdale Shopping Center, 1956. Courtesy Time Life/Getty Pictures.

ground with Southdale. One proved to be an overnight success and the other a horrible failure. Gruen designed Southdale to be a completely covered market, and after it opened developers and architects across the country took Gruen's concept of an enclosed shopping center and ran with it. But he also designed it as one part of a larger development, and few followed that piece of his plan.[3] In due time, Gruen would pin many of suburbia's problems on this one piece of overlooked advice. In 1956, however, Gruen basked in the spotlight of his success with Southdale.

In October 1956, Southdale opened its doors as the first enclosed shopping center in America, progenitor of the ubiquitous mall that in twenty short years would come to dominate retailing. With seventy-two stores on two floors, 810,000 square feet of retailing, 5,200 parking spaces, a soaring garden court, and two full-size department stores, the $20-million Southdale was a wonder on many levels. Not only was it the ultimate and largest expression of retail's move to the suburbs, but as an enclosed shopping center, Southdale created an entirely new retail environment, a new commercial palace for suburbanites.

Journalists from all of the country's top magazines came for the Minneapolis shopping center's opening. *Life, Fortune, Time, Women's Wear Daily*, the *New York Times, Business Week*, and *Newsweek* all covered

FIGURE 31. View of the interior court at Southdale, c. 1956. Courtesy Time Life/Getty Pictures.

the event. The national and local press wore out superlatives attempting to capture the feeling of Southdale. "The Splashiest Center in the U.S.," *Life* sang. The glossy weekly praised the incongruous combination of a "goldfish pond, birds, art and 10 acres of stores all . . . under one Minnesota roof." A "pleasure-dome-with-parking," *Time* cheered. One journalist announced that overnight Southdale had become an integral "part of the American Way." Another magazine declared that with Southdale

FIGURE 32. View of the interior of the Southdale Court with pond in fore-ground and bird cage to the left, c. 1956. Courtesy Southdale Shopping Mall.

FIGURE 33. Gruen giving a tour of the newly opened Southdale Shopping Center, 1956. Courtesy Time Life/Getty Pictures.

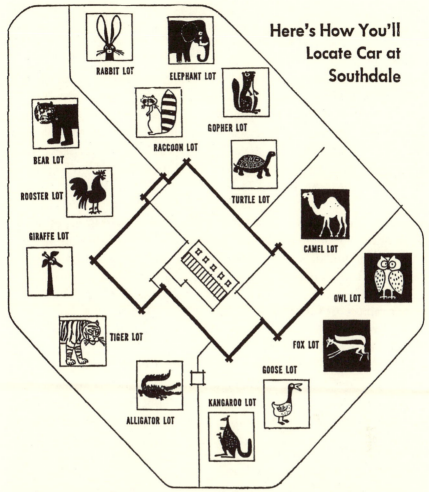

Here's How You'll Locate Car at Southdale

RABBIT LOT

ELEPHANT LOT

GOPHER LOT

RACCOON LOT

BEAR LOT

ROOSTER LOT

TURTLE LOT

GIRAFFE LOT

CAMEL LOT

OWL LOT

TIGER LOT

FOX LOT

GOOSE LOT

ALLIGATOR LOT

KANGAROO LOT

FIGURE 34. The fifteen parking lots of Southdale with their animal signs. From Southdale directory, c. 1956. Dayton-Hudson Archives, Minneapolis.

you had the creation of "America's newest institution, the suburban shopping center."[4] With its sculpture, glass mosaics, fountains, exotic birds, and tropical plants, it was also the most sumptuous.

Minneapolis newspapers—as direct beneficiaries of retail's advertising dollar—had many kind words for Southdale. From the beginning of 1956 until the center opened in October, forty-one stories appeared in the Minneapolis papers—about one a week. Highlighting everything from the central heating plant and artists' decorations to the parking lots' animal names and store leasing, the papers produced a stream of articles to whet shoppers' appetites.[5] The publicity worked well. On its first day of business, 75,000 sightseers flocked to Southdale. Journalists focused on what seemed to be its most novel feature: its interior court. One local reporter put Southdale on a domestic scale—"the equivalent of 650 two-bedroom houses."[6]

For Gruen, Southdale represented the fruition of what he could only dream about thirteen years earlier. It is difficult to capture how novel an enclosed mall was for 1950s Americans. Southdale, *Business Week* explained, "has an unusual layout—all indoors, with stores arranged around a huge roofed court" which provided "July Heat for January Shoppers." The enclosed shopping center made "a Better Outdoors Indoors," *Architectural Record* marveled. "The Garden Court is one of the largest indoor public areas in the United States," one local paper boasted.[7] Southdale's enclosed court and malls represented the most lasting of Gruen's many contributions to American retailing.

If Northland had relied on twirling mobiles, blooming tulips, and resting places to satisfy the shopper, at Southdale Gruen went much, much farther. At its center Gruen designed the fanciful and immense "Garden Court of Perpetual Spring." Five stories high and a block long, the court seemed a gigantic space. It was not, however, a vast, empty one. Like a carnival, it contained much to distract the eye. *Architectural Forum* fell into a reverie listing the court's many attractions: "sculpture, sidewalk cafe, marble mail-drop to post office below, newsstand walls with abstractions in glass mosaic, cigar-store Indian, 42'-tall eucalyptus, birdcage [with] fifty brightly plumaged little birds, a children's carnival with real zoo." One journalist guided readers through Southdale's "huge retail tunnel." With "store after store . . . stretched into the distance," crowds "sipped coffee at Woolworth's sidewalk cafe or stared through the [stores'] glass walls" while "Hawaiian singers, in costume, crooned softly" and everyone drank "free Dole pineapple juice." Gruen filled the garden court with stores, vistas, color, and light. Natural sunlight poured through the skylights. Fifty-foot-high trees grew in the court. Gruen proudly explained that Southdale's "artificial climate" allowed for the "growth of California flora with magnolia trees, a eucalyptus tree, and even orchids."[8] The court also contained a juice bar, a newsstand, a tobacco store, an airlines kiosk, and a radio booth. "In the mall itself are spirited kiosks [that have] glass mosaic murals with porcelain enamel surround on both exterior walls," *Architectural Forum* reported.[9] Pedestrian bridges criss-crossed the court and two escalators glided people up to second-floor stores. Woolworth's operated a little cafe with wrought-iron tables and umbrellas. *Life* waxed ecstatic about a fifty-foot-high sculpture "of bronzed, lacquered steel plates" which created "FUTURISTIC FRILLS" for the shopper.[10] Just as Gruen had hoped, people came to Southdale as much for the crowds, art, and entertainment as for the shopping. During its first year, the center averaged 50,000 visitors a day.

Though Gruen had suggested an enclosed shopping center in his 194X exercise and had expanded on the concept in 1950 for Montclair in Houston, the idea as realized in Southdale appeared unheralded to everyone else. In Southdale's soaring court, Gruen created a space both overly determined and overly distracting. "The visual result," one writer perceptively observed, "is a tremendous variation and liveliness held together by the strength of the central plaza court with its escalators." One retailer even complained that Southdale's majestic interior so overwhelmed people that they forgot to shop. *Time* announced that, at Southdale, Gruen had created a "Carnival Atmosphere." In one interview, Gruen explained the underlying purpose of an enclosed mall. He wanted people to "feel that they are outdoors—to provide psychological as well as visual contrast and relief from indoor shops." Shoppers, he added, would also be "provided with . . . the visual enjoyment of landscaping, fountains, and sculpture."[11] Although Gruen sought to entertain visitors during their retail adventures, he had also devised the court to produce more profits.

"The strikingly handsome and colorful center is constantly crowded," *Fortune* happily reported. The magazine lauded the way Southdale's "good, gay design is bringing good, brisk business"; the "sparkling lights and bright colors provide a continuous invitation to look up ahead, to stroll on to the next store, and to buy." The two-story court created "a wonderfully exuberant shopping scene," *Architectural Forum* gushed. The immense court gave Gruen a way to bring gaudy colors, activity, and entertaining distractions that were both invisible to the outside and lured people inside. Gruen fashioned the atmosphere to attract, entertain, and maintain shoppers. He wanted people to enjoy buying goods. Through strategic design "shopping [will be] an easier, more pleasurable, and therefore more desirable activity," Gruen explained to Boston merchants the year before Southdale opened. [12]

For Northland, Gruen had brought people out of their cars and into courtyards surrounded by stores. Southdale took that concept to new heights. One of the most important consequences of building an enclosed shopping space was the density of shoppers and shops. At Southdale, visitors were at pains to avoid the pull of the lights, colors, and wares of the surrounding stores. *Time* described Southdale as the perfect mix of "piped music, splashing waterfalls and clanging cash registers." "Shoppers," *Women's Wear Daily* enthused, "are, in a sense, a captive audience in the clustered mall." As with his store designs from the late 1930s, Gruen designed the garden court to lure people into the retail realm for longer stretches of time. The court with its density of activity was central to controlling the shoppers' movement. "Around this garden court," he explained, "are arranged the entrances to most of the stores, and in it pulsates heavy foot traffic, comparable only to Christmas shopping days downtown." Dayton's department store was unreachable from the fifteen parking lots, so "consumers walked the mall to reach anchor stores," *Shopping Centers Today* admired. This arrangement pushed up the price of renting on the court, making the space "a valued commodity." "Only first-class retailers rented there," the article concluded.[13] The national chains Fanny Farmer and Woolworth's rented prominent locations on the court to benefit from the foot traffic.

As Southdale seemed to be the ultimate machine for selling, other professionals had ideas to make the shopping center even more productive. To create a dense commercial atmosphere and increase Southdale's pulling power, Dayton's took the unprecedented step of asking its largest downtown competitor, Donaldson's, to join them in the suburbs. Donaldson's brought in its own architect, John Graham of Seattle. One of America's leading shopping center architects, Graham had worked on Northgate in Seattle and Gulfgate in Houston for Allied Department Stores (Donaldson's parent). Graham completely disagreed with Gruen's Southdale design. He wanted to wring more profit out of the shopping center's public spaces. Over many meetings, Graham pointed out to Gruen that the immense court did not promote enough shopping opportunities.[14] "If they [shoppers] were only doing one-sided shopping around the perimeter of the square, they couldn't see what was going on elsewhere," Graham explained to Gruen. Graham recommended that the court be designed more along the lines of Gruen's three narrow malls for Southdale, so that people could window-shop on both sides simultaneously. "You wanted to expose people to as much merchandise as you could," Graham's partner recalled.[15] While Gruen won the battle over Southdale's court, Graham won the war in American retailing.

American architects and developers soon followed Southdale with other enclosed malls across the United States. However, the very aspect of Southdale that attracted so much attention, the garden court's immense size, was quickly put aside.[16] Architects and developers soon saw the commercial logic of smaller interior spaces. In other shopping centers the court became a narrow walkway, more like what Gruen labeled "malls" at Northland and Southdale. Of course, this design had the economic advantage of letting people window-shop continually. Although other architects and developers would go on to create denser retail environments, at the time Southdale brought an unprecedented density of stores to suburbia. Some observers, though, hated what they saw at Southdale.

The opinionated American architect Frank Lloyd Wright visited Southdale shortly after its opening. "What is this, a railroad station or a bus station?" he asked. "In all this there should be increased freedom and graciousness. It is wholly lacking." About the popular garden court, Wright asked: "Who wants to sit in that desolate looking spot? You've got a garden court that has all the evils of the village street and none of its charm." Not only did the famous modernist hate Gruen's design, he also thought Gruen's inspiration was misguided. "You have tried to bring downtown out here. You should have left downtown downtown," Wright complained.[17]

With kiosks, shop windows, cafes, streets, fountains, sculpture, crowds, benches, and trees, Gruen consciously re-created an aura of urbanity for white suburbanites. "Through a carefully designed psychological type of illumination, through an abundance of plants, tree groups, and ponds, through an easy-on-the-foot type of pavement, through the sidewalk cafe . . . and through a much more daring use of works of art," he bragged that he had designed "an urban space, of city-wide interest." Like Wright, 1950s journalists groping to describe Southdale's sensations turned to the most obvious example of commercial density: downtown. They wrote about Southdale as a city. *Architectural Forum* saw Southdale as "more like downtown than downtown itself": "There is nothing suburban about it except its location." Gruen had not copied downtown at Southdale, the magazine explained. Rather, the design represented "an imaginative distillation of what makes downtown magnetic: the variety, the individuality, the lights, the color, even the crowds." Further, with "a busyness and a bustle" Southdale had what "noisy and dirty and chaotic" downtown sorely lacked. The "sidewalk cafes, art, islands of planting, pretty paving" made Minneapolis's downtown appear "pokey and provincial in contrast with Southdale's metropolitan atmosphere."[18]

Ironically, Gruen was using the best of downtown just at the moment when downtown had lost its importance. For newly arrived suburbanites, shopping downtown would have been a familiar experience. The shopping center would be clean, safe, and ordered, whereas downtown seemed dangerous and dated. "Eliminate the noise, dirt, and chaos, replacing them with art, landscaping and attractively paved streets" and you had America's shopping malls, one magazine explained.[19] Likewise, the shopping center's commercial density, pedestrian environment, cafes, and civic art suggested the aura of urbanity that suburbanites had lost. In addition, it was hardly a secret that the suburban experience, and especially the shopping center, was premised on creating a separate, private space for whites. Southdale's court provided a secure, predictable space from which white suburban men and women could feel a part of a larger civic world.

While Gruen was inspired by downtown, the emporium's developers never intended it to replace downtown retailing. Downtown, they thought, would still serve as the center of a city's retailing. The new suburban developments would simply supplement the flagship store's sales. When Dayton's president first announced plans for Southdale in 1952, he went out of his way to declare that "we do not believe we or anybody else will lose any business because of the suburban move." Dayton's continually portrayed the opening of Southdale as a symbol of Minneapolis's economic expansion and not its decentralization.[20] "The loop [downtown] isn't going to disintegrate," its president reassured the residents of Minneapolis. "It hasn't in any other city."[21] One retail analyst speaking about Chicago stores confidently reminded investors that "the central business district of Chicago will always be the most powerful retail focus within the entire metropolitan area." Similarly, *Women's Wear Daily* reported that the "expanding operation of Carson's in the suburbs does not reflect its feeling that State Street is drying up."[22]

Despite these balmy predictions, suburban branches quickly upstaged the downtown department stores. Shopping centers stole market share from downtown's retailers. In Detroit, for example, J. L. Hudson's downtown store lost 20 percent of its sales with the opening of two suburban shopping center branches. The company was more than willing to cannibalize its downtown sales, however, because the pastures of suburban retailing looked so green. The company's total sales increased by 60 percent.[23]

Downtown moved out to suburbia in another way as well. Of Southdale's seventy stores, only 5 percent were part of national chains.

Smaller concerns, often with a downtown Minneapolis connection, formed the majority of Southdale's retailers. Gruen often sang the praises of downtown merchants moving to malls, not for any idealistic reason but for purely economic ones. "A local merchant," Gruen explained, "may control a very high proportion of the market and may therefore become very important to the shopping center."[24] Older Minneapolis businesses seized the opportunity to reach suburban consumers who had recently left the city. These merchants did not abandon their downtown locations but operated both an urban and a suburban store. For instance, Farnham's sold stationery in both downtown Minneapolis and St. Paul while also encouraging customers to visit its new Southdale branch. Similarly, the Juvenile shoe store advertised four locations—downtown, Miracle Mile, and two suburban shopping centers.[25] Merchants, Gruen explained, were simply following their "best customers," who had "fled to the suburbs," like "Mrs. Fox . . . to Lake Valley, Mrs. Wolf to Beauty Acres, [and] Mrs. Badger to Sunnyside." While Gruen drew inspiration from downtown, he wanted to avoid some of suburbia's pitfalls. "Decentralization," Gruen explained to one reporter, "for the sake of decentralization was unhealthy."[26]

Gruen touted his high-minded goals for Southdale. On numerous occasions, he spelled out how the shopping center could reform the suburban landscape. In one article, he detailed how creeping commercial strips offered "poor shopping conditions and a depressing shopping atmosphere." The strips were successful in one respect, Gruen allowed. The rows of stores "succeed beautifully in a step by step deterioration of the surrounding residential areas by their appearance, their noise, their smells, their traffic congestion." One architect lamented that "mile upon mile of highways are 'stripped' with excessive zoning for commercial use. 'Strip' zoning with its curb parking has become a curse upon the urban environment."[27] Indeed, commercial strips were zoned for business, not beauty. And, yet, Gruen insisted, refinement and retail could coexist.

For Gruen, there was no greater symbol of Southdale's reform ideals than its blank facades. Reviewers rarely noticed the windowless walls facing the parking lots; the interior was too distracting and novel. But those blank walls were a very deliberate part of Gruen's design. No signs, no lights, no show windows, and no decoration—the exterior was supposed to be serene and uninspiring, a reaction to the bright lights of the commercial strip. Since the 1920s, the stores on the strip had been rich with signs, colors, lights, and show windows. But at the shopping center, Gruen turned the prevailing trends of retailing on their heads. Unlike his Grayson's stores, the shopping center sought to attract customers not through loud appeals but through quiet architecture. In Detroit, however, Hudson's found the lack of a sign to be a bit too risky and soon installed a large sign on its Northland branch.

To improve America's cities and suburbs, Gruen originally planned Southdale to halt sprawl. Shopping centers were the best weapon to "Fight Against the Commercial Slum," Gruen informed real estate appraisers.[28] In this respect, Gruen followed early shopping center advocates—like Clarence Stein, Catherine Bauer, and J. C. Nichols—who fervently believed that the shopping center could deter future sprawl by bringing retailers together and stopping the spread of commercial strips. The shopping center, the reformers promised, would clean up America's crass commercial streets, provide needed services to suburbanites, and turn a profit.

Gruen first conceived of Southdale as the social and commercial center for a five-hundred-acre "blight-proof neighborhood." "We are planning to create a community," the president of Dayton's department store announced.[29] "The development will offer a pleasant place in which to shop, a good spot in which to work, and a fine neighborhood in which to live."[30] Dayton's worried endlessly about public opinion—especially since it needed a zoning change. Dayton's thus used this "community" rhetoric in an attempt to appease any opposition and portray the shopping center as a benevolent neighbor. How sincere the store was about this lofty mission remained to be seen.

In 1953 Gruen completed a Master Plan for Dayton's five-hundred-acre development. It was a high-handed European modernist scheme, with apartment towers, office buildings, the shopping center, a medical center, and wide highways. Gruen placed all these modern buildings in a landscaped park featuring a man-made lake and walking paths.[31] The Southdale development, he grandly proclaimed, symbolized "the first large scale planning effort made by the forces usually considered as upholders of rugged individualism." As he complimented his clients, he also revealed his naive belief that capitalists could undertake a large-scale planning effort benefiting everyone, instead of just their pocketbooks. Instead of encouraging sprawl, the developers of Southdale chose to complement "the surrounding environment in matters of traffic, usage, protection, and aesthetics." In this manner, the shopping center would be the most important city planning strategy developed in the twentieth century, Gruen predicted.[32] He applied the simple theory that retail businesses and residences needed to be separated. This would keep the gaudiness of commercialism away from houses and preserve residential property values.

In order to achieve this massive reform, Gruen stressed the need for more systematic planning of the entire American metropolis. "Planning is as old as mankind and of divine origin," Gruen asserted. "*Laissez-faire* planning is a luxury we can no longer afford."[33] Gruen saw the remedy to most social problems as more stringent planning—be it undertaken by corporations or the state. Once, during a debate with New Dealer Rexford Tugwell, Gruen asserted that meticulous planning could solve all of America's most pressing social ills. Gruen wanted the government to plan and build entire towns in the Western desert. These public towns would bring people from different races and classes together to solve all of America's problems with discrimination and poverty.[34] For Gruen, the difference between government towns in the desert and private developers' shopping centers was slight. They both could represent, Gruen believed, an effort to plan America's environment—cities and suburbs—in a more systematic way. However, the reality turned out to be very different from Gruen's or Dayton's noble promises.

Not surprisingly, when shopping centers were built, they inevitably had an impact well beyond their property lines. In an extremely prescient comment, one of Gruen's partners worried about the impact shopping centers would have on surrounding land values. "The mere existence of the shopping center creates high land values in the area immediately surrounding it," Karl Van Leuven correctly explained before they had even built one shopping center. "These high land values" would have a decidedly negative effect, he continued, by creating "demand for more intensive use than the residential purpose for which it was probably originally zoned."[35] In other words, when the shopping center succeeded and land values began to rise, people would begin to see opportunities in land speculation. This might eventually lead to future commercial blight, as had occurred in the 1920s with single-story taxpayers. Van Leuven's prophecies proved correct. Strapped for cash, Dayton's began selling off surrounding land to other developers for residential or retail projects. Even before Southdale opened for business, new home building in Edina took off. To realize quick profits, Dayton's sold off 208 acres to other private developers for single-family homes. The Thorpe Brothers, who had helped Dayton's close the original purchase, bought land to begin constructing single-family homes. They advertised their development as following "nature's planning" and as "ideal for modern living."[36]

While realtors and developers applauded rising land values, the situation made city planners a little nervous. Since shopping centers had originally been advanced to control speculation in commercial real estate, their encouragement of more speculation flew in the face of their proponents' stated goals. In one pointed exchange with social critic Jane Jacobs, Gruen strongly denied that shopping centers led to "scatteration" or sprawl: "scatteration was not in suburban [shopping] centers but in suburban areas." He maintained that large shopping centers were "planned against scatteration," not to encourage sprawl. Once, Gruen was asked after a speech in New Jersey, had his shopping centers contributed to "this very maze of sameness?" Gruen gave his standard answer. "The regional shopping center," he said, "is one of the indications of recenterization that we are observing." He went on to explain, "I believe that it will be necessary to inject in our sprawling metropolitan regions which are basically centerless, new central facilities which slowly will grow into being cores of the regional area" and, as a result, would discourage sprawl and blight.[37] While Gruen argued for his noble intentions, his justifications were less than convincing, especially in the face of developers' needs for more profits.

Department stores first became developers as a way of moving their retail businesses to suburbia. They saw quick profits, however, in selling off their real estate holdings and in owning the malls. Most shopping center developers—including Gruen's clients, Hudson's and Dayton's—remained hesitant to let go of real estate profits for future retail profits. In one instance, a Gruen client became excited about the prospects for real estate profits. The Philadelphia department store Strawbridge and Clothier wanted to sell off "fringe property" around its new Gruen-designed Cherry Hill shopping center. "It is our feeling," the Strawbridge president wrote, "that we should pursue the so-called hit-and-run course of action in the development of this property." The president wanted to sell the land "to realize as quick and substantial a cash return as circumstances permit." The department store asked Gruen's associate, Larry Smith, for advice for "unloading the property for the highest possible dollar return." Even while pursuing this hit-and-run strategy, the department store still wanted to control the future development of the property to safeguard its own interests at Cherry Hill. So the lots, the president wrote, should be sold "with the proper protective restrictions imposed upon the purchaser, insuring that whatever development takes place will be compatible with and not competitive to the shopping center." Strawbridge needed this strategy to raise more money "to avail ourselves of the limited real estate opportunities remaining in the so-called inner perimeter trading area of the Delaware Valley."[38]

While Gruen might regret uncontrolled development beyond the shopping center, such development was often undertaken by the very same developers that employed him. Though Gruen might disagree with the policies of developers like Strawbridge and Clothier, which sold land for quick profits, he nonetheless continued working for them. Gruen kept his protests strictly private—at least before 1968. And, most symbolically and practically, Gruen never found a way to create a shopping center that was not an island in a sea of parking. His shopping centers were always physically isolated from the surrounding community. In 1965, Gruen returned to Detroit for the opening of Hudson's third shopping center, Westland. While there, he visited Northland. In a personal letter, Gruen described his disappointment. The sight was "a severe emotional shock to me." The "wild disorganized growth" around the eleven-year-old Northland assaulted Gruen's standards. If Gruen had imagined Northland stopping commercial sprawl, he had clearly failed; Northland's commercial success had spawned many other developments along the major roads. Gruen bemoaned that "we all should have known better when we planned Northland." However, he excused himself from blame, saying that "at the time Northland was created nobody in the United States had the slightest inkling that such formidable, dynamic growth could take place around a shopping center."[39]

In a more optimistic moment, Gruen argued that the growth around Northland represented a positive, if unplanned, development. With "high rise apartment buildings, hotels, a legitimate theater, office buildings, exhibit buildings, laboratory buildings, a hospital," Gruen asserted that the Northland area functioned as a dense downtown for Detroit's suburbs. "Northland," Gruen wrote, "has thus furnished proof that the existence of a strong commercial center can be the beginning of a sub-city center serving all human functions." "I am also convinced that in the long run the concept of the urban sub-center," Gruen wrote to Dayton's, "would decisively economically prove more advantageous than the one of the conventional regional shopping center."[40] In other words, Gruen now imagined convincing department stores to make shopping centers more dense, not less. He pushed for more uses to be incorporated into the shopping center. He wanted to build an entire downtown in suburbia, but he was unable to develop a sound solution. Instead, he became shrill, advocating for tighter and tighter controls that had little to do with the reality of suburban development.[41]

The proliferation of strips around shopping centers may have aggravated Gruen, but it did not devastate him. He became louder in his calls for tight control over retail development, but he studiously avoided calling on the one body that shaped the commercial strip's appearance: the developers themselves. Even in the face of contradictory evidence, he continued to rely on his belief in a benevolent capitalist who would place society's goals above personal profit. Gruen's blind confidence in the enlightened corporation caused some difficult predicaments. He was quite aware of how and why his shopping centers were soon surrounded by sprawl; developers either sold or developed the surrounding properties. But he never attacked developers for taking quick profits or ruining his plans. Even his few critiques against developers remained vague. Rather, he continued with the same refrain that he had been singing for the last ten years: shopping centers could halt the spread of formless, soulless suburban strips. At the same time, however, he privately acknowledged that shopping centers directly contributed to the type of suburban sprawl he set out to fight. In this respect, Gruen's continued rhetoric about malls' positive environmental effects became a perfect smoke screen for their failures. For the first time in his career, he seemed to duck an issue out of deference to his clients and respect for his own accomplishments. He had become an excellent public relations man for shopping centers—championing their noble purposes while realizing their profound failures.

The majority of Americans saw the indoor mall as a magnificent new creation. They loved Southdale's soaring spaces, its convenience, and its entertainment value. And yet, even at its beginning, the suburban shopping center fell far short of Gruen's original promises. He had wanted Southdale to be one part of an entire planned community of office towers, apartment buildings, parks, and lakes. Instead, what emerged was a suburban development of single-family houses with a commercial strip surrounding Southdale. But how could Gruen see the failures of Southdale when it represented his greatest professional success? He would never fully acknowledge the degree to which Southdale must have disappointed as well as pleased him. He spoke of it only in glowing terms. Most tellingly, he never criticized his own role in creating more suburban sprawl. While Gruen later attacked developers for misusing his shopping center concepts, he never publicly acknowledged his own failures.

After his Northland and Southdale malls, Victor Gruen became the most acclaimed architect of shopping centers in America. Shopping centers would become larger and enclosed, as he had dreamed so many years before, and their spaces would become the de facto centers for suburban communities. Gruen did not always feel comfortable with his position, however. He was greatly limited in his vision by economic constraints and stuck largely to the program that his clients wanted; he never realized the most idealistic of his grandiose schemes. Like other professionals that shaped middle-class dreams, Gruen accomplished his greatest expressions within the commercial sphere. The land of capital and consumption, building and buying, was the place that gave him the opportunity to express his architectural ambitions, even if the grandest of those ambitions—the shopping center's communal potential—went largely unfulfilled. In a strange way, however, his writings about shopping centers allowed him to realize the reforms he desired. Indeed, what became impossible in his shopping centers (their potential to reform) became more prominent in his rhetoric about shopping centers. And what he achieved in his architecture (commercial success), he rarely elaborated upon in his writings. For instance, while his 1940s writings continually emphasized how good design could boost sales, in his later writings Gruen never linked sales with aesthetic decisions. By the 1960s, he rarely mentioned how profits were connected to shopping center designs, emphasizing instead the public functions of his buildings. Substantial profits had become a commonplace, and Gruen turned his attention to bigger issues.

The year 1956 was a very busy one for Victor Gruen. As in other years, he gave his opinions freely. He delivered numerous speeches. He lectured to diverse groups, like the San Francisco Planning and Housing Commission, Cooper Union Art Students, California Council of Landscape Architects, and Oakland Chamber of Commerce. He spoke about parking strategies, financing shopping centers, city planning for the year 2000, and his European vacation.[42] His shopping center commissions took off. In the spring developers broke ground for two new shopping centers outside Oakland and Los Angeles, both designed by Gruen. Three additional Gruen projects opened in Detroit, Honolulu, and Tempe, Arizona. Gruen also branched out beyond commercial architecture. He completed an office building for the New York developer Lawrence

Tishman on Wilshire Boulevard in Los Angeles.[43] And the year before Gruen had worked with the dean of the University of Southern California's architecture school, Arthur Gallion, to complete designs for public housing in Los Angeles.[44] His firm designed tract houses for the growing suburbs of Los Angeles and Pasadena.[45] Most significantly, he also began to move in a new direction by exploring downtown redevelopment plans for various cities.

Gruen was also becoming something of a national celebrity. *Life*, *Time*, *Business Week*, *Glamour*, and the *New Yorker* all ran fawning articles about him and his work.[46] One magazine profile celebrated Gruen for being that rare combination of "a practical visionary who has the happy faculty of being able to translate his dreams into brick and stone." The article concluded by characterizing the architect as "a leading authority on planned shopping centers in the United States [whose] theories on city planning reflect his concern with social problems and the years he has spent in business design."[47] By 1956, the Viennese immigrant had achieved the national prominence he had so long hoped for. Of course, Gruen did not rest on his laurels; rather, he used his new national stage to advocate even bolder plans.

A mere three months after Southdale's opening, Gruen had already begun to worry over its success, or more precisely, its successors. At a *Progressive Architecture* awards ceremony in New Orleans, he gave the keynote address, in which he attacked the architectural profession. With his usual verve and eye for controversy, Gruen delivered a searing speech to his fellow architects. "We close our eyes," he warned architects. "We engage in philosophical conversation as we pass through the avenues of horror," he cried. The endless miles of suburban sprawl were "flanked by the greatest collection of vulgarity—billboards, motels, gas stations, shanties, car lots, miscellaneous industrial equipment, hot dog stands, wayside stores—ever collected by mankind."[48] He even went so far as to lampoon *Progressive Architecture*'s prizewinning designs. He dubbed the winners a new style of architecture—"the 'running-away' or 'escapist' introvert movement." Architects were designing isolated architecture and he saw it as morally and aesthetically reprehensible. "Our buildings," he declared, "flee the companionship of structures other than their own kind. . .and thus we architects have followed the merchants and the commuters." Elsewhere Gruen regretted that the beauty of architects' buildings was "seen only through the wraparound windshield or the rear view mirror of automobiles going 30 to 60 miles an hour."[49] He then delivered the harshest criticism he could fathom: "We have become suburbanites and exurbanites." For Gruen, a defender, lover, and champion of cities, to label architects "suburbanites" was a scathing critique. And yet, the characterization was a self-critique as well. For he was, arguably, the most prolific suburban architect in America.

Indeed, it was his suburban successes with Northland and Southdale that had brought him to *Progressive Architecture*'s awards ceremony. He was in New Orleans to receive a Merit Award for Southdale's design. How paradoxical, then, that his speech should criticize other architects for their neglect of cities. He knew better than any other architect the fruits to be gained by working in the suburbs. His career was built on the profits from shopping centers. His invective was most likely directed as much at himself as at any other architect at the New Orleans conference.

Concluding his remarks, Gruen asked his colleagues, "Do we, as representatives of a profession concerned with the shaping of the man-made environment, have a right to enjoy the luxury of discussing from Olympian heights the merits and demerits of styling certain aristocratic buildings—which stay away from the plebes?" He answered his own question not by offering a quick solution to suburban sprawl, but by calling for a recommitment to America's forgotten cities. He told architects to return from the stylish, isolated suburbs to the difficult issues of the city. It was almost as if he had completed the canvas of his suburban work and now wanted a new one. "We should take, with strong hands, the reins in urban planning endeavors," Gruen advised his fellow architects.[50] As the suburban shopping centers had reproduced downtown for suburbanites, the dilemma now, according to Gruen, was how to remake downtown. What those new cities would look like and whether grand plans would work was an unanswered question in 1956. But at that time, it seemed that America's downtowns would be given new life by a commercial architect who had created his reputation in the suburbs.

CHAPTER SEVEN

Saving Our Cities

The questions "Can our cities be saved? Will they be saved? Are cities worth saving?" are merely academic. They not only can be saved, but they must be. The question before us is how.
—Victor Gruen, 1955

Though they earned him a national reputation, Gruen's immensely popular shopping centers left him only partially satisfied. He thus set his sights on an even more formidable retail challenge. With shopping malls, Gruen had sought to create a new way for suburbanites to shop, and he had largely succeeded. Now he turned his attentions to one of the inspirations behind the suburban shopping center: downtown. As Gruen enjoyed the fruits of his work in suburbia, urban politicians and businessmen across America began to worry about their futures. Once again, Gruen turned first to writing to stake out a new area. In articles and speeches, he began to suggest a few simple plans to rejuvenate downtown. His strategies were the same as those that had spelled success in suburbia. He wanted to provide parking, entertainment, pedestrian malls, landscaping, and modernized stores for downtown. This plan, Gruen confidently promised, would help downtown hold its traditional place as a region's economic center.

By the mid-1950s, American downtowns had run into hard times on a number of fronts. First, there had been little new construction in cities since the 1920s. Moreover, through the Depression and World War II, existing buildings—especially housing and apartments—had received little attention. Additionally, infrastructure improvements in roads, highways, or trolleys had also come to a halt. All these problems led to a dire situation that was compounded after the war. In particular, returning GIs and exorbitant rents created an extremely tight urban housing market, with the result that it was easier to buy a house in the suburbs than rent in the city. In response, new construction largely occurred outside the city limits; both businesses and residences began to leave cities in great numbers. Because of all these events, downtown business owners, city politicians, and urban planners all sought a radical remedy to their declining prospects. One optimistic author provided a recipe detailing how "the city fights back" against the ever-growing suburbs.[1]

For Gruen, switching his focus from suburban shopping centers to central business districts was not difficult. Indeed, when he had first proposed a suburban shopping center to Hudson's in 1950, he was reacting to downtown's declining prospects. Now he wanted to shore it up. Writing for the *Harvard Business Review* in 1954, Gruen portrayed downtowns and suburbs as interchangeable spaces that begged identical solutions for their merchants.[2] He attempted to answer the increasingly urgent question: how could Americans save their cities?

He first described the dramatic changes in American cities. The single most important factor since World War II, Gruen maintained, was the phenomenal growth of suburbs. Suburbanization had long been a topic of interest for academics, but retailers were just starting to wake up to the implications. The affluence of the postwar period—seen in America's "building boom, higher incomes," and proliferating automobiles—should inspire merchants to look for a way to profit from the prosperity. But, a "turbulent disagreement" about the best road for downtown revitalization had stalled their aims.

Gruen posed the disagreement as a life-and-death battle between suburban and downtown merchants. He presented the two camps—the decentralizers and the downtowners—as intractable and contentious. The decentralizers enthusiastically fled the city. "Just build more shopping facilities in the suburbs, they say, and forget about the metropolis." Decentralizers lacked empathy for the plight of downtown merchants. Interested only in capitalizing on the new suburban opportunities, they did not care if downtown merchants slowly died.

Downtowners took an equally inflexible stand. Opposed to any and all change, this group fervently believed in the matchless strength of downtown merchants. Even plummeting sales did not shake their faith in downtown's economic dominance. They saw further decentralization only as "a satanic device to ruin them." As decentralizers did not care about the future of downtown, Gruen explained, so downtowners ludicrously believed in "the fantasy that somehow people will stop building in the suburbs." As downtown merchants' anxieties grew, they turned to ineffectual sales gimmicks. Gruen belittled retailers who plied customers with "free bus rides, lunch-box service, special downtown shopping days and parades." These desperate efforts would fail to halt the march of customers to suburbia. "Business," Gruen quoted one merchant explaining, "literally walks in by itself in branch stores."

To Gruen, both groups—suburban and downtown merchants—lived in a fantasy land. Both were disconnected from America's social and economic realities. "The hostility between the decentralizers and the downtowners is a phony war," he explained. The disagreement, Gruen ventured, was symptomatic of a larger economic dilemma. "The health of our entire retail establishment is at stake," Gruen warned. Whether downtown or on the fringes, merchants had constructed unattractive and profitless stores. With such horrific retail environments, Americans would soon despise shopping. Gruen predicted dire consequences: the unpleasant retailing situation would break the consumption and production cycle. He invoked the recent specter of the Great Depression. The national economy, Gruen claimed, would founder unless retailing was radically updated. All merchants—whether in suburbia or downtown—would be equally ruined.

After dramatizing the dire economic issues at stake, Gruen took his readers on a tour of America's horrible retailing conditions. Whether downtown or in the suburbs, one word symbolized retail's problems: the car. Cars clogged the streets, required parking spaces, overwhelmed pedestrians, and spewed filth and noise. Gruen catalogued the "Trouble Downtown." Narrow streets, left over from the horse-and-buggy era, could not accommodate automobiles. "The tyranny of the automobile in urban areas," Gruen intoned, "must be regarded as the main factor in downtown's increasing difficulties." Merchants in New York City lost $100 million in sales due to gridlock, Gruen pointed out. And in Boston nearly half of all suburban women avoided downtown because of their anxiety over traffic problems. Yet all was not gloom and doom for downtown. In another study, almost half of suburban Boston women would shop downtown if parking were easier. While the 4,688 women surveyed did their shopping in suburbia for "standardized and branded merchandise," they preferred downtown for "style and luxury items." All because of parking problems, downtown shopping had degenerated from "the national sport of women" into an "intermittent chore." Downtown shopping had become merely "necessary," rather than pleasurable.

In Gruen's eyes, suburbia was not immune to the automobile menace. Because of inadequate planning, it unwittingly replicated downtown's failures. "Honky-tonk strips" on traffic-choked roads with inadequate parking were forming a "vast desert of unhappy shopping." "Pure avarice" and "ruthless competition" led to "more and more stores, not better and better ones," Gruen complained. The planned shopping center was the answer. With a single owner, architectural unity, and generous parking, the shopping center could control the strip's chaos. Just as he would arrange a show window, Gruen wanted to employ a "criterion of quality, not quantity" to suburban retailing. Never shy about promoting his own work, he held up Northland as the epitome of such wise development. Beauty, Gruen suggested, held the secret to Northland's popularity and prosperity. By uniting "commerce and beauty," "art and economics," Northland proved how retailers could restore "peace, leisure, and relaxation" to Americans' lives and make a profit to boot.[3] At Northland, Hudson's actual sales had exceeded anticipated sales by a third.

Gruen wondered if the same principles could not be applied to downtown. His proposition was hardly outrageous. Indeed, when Northland opened in 1954, *Architectural Forum* hailed the development as "a new thing in modern town planning," rivaling Rockefeller Center or the planned community of Radburn, New Jersey. "Its flexible market-town use of open spaces looks like a natural for coping with rehabilitation of blight-spotted decaying shopping districts," the magazine predicted. "The Best Hope for Our Big Cities" was another journalist's optimistic appraisal of Northland.[4] Gruen wholeheartedly agreed—by bringing suburbia back downtown, he believed he could spur an urban renaissance.

To conclude his *Harvard Business Review* article, Gruen made one final plea for revitalizing downtown. Using lessons learned from World War II rhetoric, Gruen appealed to Americans' patriotism and cooperative spirit. Saving declining downtowns was a "*democratic* responsibility." For America to realize its full potential, he wrote, Americans had to clear their urban slums, improve traffic patterns, create parks, and provide parking. Only with these reforms would Americans enrich their "social, cultural, and civic life." The article was Gruen at his most convincing. He neatly distilled the problems with America's cities and suburbs, provided concrete examples, and pointed the way to a better future through a combination of planning and retailing. For the rest of his American architectural career, he would continue to hit on these issues and call for more stringent planning to improve America's cities and suburbs.

Gruen's recommendations struck a chord with the American press. *Business Week* hoped that his ideas would help revive America's "Sick Old Downtown." The Associated Press summarized his recommendations, and at least thirty-five newspapers ran the wire piece. "Downtown Stores Gird for Battle," a Syracuse newspaper reassured its readers. "Main Street and downtown," a Providence, Rhode Island, article predicted, "may recoup by facing the facts of the motor age and modernizing accordingly." The *Des Moines Tribune* quoted extensively from Gruen's article to explain how "Dynamic Planning Can Modernize Retail Shopping Districts."[5]

Gruen was not alone in his push for urban revitalization. Across America, politicians and planners pushed for remaking downtowns. The federal government had just approved massive funding for urban redevelopment. First, the Federal Highway Act, which had failed to pass in 1955, did so a year later largely because big-city mayors thought that highways could help eliminate downtown congestion. Second, the Federal Housing Act of the same year allowed cities to undertake limited commercial redevelopment projects. Immediately, cities began lining up with plans to remake themselves. One text observed that seven hundred cities had published central business district plans by 1959.[6] "What is needed to cure the deep-seated disease of our urban areas," Gruen recommended in 1959, "is much more than stop-gap measures." He advocated "a basic planning philosophy" that "accomplishes in the physical sense what legislation does in the moral realm . . . freedom and liberty." Gruen declared that the planning of cities would be a way to "stimulate civic pride." Gruen insisted that a "creative, imaginative planner" had to hold "a deep conviction that the reshaping of our man-made environment is today's most urgent task."[7] As welcome as the extensive press coverage of Gruen's urban planning philosophy was, his self-promotion in the *Harvard Business Review* proved even more rewarding. He quickly landed a client that most architects only dreamed about: a progressive man with money, foresight, and his own lofty aspirations.

After reading Gruen's article, J. B. Thomas, president of Texas Electric Company, called the Los Angeles office of Gruen Associates. Gruen's argument and vision so impressed Thomas that he wanted to hire the architect immediately to undertake a metropolitan survey of Fort Worth in order to plan the city's future growth more efficiently. It was the perfect opportunity; the Texas businessman charged Gruen with putting his theories about cities and suburbs into practice.[8] Working on a large city and with a large budget, Gruen could afford to extend his proposals for American cities farther than ever before. With Thomas's backing, Gruen hoped to realize his grandiose theories at last.

The growing gulf between downtown and suburban retail would

remain the most pressing issue of Gruen's career. He never came up with a satisfactory solution. "The healthier the central district, the healthier the outlying districts. A sick urban area inevitably means a sick suburban area," Gruen frequently insisted.[9] As in the past, his first instinct was to prescribe architectural and planning solutions. He provided economic rationales for his plans. He browbeat planners, politicians, and retailers to undertake dramatic downtown campaigns. And through all his efforts, his belief in the need to reform American cities remained at the forefront. "We are swamped," Gruen told fellow designers in 1955, "with an avalanche of new inventions, discoveries, machines and gadgets." Modern suburban life was ruining Americans. Men were "enervated" from their long commutes to work; women were bored and isolated. Worst of all, according to Gruen, Americans could find no place for peace and quiet. Driving frayed their nerves; public life consisted of television. There was no refuge anywhere. "Our outlook is blurred by daily papers, television, magazines." Playing the curmudgeon, Gruen felt assaulted by "philosophy, art criticism, analytical psychology, nuclear fission, spiritualism . . . abstractivism, non-objectivism, new realism, surrealism." The competing fads made Americans feel like they were "swimming in the middle of a big pot of 'genuine, kosher, Hungarian goulash, dixie style.'"[10] Americans' anxiety was made even worse because of America's ugly, chaotic cities and suburbs.

Only strict planning measures could stem the tide of decay, defeat, and disorder and wrest American public life back from automobiles, bureaucrats, and technocrats. In his Fort Worth commission, Gruen saw an opportunity to put in place precise planning measures for the city's future growth, but he also saw in this work a further opportunity. He took his colorful urban concepts to the national media, first unveiling his plans to revitalize Fort Worth at the Aspen Design Conference in 1955. Gruen walked his audience through a remade downtown for a city of five hundred thousand, resplendent with courts and malls, sculpture and fountains, stores and parking. When the Aspen audience pressed for the city's name, Gruen coyly responded, "City X." The audience pressed for more details and Gruen asked them to wait. The wire services crackled with the story of Gruen's plans for City X. The unnamed Fort Worth appeared in newspapers across the country. The story focused as much on the mystery city as on Gruen's recommendations. Playing not to his peers through *Architectural Forum* or *Architectural Record*, Gruen addressed his proposals directly to the business community.

Business Week, familiar with Gruen from its coverage of his *Harvard*

Business Review article, ran a lengthy endorsement of his City X plan. The magazine presented Gruen's concepts as a much-needed antidote for all of downtown's woes, from declining tax revenues to white flight and deteriorating businesses. It hailed Gruen's plans as suitable for any American city, thus driving home the point that all American cities could profit from Gruen's lessons.

Business Week's article focused as much on Gruen as on City X. A photographer captured Gruen gesturing and explaining his ideas in six illustrations. *Business Week* saw no problem with Gruen's lack of experience in city planning work; in fact, the magazine saw his inexperience as a decided benefit. Gruen came not from the ivory towers of academe, but from an unconventional but more practical background in "candy stores, specialty shops, and department stores." Here was an architect who could help retailers devise a strategy to turn a profit. The article listed his shopping center projects in Detroit, Minneapolis, Oakland, Indianapolis, and San Jose. Any paradox in the fact that Gruen might be translating his suburban concepts into urban solutions was glossed over; *Business Week* presented the two projects as naturally related and nearly identical. The article repeatedly emphasized how Gruen's City X concepts were economically feasible, as Gruen had shown in his enterprising shopping center designs.[11]

Amid the publicity surrounding the release of the City X plan, Gruen himself became a celebrity. "Considerable speculation," a Fort Worth newspaper observed, "was stirred in planning and business circles across the nation." Of course, all of this attention did not occur naturally. Gruen did all he could to refashion himself as he remade City X. As a natural actor, Gruen reveled in giving presentations, interviews, and speeches. His PR savvy was not lost on the author of one article in *Progressive Architecture*, "What Can a Public Relations Counsel Do?" The article pointed to Gruen as an exemplar of an architect who marketed his expertise and generated newspaper coverage, creating "authority" through his public relations. "It soon," the article stated, "becomes very natural to see these people quoted whenever their fields of activity are mentioned."[12] Gruen had transformed himself from a commercial architect into a national expert in urban design. Five months after *Business Week* had publicized the plan nationally, Gruen unveiled it locally.

As Gruen gave speeches describing a glorious new City X, his partners and employees, led by the Italian engineer Edgardo Contini, took to the Fort Worth streets with their tape measures, cameras, and sketchpads. For nine months they undertook a painstaking "complete study of the area to be overhauled," one newspaper explained. The six-man team drew detailed city maps and generated extensive demographic information. Working from the city's street grid, the architects catalogued the condition, building material, function, and location of every downtown building. They covered maps with notations describing the city's physical and functional conditions. The "Gruen men," as the papers nicknamed them, approached the city as a problem to be solved.[13] The visiting architects ignored the city's growing suburbs and focused instead on downtown. Downtown—because it seemed finite and measurable—became an object that planners and politicians could manage, rearrange, and correct. From these surveys, the team searched for solutions.

A powerful streak of boosterism informed the architects' conception of Fort Worth. Where they catalogued problems, they also saw possibilities. Traffic congestion represented potential customers; dilapidated buildings were sites for new structures; clogged streets could be turned into sidewalk cafes. While the team measured, calculated, and quantified the city's physical elements as they were, the architects continually saw the city as it could be. Indeed, the fantasy of the future city was more compelling to them than the present reality.

J. B. Thomas flew out to Los Angeles to meet with Gruen's men and look over the proposed solutions. After stressing that they had worked on and rejected over two hundred proposals, Gruen told Thomas that the plans would ensure future prosperity for downtown Fort Worth. Over two days, Thomas contemplated the proposals and pondered the economic predictions. Convinced, he enthusiastically signed on and decided to have Gruen and his men present their proposal. Thomas hoped that Gruen's plan would serve as "the basis of concerted community effort to modernize our city."[14] In fact, Gruen's plan would do more than modernize Fort Worth; it would completely rebuild, rearrange, and change its functions.

On Saturday, March 10, 1956, J. B. Thomas stepped onto the stage of the prestigious Fort Worth Club and introduced Victor Gruen and his partner Edgardo Contini. Thomas began by striking a sober tone. "This is going to take vision, brains, guts, hard work, and money," he counseled the city's leaders.[15] Thomas explained that Texas Electric had hired Gruen in order to "stimulate sound development." He also stressed that the plan was "*A* plan for Fort Worth. It is not *THE* plan." Thomas, a bit nervous about Gruen's flights of fancy, cautioned the audience to have an "open mind" because the ideas would "challenge your imagination."

Thomas then turned the floor over to Gruen and Contini—"who have devised and set down in word and picture this plan . . . and whom we regard as highly competent."[16] The Los Angeles architects stepped into the spotlight and unveiled their plan for Fort Worth's future. With the presentation, the City X mystery was solved; Fort Worth would be America's shining example for tomorrow.

Gruen gave a grand performance. With films, color slides, charts, graphs, maps, and architectural drawings, Gruen and Contini performed with "the pomp, drama, and fanfare of a Broadway production." The civic and business leaders "sat spellbound" as the architects outlined "a series of startling proposals to re-shape Fort Worth into the dream city of America." Gruen and Contini "argued and waved their hands violently to hammer home points to their listeners." Reporters described Gruen as the consummate artist, "a plump, restless man with a decided accent," and Contini as a "handsome, eager, and dynamic" sidekick. With "Roots in Old World," Gruen had assembled "a junior-grade United Nations," one newspaper reported. The influential crowd was delighted and gave the partners a standing ovation.[17]

Gruen was not only an entertainer—he also used facts to sell his vision. His utopian dreams for a future Fort Worth with flowers and super highways seemed built on a foundation of objective, empirical data. Both to disarm critics and to convert the more economically minded businessmen, Gruen overwhelmed his audience with figures, facts, and economic predictions. Needless to say, his strategy relied heavily on his background in retail planning. He provided sales figures, tax revenues, rental rates, traffic patterns, and parking requirements. The information forced the audience to imagine that they saw their city anew through Gruen's statistics. Those that he presented were all-encompassing; they were not disembodied social minutiae that people could not comprehend. Here was someone explaining to them the exact number of parking spaces required to alleviate downtown's shortage, the precise cost of building a highway, the anticipated population of the city in 1970.

If the Fort Worth plans were to move forward, Gruen needed a broader base of support than Thomas. He hoped the plan for "A Greater Fort Worth Tomorrow" would be "a catalyst." His proposal was intended to galvanize "the varied interests of citizenry and government to evoke interest, thought, and action."[18] Through his presentation, he sought to forge a political and financial power base. Playing to "men noted for their ability to make an investment pay off," Gruen and Contini under-

FIGURE 35. Imaginary aerial view of the redeveloped downtown Fort Worth with a ring highway and pedestrian center. From Victor Gruen and Associates, *A Greater Fort Worth Tomorrow* (Los Angeles: Victor Gruen Associates, 1956).

scored the good business sense of their plans. Gruen outlined two steps essential to realizing the plan. The first was the will to revitalize; the second, a powerful organization that would step forward to push for the plan.

The audience answered Gruen's call and took up the challenge of urban renewal. "Not a single adverse comment was voiced from the leaders of government, business, industry, finance, and civic groups," one paper glowed. Another article quoted nineteen prominent Fort Worth citizens who supported the plan, including the president of the Chamber of Commerce, the presidents of the largest downtown retailers, and the police chief. The city fathers immediately formed a Greater Fort Worth Committee.[19] Headed by the president of the First National Bank,

FIGURE 36. Gruen Associates drawing of the pedestrian downtown Fort Worth filled with festive people. From Victor Gruen and Associates, *A Greater Fort Worth Tomorrow* (Los Angeles: Victor Gruen Associates, 1956).

it pledged to find "the skill, money, and guts" to begin.[20] The committee promised to move the plans from Gruen's drawing board to the city's streets. "Let's do it and quick," a Chamber of Commerce publication declared.[21]

Overnight, it seemed, Fort Worth was a city worthy of national attention and national acclaim. "Fort Worth became the most famous city in America," the Chamber of Commerce committee chair enthused. *Business Week, Time, Newsweek*, and the *New Yorker* all ran articles spotlighting the Fort Worth plan. *Architectural Forum* and *Architectural Design* carried the proposal as an urban planning innovation. The magazines saw it as a possible prototype for saving all of America's downtowns. Politicians cited Gruen's ideas, and other planners imitated his work. One article claimed that plans for eighty other cities were directly inspired by Gruen's Fort Worth work.[22] Even the women's magazine *Glamour* ran an article about how Gruen would reshape America's downtowns.[23] The idealistic developer James Rouse, who would himself go on to have a long career in downtown redevelopment, called Gruen's Fort Worth plan "the largest, and the boldest, and most complete dealing with the American city"—"the most magic plan," which provided "a wonderful image of what the city could become."[24] For better or worse, Gruen and the Fort Worth plan had become synonymous.

More applause followed Gruen's proposal. The *Fort Worth Star-Telegram* and the *Press* took their Sunday readers on a guided tour of the "Gruenized" city. Even the *Dallas Morning News* had to admit that the plan was "by all odds the most challenging and imaginative that has yet been advanced for any American city."[25] At the very least, Fort Worth was poised to step out of Dallas's shadow. A local columnist and city booster, "The Home Towner," saw "something brand new and exciting in city planning." He pushed for immediate action. Citizens were "ready to pitch in their energies and their own dreams to make it come true," he wrote. "What a challenge! Man, oh man!" Fort Worth journalists prematurely heralded Fort Worth as the "City of Tomorrow." "It's the first city dream plan in the United States," one paper declared. [26] The flurry of praise for Gruen's Fort Worth plan flattered him deeply. He was now a commercial architect who was being taken seriously as the savior of downtown.

J. B. Thomas, as Gruen's sponsor, also received immense praise. The Babbitt-like Home Towner piped up that the plan was a "prettily-packaged gift" and "a fine piece of forward-looking citizenship, of generosity." Of course, as a business executive, Thomas had additional motivations and his own worries about the future direction of his hometown. He wanted the advice of someone "with a broader viewpoint and a wider contact with this sort of problem"—and he ended up with Gruen and City X.[27]

Fort Worth was familiar with businessmen guiding the city's planning efforts. In 1928, after a failed public effort to implement planner Harland Bartholomew's city plan, the Chamber of Commerce announced a five-year program of its own. With a million-dollar price tag, "Five Years of Progress" called for the construction of highways, boulevards, buildings, and industries. The plan combined private and public investments to finance new offices and stores designed in the latest architectural styles, new and diverse industries, and boulevards and highways. Again, in 1945, the Chamber of Commerce took the lead in city planning. The business leaders issued *Fort Worth Plans for the Future*, which appealed to the state of Texas to give the city the legal authority to adopt a Master Plan. Private corporations would then undertake the redevelopment of blighted areas. While nothing came of the 1945 plan, its failure did not deter Fort Worth's businessmen from trying to set the city's development agenda.

In the 1950s the city's direction preoccupied J. B. Thomas and other Fort Worth businessmen. During World War II, Fort Worth's population had boomed, adding over 100,000 new residents. The suburbs grew comparatively slowly, adding only 35,000 new residents over those same years. However, from 1950 to 1960, the city witnessed a complete reversal in its growth patterns. Its population growth all but halted as new housing starts, residents, and businesses left for the suburbs. Defense-related industries, like Consolidated Vultee Aircraft Corporation's Convair plant and Bell Aircraft's helicopter factory, brought thousands of new jobs to the area. Many, if not most, of these workers made their homes in the growing suburbs of Grand Prairie, Hurst, Euless, Bedford, and Arlington. Tarrant County, surrounding the city of Fort Worth, added 177,000 people, while the city grew by only 77,000. Even that number presented Fort Worth's situation in a misleading light; in 1954 the city annexed a large tract of suburban land that added 56,000 people to the city's population. In 1940, the city made up almost 80 percent of the county population. By 1960, it had fallen to just 66 percent.[28] Further, the expansion in retailing was nearly all in the suburbs. From 1954 to 1958—the very years Gruen pushed for his downtown plan—Fort Worth added only four general merchandisers and lost fourteen apparel shops. In comparison, the suburbs gained forty-seven new general merchandisers, thirty-two apparel stores, and six department stores.

When Thomas introduced Gruen at the Fort Worth Club, the businessman alluded to a "precedent" for his city planning effort.[29] Thomas was no stranger to private planning or grand schemes. In 1941, upon becoming president of Texas Electric, he began to worry about his company's future. With West Texas as a major market, Thomas realized that the region's future depended completely on having a supply of good, cheap water. "West Texas was crying for water," was one newspaper's description of the region's dire predicament. Thomas believed that businessmen, not the government, could best solve West Texas's water problem. "Big Business had as much interest—maybe more—in the people as did Big Government," one newspaper article explained about Thomas' planning philosophy.[30] Thomas, through Texas Electric, initiated an engineering survey to find possible sources of water. Dissatisfied with the engineers' first assessment, he sent them back into the field. After receiving a proposal suggesting that artificial reservoirs presented the only workable solution, the Texas Electric Company began building lakes on the dry plains. The initiative resulted in five new reservoirs providing water for West Texas; a giant one of nearly 8,000 acres was named after J. B. Thomas. Texas Electric sold the water cheaply to towns and erected its own electric plants on the man-made lakes. This water supply would help assure West Texas's continued growth and Texas Electric Company's future prosperity.

As West Texas had thirsted for water, Thomas saw Fort Worth parched for a lack of urban planning. He wanted Gruen to develop an equally suitable and profitable plan that, in the words of the Chamber of Commerce, would "assure Fort Worth's continued growth and prosperity." But Thomas's motives were far from philanthropic. "Don't think I'm Santa Claus," he quipped. "I'm not that altruistic." He had economic reasons. The business of the electric company was "one requiring the investment and expenditure of large sums of money," and its profits relied on the city's long-term economic health. As the utility company enjoyed greater profits with suburban growth, Thomas also wanted to guarantee that his best customers—downtown businesses—remained viable. Thomas touted the Gruen plan as a way to "stimulate sound development." "I'm a businessman, and my business is supplying electricity," Thomas declared. "If the city grows, my business grows."[31] A downtown renaissance brought about by Gruen's designs promised more revenues for Texas Electric.

Gruen occasionally rhapsodized about his ideal client; J. B. Thomas nearly fit the mold. In this reverie, Gruen placed his faith in progressive corporations solving America's social problems. Gruen imagined realizing "the great dream of my life"—an "ideal plan for the urban environment." His revolutionary plan single-handedly "solved all the problems which our cities, and the people who have to live in them, are facing." Seeing himself as a salesman of new and improved cities, Gruen "had only to go out and sell it." He first turned to the government, but met with little interest. He then turned to large developers who showed "mild interest" but were unwilling to "buy" his solutions. Finally, Gruen appealed to the one corporation in his adopted hometown of Los Angeles with the capabilities and creativity to build a new city: Disney. In Gruen's daydream, Disney was his perfect client. In his mind Disney seemed progressive, well-funded, and able to carry out his plans. Of course, after seeing his fantastic plans, Disney immediately signed on and began constructing a city of 20,000. At the end of Gruen's fantasy, he proudly claimed that "my concepts proved even more successful than Disneyland."[32] Whether Gruen and Thomas could build a city more popular than a Disneyland for downtown Fort Worth remained to be seen.

Gruen most clearly articulated his vision for the future Fort Worth in a lavish brochure. His report, *A Greater Fort Worth Tomorrow*, did not read like other city planning documents. Gone were the dry statistics and architectural schematics. Instead, Gruen relied on dramatic words and colorful drawings to convey his vision. He was creating an advertisement in order to find funds to build his modern downtown. *A Greater Fort Worth Tomorrow* began with a jejune poem penned to the "young and vigorous city . . . full of flesh and blood activity." The verse depicted a future metropolis that would strike envy in the hearts of all other American cities. Fort Worth, like "all cities everywhere," had "problems." But the problems could be "recognized and solved." And through "therapy" the heart of the city could be saved. With "tall buildings, stretching spires to the sky," "broad sweeps of tree-dotted parks," and "concrete ribbons of freeways," Fort Worth would become the most envied city in America.

Neither bashful nor vague about making pronouncements, Gruen in his eighty-seven-line poem described existing problems, called for action, and promised a "fuller life" in a future Fort Worth. In the remaining pages of the report, Gruen expanded on these themes. The report first catalogued the city's problems. Stressing that all cities always had problems, the report contended that "as a natural consequence of the *amount* of city growth, every problem is magnified to sometimes terrifying proportions." These problems, according to Gruen, led to severe inefficiencies. Commercial blight, traffic snarls, delivery problems, and horrible shopping conditions all squandered time and money. "No city can, in the long run, afford this waste," Gruen warned. The inefficiencies produced "a vicious cycle, which will eventually find the central city bankrupt and the remainder of the city paying for its upkeep." Throughout the report, Gruen hammered home the theme of present inefficiency and future efficiency. For instance, what appeared to be an extravagant expense to construct underground truck tunnels would be more than recouped by the increased speed of store deliveries. All of his recommendations would create more efficient and pleasant conditions for retailing and living, he argued.

The report then outlined overarching goals for the Fort Worth plan. Implementation would foster a "gradual upgrading" of downtown and the roads. It would also bring much-needed pedestrian space back to the city. The final result would be a "stimulation of the social, cultural and civic aspects of downtown." Of course, these goals reinforced each other. For instance, once cars were provided with parking, the streets could be turned into pedestrian malls. An increase in pedestrian traffic, Gruen maintained, would lead to more valuable real estate downtown, which would in turn encourage landlords to improve their properties. Evoking the accepted theory that aesthetic blight led to economic blight, Gruen linked physical improvements to future economic growth. It was not simply a matter of making downtown pretty; rather, a pretty downtown would pay for itself. Gruen provided plenty of statistics to back up his contention. There were numbers for everyone: retail statistics, evocative drawings, organizational charts, highway statistics, population figures, and detailed maps.

After quickly sketching Fort Worth's problems and the plan's goals, the report turned to the city's glorious future. Whereas Gruen drew Fort Worth's problems and goals with a broad brush, he made the future specific. He offered these specifics in the form of simple stories that followed three hypothetical citizens—two businessmen and a homemaker. The tales put a human face on the proposed revolution in urban life and emphasized how downtown's physical changes would lead to economic and cultural improvements.

The first story looked out over Fort Worth from an aesthetic point of view. During a business executive's commute downtown, he boasted about "the elimination of vehicles from the central district." The businessman admired the way cars had been banned from downtown and replaced by electric trams and sidewalk cafes. The new city reminded him of a world's fair. A drawing showed the businessman smoking a pipe while surveying the hyperrealistic remade city below. Through plate-glass windows, he magisterially gazed out on towers rising from the city, new highways in the distance, pedestrians walking below, covered sidewalks, pools, courts, and parking garages. "Fort Worth had grown at an incredible speed," the story boasted. While this had been expected, the amazing aspect, to the businessman, was that the growth had followed a "framework," meaning Gruen's plan. This strict framework—of parking garages, highways, and pedestrian malls—had given rise to "the flourishing city."

If the first story emphasized how even a businessman would be able to appreciate the aesthetic improvements to the city, the second story spoke to the economic benefits. Following a downtown retailer, it described a merchant whose sales had been enhanced by city beautification. Once again, the pedestrian mall proved the centerpiece. "On the day the first downtown street was blocked off as a test," the merchant remembered, "the experiment proved to be an unprecedented success." The merchant explained that the city's improvements attracted new corporations, businesses, and factories, which further fueled the city's economy. For instance, more office buildings had been built downtown, which meant more workers, visitors, and shoppers. The improvements now formed "a part of everyday living," but "the excitement and pride of being the first city in the world to put such a program into effect had never dulled." The story imagined the best of all possible worlds where both downtown and the suburbs profited.

The third story followed a housewife who was taking the bus downtown for a leisurely day of shopping and errands. Whereas the other two stories focused on economic growth, the housewife's tale revealed the domestic engine behind that boom: consumption. Since she was defined above all as a consumer, the housewife's primary duty was shopping. Her activity would fuel the city's growth and affluence. She spent her day at the bank, an attorney's office, back to the bank, having coffee, shopping for an hour, taking lunch, resuming shopping (for the kids), and watching a movie. The entire day's activities, some of which were formerly done by her husband, gave the housewife "an added sense of responsibility and accomplishment." The housewife's productive day of shopping was made possible by "the smoothly flowing traffic, the compact groupings, the absence of cars and traffic signs," that Gruen recommended for a modernized Fort Worth. The salvation of downtown, Gruen argued, rested on convincing white, middle-class females to return to the city center for shopping.[33] As if echoing the plan's prescription for women in Gruen's future Fort Worth, one newspaper article gave what it saw as "the pattern for women's reaction." "I'd want to stay in town shopping all the time," Councilmember Spurlock declared. "My husband would have to increase his income to pay for the extra purchases," she joked.

Gruen presented a forceful and fanciful narrative of the city's future. The three stories measured the city of Fort Worth by standards of beauty, efficiency, and retail profits and enabled Gruen to condense hefty theories into concrete assets. The white, suburban characters gave his middle-class audience, like the elites of the Fort Worth Club, roles in which they could see themselves. The report also recommended a plan of action, stressing the need for public-private cooperation. Gruen wanted his plan to "shock" these sometimes antagonistic sectors into joint action. Like many other 1950s city planners, he hoped that public investment in infrastructure–highways, pedestrian malls, and parking garages–would lead to private investment in new buildings. Gruen specifically pointed to the success of Philadelphia, Pittsburgh, New Haven, and Chicago as examples where joint ventures between the government and businesses were remaking the city. In these cities, Gruen applauded the way that citizens were forming councils to implement urban renewal proposals.

The same week that Gruen performed for the Fort Worth cognoscenti, the *New Yorker* ran a laudatory profile of him. The author described Gruen as "one of the best-known architects in the country" and asked the architect how he might go about remaking "the beloved but exasperating" Manhattan. Speaking from his cluttered study in a newly purchased Stanford White townhouse on West Twelfth Street, Gruen had no shortage of opinions. He lamented that Americans treated "planning" as if it were a dirty word invented by the Communist Lenin. Without planning, New York would wear people down. "Wherever we turn, it's jostle and bustle and frayed nerves and bad tempers," Gruen complained. As in his Fort Worth plan, Gruen based his recommendations for Manhattan on his 163–acre retail creation in Detroit of two years before. Painting an idyllic picture of Northland for readers, he promised that he could create the peace and quiet of the suburbs in the city. Northland would teach Americans "that it's the merchants who will save our urban civilization," Gruen concluded.[34]

The *New Yorker* provided tempting details of Gruen's extravagant plan for Manhattan. He would banish factories and warehouses to New Jersey; "how ridiculous for this show window of the world to have block after block given over to factories!" Everyone would walk in Gruen's Manhattan. He would build tunnels to hide all automobile traffic and convert the streets into lovely malls. "When our feet get tired," he raved, "there will be thousands of comfortable benches and scores of charming sidewalk cafes." A year earlier Gruen had recommended turning the Herald Square area of Thirty-fourth Street into a mall. The *New York Times* had cheered Gruen's proposal, predicting: "Merchants Lose Downtown Blues."[35]

His plans for Fort Worth were just as "futuristic" and "daring" as those he dreamed up for Manhattan in the *New Yorker.* They featured heliports for personal helicopters, air-conditioned streets, electric people movers, underground truck tunnels, pedestrian bridges, and giant sculptures. Downtown would have a new freeway, six giant parking lots, new office buildings, new stores, and a new civic center. Just as his first shopping center plans—like Montclair or the Olympic Circle—proved overly ambitious, so his initial downtown proposals attempted to accomplish everything with few concessions to practicality.

Gruen also drew generously on his earlier retail work to remake Fort Worth as a consumer mecca. Urban renewal plans, like a large-scale store modernization strategy, promised to attract people, improve sales, and raise property values. The Fort Worth plan would "dress up the downtown area," Gruen explained. The *Fort Worth Star-Telegram* explained how retailers would "have a big stake" in turning Fort Worth into the "city of tomorrow." The merchants should "expand, modernize, and improve their business establishments," the paper recommended. "The Gruen Plan for redevelopment of the downtown area . . . [would] unfold" only through retail improvements and expansions, the article concluded.[36] Retailing was central to Gruen's vision for a new Fort Worth and retailers would be the main economic beneficiary.[37] With boundless optimism, Gruen prophesied that by 1970 Fort Worth would need six million more square feet of retail space. This was an astonishing prediction—nearly seven times the square footage of Southdale Shopping Center. He envisioned that after the plan's implementation downtown real estate values would skyrocket. Wholesalers, machine shops, thrift stores, and factories would be driven from this "shopping paradise."[38] Retailing, which had been located downtown since the turn of the century, would stay put.

Even the New York author Jane Jacobs, archcritic of all urban renewal plans, embraced the Gruen Plan for Fort Worth. Writing for *Fortune* in 1958, Jacobs denounced urban renewal efforts: "these projects will not revitalize downtown; they will deaden it." The costly projects would fail, Jacobs predicted, because they destroyed urbanity. "They work at cross-purposes to the city," Jacobs wrote. "They banish the street. They banish its function. They banish its variety." But when the Gruen plan came along the foremost critic of urban renewal embraced her enemy. By outlawing automobiles from downtown, the Gruen plan, Jacobs believed, would bring back the original walking city. By building "sidewalk arcades, poster columns, flags, vending kiosks, display stands, outdoor cafes, bandstands, flower beds, and special lighting effects," Gruen would resurrect "downtowns for the people." Jacobs imagined the plan leading to a rich public life of downtown "street concerts, dances, and exhibits." "The whole point," Jacobs explained, "is to make the streets more surprising, more compact, more variegated, and busier than before—not less so." America's most complete statement on the urban condition to date, Jacobs called it. Impressed by the plan's boldness, she penned what she called "a fan letter" to Gruen and Thomas. "The service done by the Fort Worth plan," she wrote, "is of incalculable value." Gruen's plan, according to Jacobs, had "set in motion new ideas about the function of the city and the way people use the city."[39] So taken was Jacobs with Gruen's vision of a modern, walking city that she skipped right over his recommendations for six giant parking lots and a new highway.

For Gruen, people could only walk around downtown if they had a way to get there. Thus, highways and parking lots were an essential part of his plan. Since Gruen's ideal audience lived in the suburbs, providing ways to drive downtown was key to his plan. Instead of extending his futuristic ideas to mass transportation, he endorsed monumental freeways and massive garages. As at a department store or a shopping center, accommodating cars and drivers was of paramount importance to downtown as well. He based his traffic system on an optimistic scenario. By 1970, Gruen claimed, 152,000 cars would need to move in and out of the downtown area daily. These automobiles would require a phenomenal 16.2 million square feet of parking, or four times the total area of downtown's present buildings. Devoting that amount of downtown land to parking seemed impossible.

Gruen saw two ways to tame this traffic tangle—either construct downtown highways or eliminate cars from downtown. He warned that constructing more highways would severely displace downtown businesses and ultimately exacerbate congestion. The second option seemed perfect. Downtown could be cordoned off from the rest of the city to create a pedestrian enclave. Of course, carving out pedestrian malls still depended on new highway construction. Instead of ramming highways through downtown, Gruen proposed a belt highway to ring the city center. The Belt Line Highway would connect to existing highways running to the suburbs and provide, in Gruen's words, a "total solution of the downtown traffic problem." Gruen's highways did not drop people onto the crowded downtown streets; rather, the highways whisked suburbanites directly into the six massive parking garages—a novel approach. These huge garages, with sophisticated electrical devices that identified empty spaces, would ensure that drivers never had to fight for parking. While Gruen promised efficient, car-oriented transportation for Fort Worth, the plan also stressed the importance of pedestrians. By banning autos from the city center, Fort Worth would gain 4,500,000 square feet of land that could be transformed into "landscaped areas with fountains, flower beds, trees, and public walkways."[40]

Gruen never had an ambivalent relationship with cars; he always hated them. Even when he designed stores for the Miracle Mile or for shopping malls in a sea of asphalt parking lots, he criticized Americans' love affair with their cars. "The most evil machine in Mr. Gruen's garden is the automobile, and he heroically proposes that we outlaw it from our urban cores," one journalist explained in *Harper's*. "He hated automobiles more than anything else," one partner remembered.[41] "This automobile population infringes on the rights of humans in a violent manner," Gruen asserted. They turned the American city into "an unlivable environment, inefficient, and ugly." Americans' 40 million cars left in their wake ugly strips of "markets, chain stores, automobile showrooms, used car lots, gas stations, hot dog stands, roadside restaurants, cocktail bars."[42] In one fantastic proposal, Gruen imagined hiding all automobiles in vast underground parking garages, which would store thousands of cars, leaving no aesthetic or emotional scars on the city. He wrote many other articles about the "invasion" of the automobile, and all this anti-car rhetoric gained Gruen much attention. Cars ate up too much space.

One especially bizarre anecdote, which Gruen repeated on many occasions, was his horror story about the faraway planet "Motorius." Gruen reported that astronauts had discovered another civilization, not unlike Earth. The information was being kept under wraps, however, because it might "threaten our national economic security." The "Motorists" of "Motorius" had "ingeniously engineered" an "86–lane expressway system." They "lived, slept, and procreated in their machines," he informed his audiences. Speeding around their planet in perfectly synchronized traffic patterns, the Motorists spent their entire lives behind the wheel, watching life through their windshields. They demolished all their buildings for more and more highways, eventually covering 92 percent of their planet in asphalt. Then, one day, tragedy struck, in the ominous form of a blowout. One flat tire, changed inefficiently, led to gridlock, and all the Motorists starved in their cars. Of course, the government kept this information classified because the knowledge would have "disastrous results on the progress of the national freeway program, on the employment situation in Detroit, on traffic improvements within our cities, and on garage construction projects." In the Motorists' demise, Gruen saw a moral for Americans. "Spread causes further spread, congestion causes further congestion, freeways bear new freeways, and anti-city begets more of its own malformed type," Gruen lectured.[43] But for all his railing against the automobile, Gruen's criticism and designs stopped far short of either relying on mass transportation or not accommodating cars.

When journalists characterized Fort Worth's proposed redevelopment, they looked to the 1950s apotheosis of retailing: the suburban shopping center. According to *Business Week*, Gruen's Fort Worth plan would result in a perfect mix of suburbia and urbanity, "a cross between New York City's Rockefeller Center and the most modern shopping centers in the country." "TODAY—vast suburban centers with easy parking TOMORROW—pedestrian plazas in downtown sections," *U.S. News and World Report* optimistically predicted.[44] "Downtown," one journalist explained, "is treated as Big Shop center" because it is "the biggest center of them all." Gruen, the article went on, felt that "the same techniques that have made shopping centers so successful can be applied with equal value to downtown areas." "Like suburban centers, city shopping centers can be planned to keep service traffic underground, with covered sidewalks and benches, landscaped gardens, sculpture fountains," *Glamour* told its readers. "Shopping," the magazine continued, "doesn't have to be drudgery; it can be fun."[45] In this way, suburbia would save downtown.

For the planning of Fort Worth, Gruen borrowed from his successful shopping center designs. Out where the automobile ruled, he had reintroduced spaces where people could get out of their cars, walk about, and window-shop. He wanted to create the same experience in downtown. The concept of re-creating a walking city would shape Gruen's urban plans for the next decade. For Fort Worth, Gruen and his partners had "tried several ideas. They argued, they rejected, they redrafted, they talked, and they planned." But in the end, they always returned to their own success with Northland because it "would fit ideally into Fort Worth."[46] By banning autos from the city center, Fort Worth would gain land that could be transformed into "landscaped areas with fountains, flower beds, trees, and public walkways."[47] "The pedestrian is king," the public relations firm for the Fort Worth plan announced.[48]

Gruen had advocated taking suburban malls downtown as early as 1952, which was remarkable, since he had no suburban successes to point to at that time. "In recent years," Gruen explained in a Minneapolis interview, "people have become discouraged from using the 'city core' for cultural and civic gatherings." He hoped to re-create the hustle and bustle of a suburban shopping center to bring the white middle class back downtown. "The lessons learned and the experience gained in the planning of regional shopping centers will contribute immeasurably to the successful carrying out of this task," he argued.[49] If shopping centers threatened downtown, what better way to save them than by stealing its competitor's strategies? And, Gruen hoped, what better strategy for beleaguered cities than to hire the architect who had perfected the suburban shopping center? Quite effectively Gruen wrapped himself in the aura of his highly profitable and popular suburban shopping centers. Virtually everyone was prepared to believe that he had a Midas touch with retailing.

Journalists trotted out Gruen's financial success in suburbia as his best credential for improving downtown. They emphasized that Gruen could perfectly balance economic concerns with visionary plans. "Trees and benches sell merchandise—so thinks Victor Gruen. . . . And he has proof." A "shopping mall similar to this is now being built in Minneapolis," one article explained.[50] Another article even predicted that Fort Worth's beautification plan would be more profitable than Northland, because in Texas flowers would bloom longer and people would enjoy being outside more.[51]

One obvious critique that might have arisen was that although Gruen's suburban ideas might work downtown, it was also his suburban malls that were killing downtown. In an astonishing twist of logic, however, Gruen argued that shopping centers did not threaten downtown, even going so far as to suggest that shopping centers actually benefited downtown merchants. They would act as a much-needed "shock treatment," forcing downtown to modernize and providing a model for doing so. Shopping centers were "an experimental workshop leading to the salvation of downtown," Gruen preached.[52]

Rarely did Gruen admit that his shopping centers might be responsible for downtown's decline. Once, on a late-night New York radio talk show, the host asked Gruen about the competition between shopping centers and downtowns for consumers' dollars. Gruen momentarily let his guard down. He hesitantly conceded that shopping centers stole cities' retail dollars and characterized the relationship as "paradoxical" at best. Still, he insisted, shopping centers provided the best model for better downtowns. "They will ease the pressure" on overcrowded cities and act as "a psychological shock treatment." Employing strained logic, Gruen predicted that only when suburban shopping centers became more popular would people recognize downtown's dire straits and care enough to rescue it. Gruen hoped that shopping centers might awaken people to "the dangers that we might lose our cities."[53] Why Gruen, the shopping-center architect, felt so strongly about America's downtowns, he never explained. But he wrote often about them, and often disliked what he saw.

In one speech, Gruen summed up his opinion of American cities: "Our cities are sick—very sick!" While he raved about European squares where Americans enjoyed their summer vacations, Gruen never celebrated American downtowns in the same way. A deep strain of antiurbanism ran through his attempts to remake the city. "We have made our cities," Gruen complained, "unlivable and unworkable, until they have become economically impractical and have ceased to give human enjoyment." No surprise, then, that when any aspect of the American city came up in Gruen's writings, it represented a problem to be solved. American downtowns—"anonymous, dull, ugly, dirty places"—were to be remade, not admired.[54] One of the most striking aspects of Gruen's prolific writings on urban America—especially since he proclaimed himself a champion of cities—was his complete inability to see anything beneficial in America's downtowns.

The year before Gruen proposed the Fort Worth plan, he engaged in a little fanciful dreaming about the future of America's cities. Writing for a television special that attempted to predict life in 1976, Gruen authored a little manifesto on how to improve society by improving the country's environment. He indulged his fantasies and painted a glowing picture of a well-designed America, not limiting his prophecies to the metropolis but examining everything from machines and shopping to nature and working. He disparaged the typical 1950s American suburban family as living a monotonous, dull, and exhausting life. The father worked all day, came home for dinner, and promptly retired to bed. The mother "felt that her life was empty and boring" because "there was nothing to do in the suburb." In Gruen's brave new world of 1976, the father pursued meaningful work while the mother explored cultural interests. She painted, played sports, and attended discussion groups. Most significantly, visiting "one of the new shopping centers where things can be done leisurely in beautiful surroundings" provided the highlight of her week. In Gruen's 1976, factories produced no smoke, fumes, smog, or noise. Americans loved their jobs. Machines completed routine tasks leaving "only creative and directional work" for Americans. In 1976, people shopped for necessities over "interactive televisions," spent their leisure time in beautiful green parks, and ate fresh vegetables. "We have reunited the family and we have reunited man and nature in an integrated environment," Gruen boasted. When he turned to the future metropolis, Gruen focused on the shiny new downtowns.

Here his predictions ran away with him and his exaggerations of the better life to come grew ever more fanciful, especially in the face of America's massive urban problems. "We have torn down the slums," Gruen predicted. "We have wiped out the blighted areas." With a theater, city hall, shops, amusements, shopping, and offices, downtown satisfied everybody's desires. When Gruen turned to the 1976 suburb, however, it appeared to be very similar to the ones being built in 1955. People lived in single-family residences. "Nuclear centers," which appeared to be glorified shopping centers, provided families with pleasant venues for strolling and shopping. Gruen's goals for rearranging the metropolis were noble indeed. He declared that all the improvements should be "consistent with the ideological theme that the world of tomorrow might be one of greater human happiness."[55]

Gruen hoped to create this type of life for Fort Worth. He predicted that his plan would boost the city's image, turning it into "a good product to see," in the words of the Chamber of Commerce.[56] One booster enthused that the plan "would be the talk of the country for a long, long time." And journalists declared that Fort Worth would be transformed into "one of the show-places of the world."[57] But newspapers also had plenty of practical questions for Gruen: Was the plan possible? How much would it cost? How long would it take?[58] For the most part, these questions were rhetorical and the papers often went on to explain that, despite the plan's far-fetched appearance, it addressed present-day problems. For every description of electric shuttles scooting noiselessly through a pedestrian oasis, the papers gave two lessons in municipal economics. Each improvement, the papers promised, would lead to further economic growth and stability. "For what at first impression may appear highly visionary," a *Star-Telegram* editorial declared, "could turn out upon closer examination to be hardheadedly practical and feasible."[59]

While the press applauded, businessmen signed on, and politicians pledged their commitment, support for the Gruen plan was not unanimous. In fact, it had many critics. Some Fort Worth residents incensed by "this impractical, wide-eyed idea of a Gruen Plan," took up their pens in protest.[60] Expressing a mixture of astonishment and outrage, they attacked the grandiose Gruen plan for being too costly and ignoring the city's real problems. People worried that the exorbitant cost would prevent the city from completing much-needed work on infra-

structure and basic services. They wanted more practical improvements—like paved roads, streetlights, garbage pick-up, clean drinking
water, and better schools—before the pie-in-the-sky Gruen plan.
Gruen's flamboyant ideas appeared to be putting the cart before the
horse. One "housewife" eloquently expressed her concerns: "What with
water and school needs as serious as they are, perhaps a program for
the city may be a luxury." Clean drinking water and working schools
were a city's "meat and potatoes," while the Gruen plan was "more like
whipped cream that you can do without." Even *Newsweek,* in a gener-
ally glowing review, admitted that the $150 million Gruen plan "will
have to await construction of an even more urgently needed $52 mil-
lion water-supply system."[61] While some citizens expressed their hostility toward the overreaching plan, others had more selfish
reasons—like their own business interests or their own plans for city
development—for fighting the city planning efforts.

Even with the enthusiastic endorsements and Gruen's heroic marketing efforts, the Fort Worth plan stalled. It was not for lack of official
support—the city council approved the plan's framework—but for lack of
funding. Footing the $150 million bill for Gruen's parking garages,
pedestrian malls, and highways remained a thorny political issue. As
with most urban renewal plans, Gruen's vision for Fort Worth was built
on a premise of extensive public funding. The city pushed for two bills
in the state legislature. When passed, they would give the city power to
condemn buildings, sell off property, and oversee redevelopment, as well
as to operate parking garages.

Before the city could push for the bills' passage, however, Fort Worth
needed to obtain money for the Belt Line Highway. The Belt Line was
crucial, as it was the first stage of Gruen's plan and would give people
an easy way to drive back downtown. Supporters first asked the State
Highway Commission to reroute highway funds to the project. A high-
powered delegation went to Austin to plead the Belt Line's case before
the commissioners. The city manager, mayor, Chamber of Commerce
president, and J. B. Thomas put on a slide show. The colorful images
were unconvincing, however, and the Highway Commissioners stuck
with their earlier plans for an elevated East-West Freeway. (The Belt Line
was a more expensive depressed highway.) When the commissioners
told the delegation to apply again the following year, the chair of the
Greater Fort Worth Committee tried to put a positive spin on the crush-
ing blow. "The decision," he announced, "in no way diminished the
enthusiasm and dedication of purpose of the Greater Fort Worth Plan-

ning Commission for the early implementation of this initial phase of the Gruen Plan."[62] While the committee's spirits may not have been dampened, their goal of implementing Gruen's plan by constructing a ring road around downtown seemed well out of reach.

The passage of the urban renewal bill through the Texas legislature represented the next big hurdle for the Gruen plan proponents. Nicknamed "the Gruen Bill" by journalists, the legislation would have given Texas cities the power to condemn and clear blighted areas. The land, rearranged into larger tracts, would then be resold to private parties for redevelopment. This type of bill was common practice across the nation as cities pushed for federal urban renewal funds. "Texas," the Greater Fort Worth Committee emphasized, "was one of the few states without such legislation—thirty-seven other states already have it." Essentially, the bill was a rubber stamp for municipalities to begin applying for federal urban renewal funds. When approved on a state level, the federal government would pay up to two-thirds of the cost for land acquisition. Many Texas legislators remained suspicious, however. The supporters from Fort Worth stressed that the Gruen Bill would not force the city to take action; it would simply give them the option. The Gruen plan supporters promised that the city's voters would still decide when or if to begin the implementation.[63] Even with such assurances, the Senate State Affairs Committee defeated the bill by just one vote. The Texas legislators worried that the bill would infringe on the rights of property owners. One state senator, firmly against the bill, said it also created too much potential for "graft and corruption." Proponents of the Gruen plan declared that the bill had been defeated because of a lack of understanding and vision. "It is a free enterprise bill" that had "every safeguard for protection of private property," they countered, insisting that the legislation could be revived. But the committee's action sounded the death knell for any large-scale action in downtown Fort Worth.[64] Without the prospects of federal grants, the financing of the Gruen plan appeared to be over before it had begun.

Boosters for urban renewal remained optimistic, however, and sought to have at least part of Gruen's plan enacted. Parking seemed to be the one area where they could find public and political support, even with the Texas legislature. Parking was also one of the more pressing needs of downtown. Additionally, the supporters hoped that by beginning with parking they could then build momentum for the rest of the plan. Nicknamed the "Parking Bill," the legislation would give Texas municipalities the authority to build and operate public garages. The parking bill went to the State Senate nearly one year after Gruen's initial proposal, and it immediately came under heavy fire from a powerful group of private garage owners. The president of the Chamber of Commerce and two bank presidents firmly opposed the bill. They contended that if Fort Worth built garages the city would hold an unfair advantage over private operations. George Thompson, one of the bank presidents, had once been a firm supporter of the plan until the subject turned to public parking garages. Thompson, who was a large investor in two profitable downtown garages, resigned from the Greater Fort Worth Committee and let loose a searing critique of Gruen's plan. "Municipal garages would enjoy a monopoly of downtown garage business," thus bankrupting private garage operators, Thompson telegrammed the House subcommittee. The bank president also pointed out that a citywide program of urban renewal enacted for the sole benefit of downtown property owners was highly unfair. Thompson accused the backers of the parking bill of beginning down a slippery slope toward state-sponsored socialism. If cities owned parking garages, he asked, what was to prevent them from opening department stores or banks? By the end of April, the Texas legislature had come around to Thompson's position. The defeat was the final blow against the Gruen plan. "The key measure," the *Star-Telegram* regretfully reported, "for Fort Worth's Gruen Plan of downtown modernization was killed." Thompson celebrated by claiming that not one in ten downtown property owners had backed the Gruen plan. He declared the defeat of the parking bill to be a victory for private property rights and the free market.[65] With these legislative defeats, the Gruen plan proponents had no legal authority or money to build their dream city.

Three years after these legislative defeats, champions of the plan were still lobbying for action. "Let's Try Being *FOR* Something!" the editor of the *Fort Worth Press* demanded. The editor lamented the loss of Gruen's "tremendous, imaginative idea," which other cities thought was "bold, enterprising, progressive." Fort Worth citizens had "thought of all the reasons in the world why it won't work, why we can't pay for it, why it doesn't make sense." Nobody had tried to salvage parts of the Gruen dream that might be implemented in Fort Worth. "We are killing it, you and I. Every day we are killing it," the editor dramatically proclaimed. And "we offer nothing at all better."[66] Addressing all Fort Worthers, the editor's call to action fell on deaf ears. No citizens or politicians pushed for reviving the plan. The Gruen plan, at least in Fort Worth, began gathering dust. All the national publicity and marketing had come to nothing; Fort Worth constructed none of Gruen's ambitious plan.

Though Gruen lost the fight in Fort Worth, he was not easily discouraged and took some comfort in the knowledge that support for his shopping center ideas had also taken awhile to catch on. Perhaps future Americans would see the wisdom of his urban innovations. Surely the tidal wave of publicity had at least highlighted the problems of American cities. And in the process, Gruen had become a celebrity, lionized as one of the country's leading experts on downtown revitalization efforts. For the next ten years, he would work to convince a city or a developer to build his dream downtown. Even with his high-flown rhetoric and grandiose promises, it would be a difficult sell.

The Fort Worth project also inspired a new round of speaking engagements for the Los Angeles architect. Gruen toured the country—indefatigably, as was his style. He spoke at prestigious universities, local chambers of commerce, retail trade shows, and architectural conventions. Unlike other urban planners of the 1950s, Gruen appealed to a wide variety of groups. In 1956, for instance, he delivered the exact same speech to architects at Harvard, the Oakland Chamber of Commerce, and Boston retailers. A consummate salesman, he mesmerized his audiences with sweeping generalizations about America's urban decline and his bold solutions. In speech after speech and article after article, Gruen painted bleak pictures of American cities, only to show pictures of his revitalized cities. He positively glowed over what American downtowns could become.

The speeches also gave Gruen a forum in which to rehearse his larger planning ideas. He played with various strategies to reform the American environment, announcing his solutions in broad generalities. Who could oppose creating a parklike atmosphere downtown? Who could be against the need for more downtown parking? Who could object to fewer traffic jams? Gruen avoided talking about a city's particular problems; rather, he rhapsodized about his own architectural achievements. He would walk an audience through his latest shopping center or his Fort Worth plan. He described the civic progress and tidy profits to be made at Northland or Fort Worth. For Gruen, speeches were more than the testing ground for new urban theories—they promoted his own work and ideas. Whether speaking to planners, architects, businessmen, academics, or bankers, he emphasized that the architectural project he designed would be profitable, socially and economically.

With no more experience than the ambitious Fort Worth drawings, his suburban shopping center successes, and his own visions, Gruen embarked on a new phase of his architectural career. He wanted to remake America's cities and, in so doing, remake himself as an urban planner. Planning became Gruen's buzzword. "Against this terror of the robot, this blitzkrieg of technology, there is only one effective weapon. This weapon is planning," he declared. He characterized his work as nothing less than "the application of wisdom and heart to the task of organizing and regulating relations between people and people, people and nature, people and the machine."[67] He wanted to be the architect that would reorganize the entire urban environment.

When speaking in other cities, Gruen pulled out the colorful Fort Worth plan to show the possibilities of large-scale urban renewal. His drawings of carefree pedestrians and festive streets practically coerced his audience into improving their own cities. If the cow town of Fort Worth could erect this future city on the Texas plains, then surely your metropolis can do the same. (He never let on that the Fort Worth plan had failed.) In a speech to the Oakland Chamber of Commerce, Gruen equated Oakland's problems with Fort Worth's. In a speech to merchants in Kalamazoo, Michigan, once again he turned to the Fort Worth plan as his example. As he delivered these speeches, Gruen also reminded himself to "INSERT LOCAL DATA." That three-word phrase was the extent of his acknowledgment that he was lecturing in different cities with different problems. In a rare attack on Gruen's blatant self-promotion, one Miami journalist saw his slick presentation as nothing but shallow hype. "I was convinced," recounted the journalist, that "Miami architects would take Gruen to the heart of the trouble: The failure to dramatize Miami's problem."[68] To the journalist's surprise, however, no one questioned Gruen's ideas.

That Gruen fell back on the Fort Worth plan as a template for urban renewal projects across the nation anywhere was not without some justification, however. In part, Gruen was giving city leaders what they wanted. Many American cities that were beginning to experience economic difficulties because of suburbanization aspired to similar downtowns to compete with suburban shopping centers. Gruen offered cities compelling plans to modernize their older downtowns with their own shopping cities. In one instance, an urban planner submitted Gruen's drawings for Fort Worth to remake Charleston, West Virginia. Gruen wrote the newspaper, saying that he was quite flattered. He also hoped that "blindly copying somebody else's drawing for another city is no

indication for the lack of sincerity and seriousness of the entire project."[69]

Gruen wanted to do more than dream of saving downtowns; he desperately wanted to rebuild one. After the political failure in Fort Worth,
Gruen did not have to wait long before for another opportunity to test
his ideas. Learning from his Fort Worth disappointment, he offered
smaller, more manageable plans for two different cities. Just as he had
learned to focus his vision for the shopping center in the early 1950s,
Gruen now cut back on the expensive frills for his downtown plans. He
drew on the main concepts from Fort Worth but scaled them back. He
made sure to include a pedestrian mall, an enclosed shopping area, a
ring road, and plenty of parking. But gone were the giant parking
garages and other frivolous aspects. Inadvertently, Gruen also stumbled
on a way to avoid financial missteps. By adapting the Fort Worth plan
to smaller cities, he could keep costs down. Because of the desperation
that downtowns felt owing to the suburban competition, Gruen's ideas
would soon help set off a wave of renewal efforts across America.

CHAPTER EIGHT

The Suburbanization of Downtown

If we do not want the city to be destroyed, if we do not want Anti-city to bury us, we have to prepare for an all-out counterattack.

—Victor Gruen, 1964

In April 1957, as the Texas legislature shot down Gruen's dreams for Fort Worth and as Southdale enjoyed its first year of success, a second city hired Gruen to prepare a downtown plan. Inspired by both the fanfare surrounding the Fort Worth plan and Gruen's Detroit malls, the Downtown Kalamazoo Association sought to save its center city. The association asked downtown property owners to pay three-tenths of one percent of their property value. More than 120 businesses contributed a little over $40,000 to sign up Gruen's firm.

Before the ink had dried on the contract, the firm publicized its vision for Kalamazoo. Gruen and his partners cast the downtown plan as a path to prosperity for the city. "Private enterprise," Gruen's man on the ground stressed, "is the best method by which a program can be carried out." He added that the Gruen firm opposed "leveling everything and starting all over." "We prefer," he said, "to stress revitalization as opposed to redevelopment."[1] The distinction seemed minor, but it was made to calm protests from citizens, merchants, or property owners who might have their buildings tagged for demolition. The Gruen firm also attempted to create a broad base of support in order to avert the political train wreck that had finished the Fort Worth project. Gruen emphasized that with his plan downtown merchants would improve their real estate holdings and retail businesses.

A month after the Downtown Kalamazoo Association and Gruen Associates signed the contract, the local newspaper reported on the firm's methods and progress. After only ten days of collecting data and notes, Gruen's project planner, Ulrich Weil, said that downtown Kalamazoo desperately needed revitalization. The paper praised Weil's thorough study of "annexation, finances, population trends, capital improvements, people and shopping behaviors, and tax assessments and rates." He also interviewed businessmen, academics, and politicians on their thoughts about downtown improvement, even encouraged other people with ideas to call him in Detroit. Once again the Gruen firm stressed that no hardship would be experienced by retailers located within the proposed redevelopment area. Weil even predicted that Kalamazoo residents would have lower taxes because the project would result in increasing property values downtown.[2] The prospect was irresistible: a remade downtown and falling taxes.

By the end of 1957, Gruen had trotted out a scaled-down version of his Fort Worth proposal for Kalamazoo. While the Fort Worth plan had imagined remaking twenty-two of downtown's best blocks and adding six giant parking garages and two separate highways, the Kalamazoo proposal was much more modest. Once again, a pedestrian mall would be the centerpiece. With a minor ring road and parking lots, the Kalamazoo downtown would be transformed into the Northland shopping center. To make room for parking, Gruen once again recommended eliminating "industrial, wholesale, and warehouse activities" as well as some residences. Throughout the Kalamazoo proposal, Gruen's men stressed that businesses and the "free enterprise" system would take the lead in spearheading and realizing the plan. The Downtown Association embraced Gruen's proposal. Three months later, the supporters urged city officials to begin implementing the plan as quickly as possible.

The simplicity of the Kalamazoo plan was its greatest strength. With relatively little demolition or new construction, a new downtown could be easily created around the pedestrian mall. In fact, the plan appeared to be so simple that the Downtown Kalamazoo Association took over the task of revitalization from the city government. But things were not as simple as they seemed. Gruen followed the architect-client model that he knew best, and the firm worked as if it were designing a shopping center. Gruen assumed that he would be employed first to undertake planning and then to complete the building designs. Unfortunately for Gruen, the model did not transfer to a planning project so easily. For a shopping center, Gruen had only one client, the developer. Downtown he had to work with individual businessmen and contend with the city government. Furthermore, the Kalamazoo Association accepted Gruen's recommendations for planning and then pushed ahead with construction on their own. Suddenly, Gruen had no client—and he was not pleased. He did not want to leave what he saw as preliminary ideas in the hands of untrained businessmen and politicians. But the Kalamazoo businessmen remained true to their word and worked doggedly to implement Gruen's plan to the letter.

The following year, Kalamazoo's Mayor Glenn Allen, Jr. presided over opening ceremonies for the $60,000 Burdick Mall. The city had footed half the bill for its trees, fountains, benches, and decorative walkways. A special assessment on merchants whose businesses fronted on the mall paid for the rest of the improvements. The pedestrian mall had led to other new investments in downtown as well. The same morning as Burdick's opening ceremonies, wrecking balls crashed into the central fire station to make way for a new $600,000 Jacobson department store. "The mall is a symbol, a spark plug to ignite all types of business and generate new ideas," one Kalamazoo merchant excitedly declared. A third of the stores on the new mall had begun modernization campaigns. From the State Capitol came word that funds for a new parking lot were going to be available. "New Greenery: Money and Mall," one paper enthused about the opening.[3]

Journalists from across the country hailed Kalamazoo's Burdick Mall as America's premier pedestrian mall. The renovation generated a blizzard of national news stories about the small city's efforts. *Life* magazine ran a glowing review. Gruen's clipping service worked overtime to keep up with the staggering number of articles—a little over three hundred during 1959 alone. The government's United States Information Agency chose Kalamazoo as the All-American City for 1959, and a showy exhibition on the city traveled to Britain and Germany. [4]

In Kalamazoo the mall seemed a success as well. Fifty thousand people packed onto the mall to hear the Jimmy Dorsey band play. The local paper declared "the bold venture—a smashing success!" The only concern that the newspaper expressed was that the crowd might have been too large. "The crowds around the stage during the band concert were so huge that moving up and down the Mall to 'look around' proved almost impossible," the paper reported. It added that though the crowd was "well-behaved," during the celebration people had been "forced . . . up against the show windows." By the fourth day of the mall's opening, the crowd had swelled to 30,000. "The largest crowds in downtown Kalamazoo's history," *Chain Store Age* cheered. With stores selling more, crowds of people, and store improvements around the corner, *Chain Store Age* said that the Burdick Mall "held the key to revitalization of faltering downtowns across the USA." With its "fountains, shade trees, flower beds, closely cut grass, playground area, park benches, and multi-colored concrete block walkways," the retail magazine proclaimed the mall beautiful and profitable.[5]

A year later Kalamazoo was still celebrating. "The municipal officials and business people," one paper said, "are completely sold on the plan as a novel and spectacular way to improve business in the downtown area." The city dedicated an additional block to the mall. The city also pointed to the widening of East Walnut Street, the addition of 250 new parking spaces and another 250 planned, improved lighting, a uniform storefront program, and plans for a more efficient delivery system. "Just a Year Old, How It's Grown," one local journalist proudly reported.[6]

Kalamazoo's success sparked cities across America to contemplate the mall idea. The city became a must-see for municipalities considering refurbishing their own downtowns. Groups came from Lancaster, Harrisburg, and East Liberty, Pennsylvania; Champaign and Joliet, Illinois; Elkhart, Indiana; Rochester and Lockport, New York; and Cleveland, Ohio. Even New York City became swept up in the pedestrian mall craze. A mall was proposed for Fifth Avenue from Thirty-Fourth to Sixtieth Streets, with arches carrying crosstown traffic. Twenty million dollars from a merchant's association was supposedly already earmarked for the effort.[7] Downtown pedestrian malls, like suburban shopping malls, were being contemplated across America. One paper cheered that fifty-five cities were planning on improving their downtowns with pedestrian malls.[8] For urban politicians, planners, and merchants, the pedestrian mall seemed a godsend. The pedestrian mall mania took off across the country as politicians wanted to solve downtown's economic doldrums or at least show their commitment to solving downtown's problems.

Compared to other urban renewal projects, pedestrian malls were a bargain. For most politicians, merchants, and planners, a downtown mall simply meant closing a few blocks of a major street to traffic. Perhaps a few merchants would come together and pay for flowers, planters, or kiosks to decorate the new mall. Of course, the mall was the simplest aspect to Gruen's grandiose urban plans. A pedestrian mall was easy to build compared with constructing massive parking garages, a ring highway, or a covered shopping center. With a very small amount of capital, politicians could show their commitment to reviving downtown's prospects and begin to compete with suburban shopping centers. As one *New Republic* reviewer enthused, Gruen's "delightful pedestrian malls spell not only a renaissance of urban culture. They are also a better mousetrap." Cities saw Gruen's concept as a cheap and quick fix that would lure suburbanites and their dollars back downtown. The formula for downtown revival became quite simple: "Money and Mall," as one Kalamazoo paper put it.[9]

Gruen had mixed emotions about the nation's embrace of the pedestrian mall idea. On one hand, the malls were feeble, half-realized attempts to revitalize downtown, just another cheap retail gimmick. The pedestrian malls would arouse excitement but would not provide long-term planning solutions, Gruen warned. But while he dreamed of creating entire new downtowns, American cities pursued half-baked gestures of revitalization. On the other hand, Gruen, as usual, saw the bright side and was pleased that at least some of his ideas were being taken up across the nation. Perhaps the enthusiasm would lead to bigger, more comprehensive plans to reorganize downtown.

As American cities pursued strategies to save their downtowns, even stubborn Fort Worth felt pressure. After Kalamazoo's achievement, politicians and merchants in Fort Worth once again began clamoring for action. "Permanent Mall Huge Success," the *Fort Worth Star-Telegram* informed its readers about Kalamazoo. Another article quoted Kalamazoo's city manager, who praised Fort Worth for inspiring the city's mall. The articles could not avoid pointing out that Kalamazoo had succeeded where Fort Worth had failed. "Will Mr. Gruen ever see his day in Fort Worth?" another reporter wondered. The answer was a resounding no; Fort Worth seemed to have neither the will nor the wealth for a downtown mall.[10] After Kalamazoo's success, Fort Worth proposed a pedestrian mall that would be closed to cars and decorated with potted plants provided by store owners. The gesture was a far cry from Gruen's original plans for the city. Yet even this simple plan ran into opposition. The city council had to change zoning regulations for the planters and allow the streets to be closed to traffic. The test site finally opened in September 1959, over three years after Gruen had presented his original plans for reviving Fort Worth's downtown. The mall consisted of six blocks along Houston Street, and the city promoted the site as "a salvation of the downtown area." But for Fort Worth, the downtown experiment was too little, too late.[11]

After the media hype surrounding the Fort Worth and Kalamazoo work, Gruen received another commission that had the potential to be more fruitful than his work in the Texas city and more grand than the Burdick Mall. The commission came from a familiar client—two department stores in the upstate New York city of Rochester. Faced with competition from new suburban shopping centers, Rochester's two largest downtown department stores—McCurdy's and Forman's—urgently wanted to prop up the city's historic center of commerce. "This city and merchants," the department store owners explained, "are confronted with problems of decentralization." To be sure, the two downtown department stores were not forgoing suburbia's prospects; both merchants operated thriving suburban branches at suburban malls. The department stores simply wanted Gruen to help them shore up their downtown sales as well.[12]

In December 1956, after reading rave reviews about Gruen's Fort Worth plan, the owners of the McCurdy and Forman department stores approached Gruen. Like many downtown business owners, they were concerned about their commercial viability in the new suburban age. In 1956, no fewer than eight large shopping centers were planned for Rochester's suburbs. From 1952 to 1958, the department stores saw more than 400,000 square feet of competing retailers open in the suburbs. "We are watching," they wrote Gruen, "with alarm the downward trend in business in centers of other American cities." And while the city planned to build a five-hundred-car parking garage near the two downtown stores, the merchants desired a "long term policy." They hired Gruen to recommend "significant and long-lasting improvements in our downtown area."

After an extensive economic and physical survey of Rochester, to nobody's surprise, Gruen concluded that downtown was a shambles. Rochester, he reported, was a classic "example of urban blight." He was shocked to see the mixed uses of downtown, with "parking lots, shack-like structures containing workshops, warehousing and storage facilities and some economically marginal retail enterprises." Striking a familiar tone, Gruen also singled out the catastrophic changes that cars had brought. Automobiles choked Rochester's Main Street and cut into retailers' visitors. The city, according to Gruen, was barely staying afloat against "the surf of slow but incessantly moving waves of automotive traffic." Cloaked behind a thin veil of prosperity, downtown, Gruen stressed, had been wrecked by "parking lots, garages, used-car lots, widened roads, and other automotive facilities."[13] He recommended removing the cars in order to bring shoppers back downtown and restore downtown's economic dominance.

In April 1957, Gruen formally presented a revitalization concept to the two department stores. He recommended what was becoming his standard urban renewal formula: a ring road, eight multilevel parking

FIGURE 37. Model of proposed Midtown Plaza, Rochester, New York. From Victor Gruen and Larry Smith, *Shopping Towns USA* (New York: Reinhold, 1960), 271.

garages, and a fourteen-block pedestrian mall. On this occasion Gruen went a bit farther: He also proposed building an immense covered shopping center. The covered mall was a brash move to bring suburbia's greatest success back downtown. The two executives were wildly enthusiastic. They jumped behind the proposal and immediately began taking steps to realize Gruen's recommendations. Behind closed doors, McCurdy's and Forman's formed the Midtown Holdings Corporation. Almost overnight the corporation began taking steps. They gambled $5 million on acquiring seven and a half acres in the center of Rochester.

In January 1958, at a secret meeting, the department stores and the Gruen firm informed Rochester's mayor Peter Barry about their plans. They told the mayor that they envisaged an indoor shopping mall built behind their existing department stores. Midtown Plaza—as they named it—would consist of an underground parking garage, a seventeen-story office/hotel building, an indoor mall, and an outdoor pedestrian mall. In addition, the two department stores wanted to expand their own facilities. By actually adding new retailing and buildings to downtown

Rochester (rather than restoring what already existed), the proposal was unprecedented. Not only would the plan be shoring up downtown's future, but it would actually bring in new construction. Mayor Barry immediately endorsed the Midtown plan, declaring that the proposal fulfilled the city's last ten years of efforts to "restore downtown Rochester." Unlike other cities' contribution to urban renewal efforts, however, Rochester's would remain minimal. The mayor unofficially promised to help the department stores by closing Cortland Street for a pedestrian mall, constructing an underground garage for two thousand cars, and connecting downtown to the new loop road with a broad avenue. By January of the following year, the city had officially approved the plan.

A few years earlier Gruen had outlined the strategies that were put to work in Rochester. "The private initiative," Gruen explained in a 1956 speech, "must take the lead and then cooperate in the development of a basic, overall, comprehensive, master plan with all the authorities."[14] The proposed Rochester plan seemed to execute Gruen's strategy perfectly; the city must play handmaiden to the big retailers. For the mall's inspiration, of course, he had to look no farther than his own suburban work for inspiration. He took his ideas directly from his suburban shopping centers. Some journalists also picked up on a European influence. One paper told how the "Viennese-born" Gruen built "a modern version of the traditional European square to enliven downtown Rochester." Hitting closer to the mark, *Architectural Forum* declared that Midtown was reminiscent of nineteenth-century European arcades.[15] In fact, Gruen went so far as to take measurements from one of the best-known Italian arcades. Visiting Milan in 1960, he sent a postcard back to his partners in Los Angeles, in which he described the arrangement of the Galleria Emmanuel in great detail. The floor plan was a Greek cross meeting in "a large rotunda" with a fifty-foot diameter. Four rectangular arcades branched out from the rotunda for either 240 feet or 120 feet in length; the arcades were between 55 and 60 feet wide. Gruen demanded that his descriptions be typed up in a special memo and distributed to all the partners and the planning department. He wanted to use a similar layout, especially the broad rotunda, for Rochester's mall.[16]

In April 1962, Midtown Plaza officially opened. *Architectural Forum* praised it as a "carnival in the snowbelt" that "combines the ancient lure of the European gallerias . . . with the design principles of the newest suburban shopping centers." One awestruck reporter, showering praise

FIGURE 38. Drawing of interior of Midtown Plaza. From Victor Gruen and Larry Smith, *Shopping Towns USA* (New York: Reinhold, 1960), 271.

on the seven-acre, "$35 million magnet of commercial excitement," enumerated the plaza's impressive features: "two big department stores, 30 retail shops, 13 floors of office space, the city's busiest post office branch, a 78-room hotel . . . an auditorium, a sidewalk cafe, a floating restaurant-bar with 10-mile views, a central bus terminal, and underground parking for 1,843."[17]

All the hoopla over Midtown Plaza was not simply for the opening of another large mall, but for the hope that Midtown Plaza represented for all American cities. It was easily the single largest private investment in America's downtown retailing since World War II. Urban advocates hoped the construction would spur similar projects in other American cities. "The first bulls-eye answer of an aging American center to the threat of the suburban shopping center," *Architectural Forum* called Gruen's downtown mall. "Midtown Plaza," the *New York Herald Tribune* declared, "will be watched with consuming interest by other American cities with decaying centers—which is to say just about all of them." The *Washington Star*, seeing Midtown as a model for the nation's capital, called the Plaza "the Nation's most spectacular center-city revival" and went on to explain that "the big lesson for cities seems to be that downtown business districts need enlivement."[18]

City planners made pilgrimages to view Midtown Plaza's wonders. New Haven's Citizen Council traveled there to compare it to their plans for their own Chapel Square Mall. The City Planning Department of Worcester, Massachusetts, boarded a private jet and traveled north to inspect the downtown project.[19] Even Congress arranged a special trip to see the downtown mall; representatives held hearings about the state of the city on Midtown's mezzanine. Leaving little doubt about the future direction of cities, one participant in the congressional hearings intoned, "Related to an urban renewal project, Midtown, is . . . the model." The *World Book Encyclopedia* for 1962 featured Midtown Plaza as the single best answer to downtown's persistent economic problems.[20] For Rochester's department stores' worries, Gruen gave them a solution perfected in his suburban work.

"We determined," one businessman explained, "to make downtown more attractive than any suburban shopping center." As Gruen had included the best qualities of downtown in the suburban mall, now he invoked suburban malls for downtown revitalization. "How can we attract people back to the heart of the city?" Gruen asked.[21] "The Midtown Plaza project illustrates how the planning concepts which were developed in the design of regional shopping centers can be translated into the urban vernacular."[22]

One of the more influential urban policy groups, the Urban Land Institute, enthusiastically endorsed Midtown Plaza's combination of retail facilities "with hotels, office buildings, banks, a post office, a children's play area, an auditorium." The Institute predicted that Midtown's "huge pedestrian court" would establish "a Twentieth Century town square which will be utilized for concerts, exhibitions, and other public events, and which will serve as a social meeting place for the City."[23]

Remaking Rochester's downtown involved much more than a facelift; the transformations completely shifted the ways Rochester's citizens would use their downtown. "The idea was to restore some excitement, some dynamism, some life to the dying heart of town," the *New York Herald Tribune* observed. As Gruen enthusiastically described Midtown to the Regional Plan Association of New York: "the central plaza has become the 'Town Center' of the twentieth century." Rochester, the *Washington Star* said, "has created something no other downtown possesses anywhere in the world—a 'town square' under glass." Early observers saw Midtown as an entirely new type of downtown. As the *Washington Star* concluded about the Midtown Plaza: "It makes the city more lively."[24] "Now as you stroll inside Midtown Plaza, the place is crowded, day and night," one reporter glowed. "People cluster in the plaza, sitting on benches, talking, reading, as people have done in town squares for centuries."[25] The project was done with one goal in mind: to attract the suburban middle class and their money back to the city.

Rochester's downtown had been reorganized by two department stores that now offered public facilities and events for patrons to enjoy. Midtown Plaza had replaced streets with mall courts and lanes. "Every single retail tenant in Midtown Plaza is a chain operation," *Chain Store Age* bragged.[26] By excluding smaller local stores, Midtown Plaza helped the rise of more nationally oriented chains. Of course, the dominance of chain stores also made downtown look and feel more like a suburban shopping center.

The great symbol of Midtown Plaza was a large piece of twirling sculpture named the Clock of the Nations. One reporter described how the clock "stops all traffic every hour and half-hour as it puts on a puppet show to the tempo of folk dancing tunes of a dozen different countries." Gruen hoped such symbols would lend downtown Rochester a cosmopolitan feel. "Midtown Plaza has recaptured for your enjoyment—and your children's—the lively and gay atmosphere of faraway marketplaces of the world," a brochure cheered. "As the plazas of Europe, from the days of the Renaissance, had traditionally been enlivened by the town clock, so Midtown Plaza features the Clock of the Nations to mark the time of the day with a colorful pageant."[27]

The appeal of Midtown Plaza did not come without some difficulty. Even with business footing the major portion of the bill, the city of Rochester invested in and undertook massive infrastructure improvements. It built the mall's parking garage, gave two city streets to the developers, extended another street, and constructed a ring road around the downtown retail area. The final bill for the city came to $12 million.[28] Through this public subsidization, Rochester re-created its downtown for the prospect of attracting middle-class suburbanites.

Criticism of the Midtown Plaza project—and especially of the city's financial involvement—heated up during the mayoral election of 1961. With Midtown two years from completion, all the city could show for its investment was an empty hole in the middle of downtown. The hole was going to be the parking garage, politicians promised. During the campaign for mayor, Democrat Henry Gillette emerged as a vigorous opponent of Midtown Plaza. He attacked Republican mayor Barry's record on the project. "Democrats insisted that the GOP had 'given away' $15 million to Midtown Plaza," one newspaper article reported. During a televised debate, a councilmember charged that "Midtown Plaza is a partnership between the city government and two merchants." He went on to say that "we are not against the concept of Midtown but against fantastic costs." Ironically, Gillette's criticisms did not concern the city's role in this type of investment but simply Rochester's lack of forethought in failing to obtain more federal and state funds. The project had been built "without adequate planning for the people," Gillette charged. The Democrats swept the elections, largely on this one issue.[29]

The Midtown Plaza project was successfully completed; Gruen learned how important it was to have political as well as economic support for his plans. The failed public initiative of Fort Worth and the largely private financing of Midtown made it clear where the money for large-scale projects was. In Rochester, private lenders had financed a private developer. However, few department stores could afford to acquire large tracts of land in their city's downtown and turn around and construct a brand-new shopping center. The financial model of Midtown was never repeated. It also was not repeated because of the massive amount of federal funds available for urban renewal. The best estimates put the price tag at almost $20 billion for the 1949 Urban Renewal Bill, with a small fraction of that going toward commercial demolition and rebuilding downtown. Gruen may have railed to his heart's content about the need to revitalize downtown, and his audiences as well as the press may have been sympathetic to his arguments, but in the end the projects were often too unwieldy and expensive to be fully realized. Typically, cities would hire Gruen to complete a downtown plan. Then the city's redevelopment authority would condemn and demolish properties in the urban renewal area. For instance, in Lancaster, Pennsylvania, the local government used eminent domain to claim four square blocks of properties downtown. It then constructed a four-floor parking garage, a row of stores, and two large buildings.[30]

As private money built suburban shopping centers across America, public subsidies attempted to lure investors and white shoppers back downtown. City planners and politicians wanted a mall to help them sell their city as a thriving, economically viable place. They also hoped that the mall's success would spill over into the rest of the city. In many ways, urban renewal funds made cities begin to see their primary purpose as economic. City governments began to package, market, and merchandise the spaces of their cities to corporations. The future of cities became linked to the future of retailing. But for all the politicians' and planners' efforts, retail continued to flow to the suburbs; many more shopping centers than downtown renewal projects were constructed in the 1960s. Even with the government's vows to equalize the access to capital between downtown and suburbia through federal urban renewal funds, suburbia had already secured the most important source of cultural and financial capital of the 1950s: the white middle class.

In nearly every city where Gruen worked the percentage of whites in the population fell, total population fell, and the per capita income fell. In Minneapolis, the site of Gruen's Southdale mall, the central city population fell from 1940 to 1960 while the surrounding suburbs grew by one million people. At the same time, the African American population of the city increased by 155 percent; the suburbs were 98 percent white.[31] Similarly, in Detroit, where Gruen worked for Hudson's, the central city population peaked in 1953 at 1.8 million and then fell to 1.67 million by 1960 and again to 1.2 million by 1980. Over the same years, the percentage of African Americans in the center city tripled, from 20 percent to 66 percent of the total population. As one historian of Detroit observed, "White and middle-class flight strongly affected the viability of the city of Detroit."[32] A similar trend occurred in Fort Worth. Tarrant County, surrounding the city, added almost 200,000 people from 1950 to 1960. And the county's population was almost entirely white. By 1960, 95 percent of Tarrant County's African American population lived inside the city of Fort Worth.[33] The suburban shopping center's success depended on these economic and racial divides; shopping centers helped to maintain a segregated city at the same moment that laws were promising to dismantle segregation. The creation and construction of shopping centers provided white suburbanites with places in their new neighborhoods to gather together and speak the common language of consumption. Gruen never directly addressed race with respect to his shopping centers or downtown projects. Instead, he talked as if his projects would be available to all Americans.

The plans to remake downtown into a suburban shopping center suggest how pervasive the suburban lifestyle had become, especially in the minds of architects, urban planners, and politicians. The suburban shopping center captured everyone's fancy. Even those who were terrified by its impact on their livelihoods looked upon it with deep reverence and gave it the most extreme form of flattery—emulation. Gruen had wanted to remake cities by building large downtown shopping centers and attracting white suburbanites back to the city center.[34] The idea was flawed for one basic reason, however. As Gruen well knew, suburbanites had even lusher, larger places to shop: his suburban shopping centers. In an economic race between downtown and suburbia, downtown had little chance.

Gruen's accomplishments downtown were overshadowed by what he designed in the suburbs. Even as he predicted an imminent renaissance of cities, Gruen also continued designing suburban shopping centers. While many of his downtown plans remained modest or on the drawing board, his suburban shopping centers continued to grow larger and larger. Throughout the 1960s, shopping center owners competed to capture more and more of their white, affluent suburban market. And shopping malls continued to grow larger and larger. Gruen knew much about these ever-growing marketplaces. The year before *The Heart of Our Cities* appeared, he had completed the world's largest shopping center for a Chicago suburb. The Randhurst Shopping Center represented the height of Gruen's retailing dreams in suburbia. With over one million square feet of stores and three department stores meeting under a giant dome, Randhurst was an object lesson in the economic dominance of the suburbs.[35] The mayor of the suburban town of Mount Prospect laid the cornerstone of the shopping center and welcomed "this new city." "It is our wish," he concluded, that "Randhurst Shopping Center will fulfill all of the dreams of those who have been converting the cornfields of yesterday into the merchandising realities of many tomorrows."[36] When Randhurst opened, having been capitalized at $22 million, *Shopping Center Age* bragged that it was 100 percent chain stores. The developers had even included fallout shelters for the community's use.[37] The immense shopping center opened within months of Midtown Plaza, but the suburban project dwarfed Gruen's achievement with Midtown.[38]

In light of the national recognition Gruen gained for his Fort Worth, Kalamazoo, and Rochester projects, other city politicians soon began dreaming of involving him in their own urban revitalization projects. By 1963 Gruen's urban renewal career had taken off. His firm was asked to fix downtowns across America. In the early 1960s Stamford and Bridgeport, Connecticut; Lancaster, Pennsylvania; San Francisco, Fresno, and Redlands, California; Green Bay, Wisconsin; Boston, Massachusetts; Paterson, New Jersey; Urbana, Illinois; and Knoxville, Tennessee, all turned to Gruen for plans to remodel their downtowns. In Boston he worked to create middle-class, high-rise apartment buildings along the Charles River. In Lancaster, he helped plan and design a shopping area and office building complex in the center of downtown. None of the projects would be as grand as Midtown, however.

As America's politicians and planners pinned the future of their cities on shopping centers, the idea meant that other needs of the people of the city were ignored. In the early 1960s, urban renewal also became increasingly criticized from both the left and the right on the political spectrum. For instance, Herbert Gans, Jane Jacobs, and Martin Anderson all attacked urban renewal projects for squandering public funds, ruining neighborhoods, and imposing a modernist vision on the city's variety.[39] Gruen's simultaneous involvement in both urban renewal and suburban shopping centers came under increased suspicion.

By the late 1950s, Gruen had gained much experience redesigning downtowns. He turned his newfound expertise into a book on America's urban crisis and his cures. In 1963, Gruen compiled many of his speeches as his most complete statement to date on American cities. Titled *The Heart of Our Cities*, the book was a counterpart to his developer's guide for suburban shopping centers of four years earlier, *Shopping Towns USA*. In that book, Gruen had provided practical advice about planning, developing, and running a shopping center. He took readers on a guided tour of the different shapes, financing, and styles of American shopping. In *The Heart of Our Cities*, Gruen had fewer examples at his disposal. Instead of examining successful projects, he used the book as a soapbox to critique American cities' failures. In a strange twist, his argument for American cities became a jeremiad against them. Nothing was above reproach in Gruen's book. He railed against Americans' love of automobiles, the suburban wasteland, the plight of cities, blind government bureaucrats, greedy developers, and pompous architects. Whereas *Shopping Towns USA* provided exemplary and simple models to follow, *The Heart of Our Cities* gave examples of urban horror stories and planning incompetence. Even the few cities that had undertaken urban renewal were hopelessly wrong, according to Gruen. For instance, New Haven, Connecticut, with the country's largest urban renewal budget per capita, came under Gruen's fire. The project was not appreciably different from Gruen's own proposals—with a shopping center, large highway, giant parking garage, and office building—yet he called the New Haven project misguided. He then proceeded to tear into the city's immense, brutalist-style parking garage, designed by Yale architect Paul Rudolph. Gruen dismissed it as an "expression of personal ambition."[40] The garage was simply the symbol for an urban renewal project devoted solely to the automobile, Gruen declared. With *The Heart of Our Cities*, Gruen repositioned himself as an urban theorist and critic. Just as Gruen had remade Rochester, he now remade himself. Of course, as with so many moves in his varied career, Gruen was not unique. He borrowed heavily from other more eloquent critics of urban renewal like Jacobs and Gans. He was also able to use his newfound beliefs to separate himself from other urban planners. With the publication of *The Heart of Our Cities*, Gruen was now wearing many hats. He specialized in suburban shopping centers, urban renewal plans, and opinionated books on the urban condition.

Throughout the 1960s, Gruen continued his work on these seemingly paradoxical retailing projects. He designed larger and larger suburban shopping centers for private developers and then refashioned downtown as a shopping center for city governments. It was a difficult balancing act. While downtown redevelopment projects drew suburban consumers through chain stores, free parking, and larger shopping venues, many city residents were further marginalized by the massive public projects. With the beginning of riots in 1964 in Watts, Los Angeles, urban blacks became more desperate. They also began to level a powerful and violent critique at reform-minded liberals' visions of a new, modernized city. African Americans protested inadequate housing, urban renewal programs, and the general disinvestment in cities. As African Americans attempted to gain more control over urban policies and politics, both urban renewal plans and suburban shopping centers became targets of attack. For instance, Detroit, where Gruen had built four shopping centers for J. L. Hudson's, had become one of the nation's most segregated cities. In 1967, blacks in Detroit rioted for five days, leaving forty-three dead and $22 million worth of property damage. Joseph L. Hudson, president of the department store, took charge of rebuilding the city after the riots. His New Detroit Commission focused on ways to improve Detroit and its image. The idea that the head of a department store that had so successfully moved to the suburbs would replan the city more than frustrated some city residents. "They [the committee members] ought to stop fooling themselves. The white middle class couldn't possibly understand the problems of the disenfranchised black man," the president of the Detroit Student Non-Violent Coordinating Committee declared. "They could not do anything for black people. They've just discovered us." He asked, "How could they plan for us?" And then he focused his comments on the growing suburban-urban divide. "I couldn't plan for them," he said. "I couldn't plan programs for . . . J. L. Hudson if he were planning a new store in the suburbs."[41]

Working to create solutions to downtown's problems and to continue suburbia's successes, Gruen placed himself in a deeply paradoxical situation. The two projects encapsulated the increasingly violent divide between suburban whites and inner-city blacks in America. In light of both the criticisms and urban riots, Gruen's urban planning for downtown on commercial areas seemed more and more untenable. Not only were Gruen's visions for urban renewal projects no longer possible, but the very projects he had designed seemed to exacerbate class and racial divisions within the United States. By 1968, with American cities in flames, blacks reclaiming the inner cities, and critiques of urban renewal growing louder, Gruen made another career decision. He retreated back across the Atlantic to live in Vienna.

"Those Bastard Developments" and Gruen's Legacy

I have been led into the position of being a thinker and a doer at the same time. This is not a comfortable position. It is like standing on a bridge, with a view toward reality on one side and idealism on the other.

—Victor Gruen, 1973

In 1968, Victor Gruen retired from Victor Gruen Associates.[1] For seventeen years, his company had been thriving in America. The firm primarily earned its profits from shopping center commissions, although urban renewal work continued apace. Gruen had enjoyed a long, successful run in American architecture at a moment when the American landscape was changing in fundamental ways. Always increasing in size, cost and grandeur, Gruen's projects had continually progressed to the next, larger challenge. He had moved from working on single stores to national chains to shopping centers to entire downtowns. It had been an incredibly successful career, an American dream of an immigrant success story. Yet, in the end, Gruen wanted little to do with America.

After living in the United States for thirty years, Gruen returned to Vienna. For a refugee Jew, this was unusual. During the war, the Fascists had decimated Vienna's vibrant Jewish community of 175,000. Only 10,000 Jews lived in the Austrian capital after the war ended. One historian observed, "After 1945, one was much more likely to encounter Viennese Jews in Jerusalem, New York, or London than in their native city where Jews now constituted an insignificant percentage of the population."[2] Gruen's oldest friend, Rudi Baumfeld, never understood "how Victor could return to Vienna . . . because they had really gone through some horrible situations after the Anschluss." Baumfeld believed that even when Gruen chose to move back, the Austrian city was "a fiercely anti-Semitic place."[3] Vienna's hold on Gruen's imagination made returning seemingly unproblematic for him, however. His daughter ventured that he had "always wanted to go back."[4] For Gruen, the explicit anti-Semitism—past or present—did not dampen his strong feelings for the city.

In Vienna, Gruen moved back to his old neighborhood in the Central District. He also started another architectural firm, Victor Gruen International. Gruen had long been nostalgic for the Vienna he had left behind. In his American shopping centers, he had gone so far as to try and resurrect the richness of his remembered city. But he could not go back. An event one night, soon after his return, brought Gruen face-to-face with actual ghosts from his past. The night before Gruen planned on celebrating the opening of his Vienna office, he was given an unfortunate shock. Accompanied by his son, daughter-in-law, and granddaughter, Gruen gave a tour of his new office. His daughter-in-law remembered the office as a remodeled carriage house equipped with Bauhaus furniture, feeling "intimate, yet spartan." "The ambiance of the old carriage house was a joy to behold!" The office felt like "a lavish toast to a new beginning."

His daughter-in-law vividly recalled what happened after they left the office. When they walked into the chilly Viennese evening, a "shiny black Mercedes limousine glided to an abrupt halt at the curb in front of us." A man greeted Gruen, welcoming him back to Vienna. "Gruen let out a piercing cry! The blood had drained from his face," she recalled. The man had been a Nazi and had taken over Gruen's architectural firm in 1938. So distraught was Gruen that his family canceled their dinner plans. "As we sped away," his daughter-in-law recalled, "I turned to give him [Gruen] a last look, as he leaned weeping, alone."[5] The image that Gruen had cherished of Vienna, that he had relied upon to fashion his American shopping centers, had long since been destroyed. The vibrant, organic community of prewar Vienna only lived on in Gruen's mind while he was exiled in California.

On March 3, 1973, Victor Gruen turned seventy. His birthday presented a good opportunity for reflecting on his life's work. The architect's most significant work was now behind him. However, he was still as opinionated as ever. His fourth wife, Kemija Salihefendic, invited Gruen's friends, colleagues, and past clients to help him celebrate. She asked them to send reminiscences of memorable events and projects. Letters flooded into Gruen's Vienna home.

Garret Eckbo, the California landscape architect, wrote to congratulate Gruen for being "one successful architect." Eckbo marveled that somehow Gruen had "managed to combine urbanity and humanism in the rat race of American commercialism, and maintain his integrity."[6] Gruen and Eckbo had worked together designing a pedestrian mall for downtown Fresno nine years earlier. Gruen bragged that the design had awakened the community spirit in the people of Fresno. "Community is based on the possibility of communicating directly with each other," Gruen said. He wanted to bring people together in his Fresno project. With art, fountains, jungle gyms, puppet theater, kiosks, and bandstands, Gruen and Eckbo tried to bring life back to Main Street. Borrowing from his shopping center "tricks," Gruen redesigned Fresno "with excitement, with surprise, with all those elements that draw people." "The entire downtown area," he concluded, "became a meeting ground not only during shopping hours but during evening and Sundays and holidays and it became a real lively community." The Fresno revitalization project won a Housing and Urban Development Award for design excellence. And Gruen traveled to the White House to show Lady Bird Johnson a film about Fresno's redevelopment, "A City Reborn."[7] Other cards reminiscing about Gruen's past triumphs soon arrived in Vienna.

James Rouse, the Baltimore mall developer turned urban redeveloper, paid homage to Gruen's career. "You touched me and my associates at an important point of time in our individual growth and in the growth of our company," Rouse wrote. He thanked Gruen for pulling his company from "the provinces to the big time." Rouse then cast his eyes back to their shopping center project of 1961, in Cherry Hill, New Jersey. One of the first enclosed malls on the East Coast, Cherry Hill had been an extremely successful collaboration between Gruen, Larry Smith, Rouse, and the Strawbridge and Clothier department store. When the seventy-five-store New Jersey shopping center opened, 100,000 people flocked to enjoy its wonders. Five national magazines ran flattering articles. One article swooned over the fantastic Cherry Court, with its clerestory windows, a Japanese garden, jungle-like plantings, and a fanciful wood gazebo. "There is no space we have produced that is as grand and floating as Cherry Court," Rouse wrote to Gruen. "I have always felt that you built it with your own hands."[8] Gruen was buoyed by Rouse's praise.

The architect of several hundred buildings and city plans, the author of four books and hundreds of articles, Gruen had produced a body of architecture and architectural ideas nearly unequaled in its breadth and

FIGURE 39. Pedestrian mall designed by Victor Gruen and Garrett Eckbo for Fresno, California, c. 1968. Courtesy Garrett Eckbo.

impact. He had popularized several innovations—store modernization, enclosed shopping centers, and downtown pedestrian malls. "I'm not sure any of us artistic architects could do what Victor does," the eminent modernist Philip Johnson said about Gruen's ability.[9] For both Fresno and Cherry Hill, Gruen had designed environments to promote retailing by bringing people together. The formula served Gruen well throughout his American career. He had continually fashioned new strategies to entertain customers, reinvigorate retailing, and reinvent himself. Indeed, Gruen's skill at enticing the public ensured a succession of projects. He had increased the scale of his projects from stores and department stores to shopping centers and downtowns by producing popular buildings—and each of these served as advertising for new clients. Though he seemed to capitalize on his previous commercial successes, it did not always work so neatly or naturally. Gruen worked hard

FIGURE 40. Cherry Court at Cherry Hill Mall, c. 1966. Courtesy Strawbridge and Clothier Collection, Hagley Museum and Library.

to increase the scale and influence of his projects. In the postwar economy, he constantly refashioned himself: as retail theorist, critic of the strip, philosopher of the shopping center, savior of cities, and popular author. And in the last years of his career, he would reinvent himself yet again.

As he approached his seventieth birthday, Gruen made time to write a book. In *Centers for the Urban Environment*, he once again broadened his vision. He now tried to explain the growth of the twentieth-century metropolis and its relationship to the countryside. In many respects, the book combined Gruen's two earlier passions. He united his concern for improving the suburbs from *Shopping Towns USA* and for revitalizing downtown from *The Heart of Our Cities*. In addition, he expanded his frame and focused on how cities and suburbs destroyed nature. Gruen did all this by reviewing his own architectural career and throughout the book, making the case for his own significance. He provided case studies from the 1950s and 1960s—Northland, Southdale, Fort Worth, and Rochester—to describe the large-scale changes in the American metropolis. However, all was not perfect in Gruen's examination of his own past.

Gruen began with a chapter outlining the environmental decimation of America. He bluntly contrasted an automobile junkyard with a stand of trees. Once again, he showed the Miracle Mile as an example of the blighted American landscape. In response to the spread of the commercial strip, Gruen posed a Faustian bargain, arguing that Americans needed to chose between "conservation of nature—or pollution through misuse of technology." Cars or trees—thus he reduced the equation of sprawl versus planning. Gruen explained that he now realized how "urban settlements have decisive influence on ecological problems." He saw a war between man and nature, which unfortunately, man was winning. Nature did not have time to heal its wounds. "We can poison water, air, and land faster than ever before and faster than nature can purify them," Gruen lamented. "Nature will die, and man, realizing too late that he is himself part of nature, will suffocate in the stench of the corpse." He showed images of the "last tree," the "mass murder" of fish, polluted water, smoke from automobiles, smog blanketing the city, and piles of garbage. Gruen looked for a solution to these horrible problems and returned to the topic of city planning. To save the environment, Gruen said, Americans had to *plan* the urban environment. Only by stopping suburban sprawl and remaking the city, the man who had invented the mall somberly warned, could an environmental catastrophe be avoided. And where was Gruen in all of this? He had helped shape it all—from chain stores and commercial strips to suburbs and downtowns. The world of postwar America that he so lamented was, in part, his own creation. He better than anyone should have realized that the choices between planned development and unplanned sprawl were never so simple. But Gruen did not linger on his own complicity in exacerbating the sprawl that he now attacked. As before, he was more concerned with remaking himself and looking to the future.

Gruen recommended building "compact" cities to solve transportation problems, sprawl, and the loss of community. "By interweaving all expressions of human life within the urban tissue," Gruen explained, "we can restore the lost sense of commitment and belonging." He promised that large-scale "environmental" planning would "counteract the phenomena of disorientation, isolation, and lonesomeness and awaken a sense of identification and participation." Once again, the proposal revealed Gruen at his most utopian. The book's subtitle was *Survival of the Cities.* As he had promised to save cities and suburbs through monumental shopping center designs, he now proffered monumental plans to save humans from themselves. Gruen also attempted to put his new beliefs into practice. In 1970, he founded the Victor Gruen Foundation for Environmental Planning, which hoped to educate the American public about environmental problems resulting from urban sprawl. The foundation presented Gruen's *Centers for the Urban Environment* as its first statement. Tracy Susman, its second director, wrote the introduction to the book. The publication was an effort, she wrote, "to bring about a greater public understanding of the decisive role 'Environmental Planning' should and must play if the ecological balance of our planet . . . is to be assured."[10] Gruen adopted the arguments of the environmental movement to enlarge the scope of his own projects; he had moved from Fifth Avenue boutiques to shopping centers, now he wanted to reorder all of nature.[11]

Throughout the book, Gruen presented his own career as a qualified success. He trumpeted that he had built immense new buildings in America and had rearranged the nation's metropolises. The previous year Gruen had penned a letter to an author summarizing his career. "I consider my greatest achievements in architecture," Gruen wrote, "those which contribute to the quality of the human environment and give, beyond that, joy and stimulation."[12] Gruen also trained his sights on what he considered his failures. He did not hesitate, now that he was across the Atlantic, to skewer his past projects and past clients. Gruen had built his reputation and career largely with his retailing successes. This fact he now regretted. Gruen confessed that he was sorely disappointed in his retail successes. His shopping centers had two major flaws. "The ugliness and discomfort of the land-wasting seas of parking," Gruen said, scarred the landscape. And shopping centers focused too much on retailing and left out other community functions.[13] A commercial architect, Gruen liked to see and market himself as a designer of the entire city—an urban planner, an environmental designer.

By 1978, Gruen felt even less positive about his own accomplishments. In a speech given in London that year, he criticized Americans for perverting his ideas. The very popularity of the shopping mall gave him an easy target. He looked at what he had built and despised what he saw. "I refuse to pay alimony for those bastard developments," he proclaimed. Gruen said that Americans in their blind pursuit of profit had corrupted his vision. In the reprinted speech, "The Sad Story of Shopping Centres," Gruen gave his final judgment on his architectural career. After quickly establishing his shopping center credentials—by running through the 194X, Northland, and Southdale projects, Gruen asked what had happened in the last twenty years since his "pioneer centres opened." His verdict was unforgiving. With "a tremendous increase in numbers" and "the shopping centre concept all over the world," "a tragic downgrading of quality" had occurred. His original "environmental and humane ideas," he claimed, "were not only not improved upon—they were completely forgotten." Gruen accounted for this deplorable state by explaining that "only those features which had proved profitable were copied." The American pursuit of profits, Gruen bitterly insisted, had derailed his greatest hopes for the shopping center. It was a stinging pronouncement, even if it strained credulity. After all, had not Gruen promised that shopping centers would be the most profitable retail location ever? Had he not guaranteed developers, merchants, and bankers that the shopping center would produce phenomenal profits? Yet, of course, along with being profitable Gruen had also hoped that successful retail ventures, if properly planned, would halt sprawl. Now, he admitted defeat. He indicted shopping centers for destroying city centers, small merchants, a rich social life, and the environment as well.[14]

To explain the shopping center's horrible failings, Gruen placed the blame squarely on the backs of developers, shirking his own complicity. He claimed that their "motives" had changed. Whereas department stores like Hudson's or Dayton's had undertaken 1950s developments "to enhance the reputations of their family empires" by being "earnestly responsible towards future generations," present-day developers, Gruen lamented, only looked at the bottom line. The developers were now "anonymous real estate entrepreneurs." In the worst cases, they were "promoters and speculators who just wanted to make a fast buck." Rather than serving the needs of a neighborhood, these developers constructed "a shopping machine large and powerful enough that it could be located almost anywhere." These gigantic developments forced people "to travel dozens of miles" and delivered "the death blow to the already suffering city centers." For an example of this bleak state of affairs, Gruen turned to firsthand experience.

When "a gigantic shopping machine" opened south of Old Vienna, the city's soul had been destroyed. "Small independent shops" were forced out of business. The city core and twenty-three neighborhoods throughout Vienna had been seriously threatened. The shopping center, Gruen explained, represented the triumph of Le Corbusier's horrible ideas of separating functions and people from one another, and the city had become nothing more than "single function ghettos."

Gruen could not acknowledge the bitter irony of his statements. For, of course, if Vienna's center had been killed by a shopping center, then surely some of the blood stained his hands. Undoubtedly, he had to recognize his own handiwork. Had not he helped the same process occur in Detroit with Northland, in Minneapolis with Southdale, in Chicago with Randhurst, and in Philadelphia with Cherry Hill? One could go on and on. Gruen, now that he felt a personal stake in Vienna, vainly pointed his finger in protest. He, however, wanted no responsibility for what he had created in America. He defended himself by dismissing American cities. They were not worth saving, already ruined, he wrote. "American cities, with their comparatively short histories and small traditions," Gruen said, "offered people little beyond traffic jams." However, "for Europe the thoughtless copying of the American shopping centre has been truly catastrophic." Since European cities were thousands of years old, the rise of the shopping center would destroy opportunities "for culture, for the arts and civic virtues," he worried. No matter how "splendidly it might be executed," he wrote elsewhere, shopping centers "cannot furnish a valid answer to urban planning for the future."[15]

Gruen retreated more and more into the realm of fantasy. He even turned to fiction. In a science-fiction novel, "Is Progress a Crime?' Gruen, playing himself, sat next to a space alien on a long airline flight. The alien questioned the wise old architect about the environmental consequences of unrestrained suburban growth. Gruen responded with explanations that blamed the car and suburbia; Earth's future hung in the balance. In this dystopic novel, Gruen characterized America, and unintentionally his own retail work, as "a 'clip-joint,' where everybody is persuaded to buy what he doesn't need with money he doesn't own in order to impress people he actually can't stand."[16] In this fictional world, Gruen voiced his complaints and imagined realizing his dreams.

In this bitter rhetoric, Gruen appeared to have experienced a startling change of heart. With his return to Europe and living in semiretirement, he brooded over the way Americans lived. Living in suburbia, driving cars, building billboards, erecting flashy signs, and abandoning cities all represented, for Gruen, Americans' lack of culture and civilization. In many ways, Gruen simply continued the critiques he had leveled at "suburbscape" since the 1950s. Indeed, the surprising aspect of Gruen's rhetoric was not that he attacked American ways of living—he had always done that—but that he now offered no solutions. Earlier Gruen had promoted various architectural projects as tools to clean up America. Modernized stores would eliminate commercial clutter and bring people into wondrous spaces. Shopping centers would control the proliferating strips, provide suburbanites with a public space, and turn a neat profit. Urban renewal plans would save downtown, generate city taxes, and modernize America's cities. Whereas before Gruen recommended appealing architectural solutions to remedy America's soulless landscape, now he threw up his hands in disgust. In the past Gruen had prescribed equal doses of criticism and solutions, but now he offered only criticism.

He no longer had colorful proposals for rearranging cities. Instead, he placed his hope in "the public." The public, he claimed, should protest the further construction of shopping centers. For Gruen—an expert who had long banked on the ability of designers, architects, and planners to shape public reactions—turning to the public was a telling admission. At seventy-five, he no longer held on to the belief that architects could plan better tomorrows. He no longer fantasized about shaping an uplifting retail environment. Gruen had reached the end of his faith in the power of architectural solutions. In his new disappointment, Gruen hesitantly admitted his own failures of vision, especially with the shopping center.

Gruen offered a depressing prognosis. He appeared to be shocked by the strength of the shopping center's victory. Or perhaps his 1943 prediction of a citywide retail center had simply come all too true. In Gruen's opinion, the shopping center had become focused solely on its primary goal of promoting retail and had abandoned its possible role in creating new communities. Gruen closed his article with a prophecy about the future. The shopping center's days were numbered, he declared. He saw "unmistakable signs of its downfall." The shopping center, Gruen predicted, "has no future at all." He wanted the public to declare a moratorium on shopping center construction. For once, Gruen's instincts were way off mark; the public did not rise up and protest more shopping centers. Gruen made this prophecy in the middle of America's largest shopping center boom. According to one estimate, from 1970 to 1990, 25,000 new shopping centers opened their doors across the United States.[17] However, Gruen's very success proved the fallacy of his argument. He had helped transform shopping from a chore to a pleasure, and there was no going back. The shopping center's juggernaut was stronger than ever before.

Of course, this last diatribe was perhaps one of Gruen's best performances to date. Over his long career, Gruen had promised a better world
to audiences and clients: better stores, suburbs, or cities. In his jeremiad
against the American scene, Gruen attempted to get in the last word on
his creations and the first word on historical interpretation. Just as he
had promised quality show windows or improved suburbs to merchants,
he now tried to sell his interpretations to the public. However, Gruen
was not simply critiquing his own creations; he was also justifying his
career. In this respect, Gruen had not changed. He was still calling for
reform and promising an improved, remade world.

Gruen's argument was an ingenious blend of self-justification and
self-flagellation. Sitting in Vienna, Gruen could not pass up an opportunity to comment on his creations. He had played this strategy before.
And it had served him well. For instance, in the late 1940s, Gruen began
attacking commercial strips as aesthetic and economic blight. Of course,
he had just designed numerous Grayson's with flashy facades and neon
lights to attract motorists on those very strips. In fact, Gruen's critiques
had been invaluable to his career. The observations and remedies had
allowed Gruen to expand his architectural range. He had critiqued his
own projects, moved on to larger ones, and profited greatly. Now, at the
end of his career, Gruen attempted the same gambit. He harshly criticized his shopping center idea for encouraging sprawl, destroying
nature, and degrading Americans. He also hoped to work on a larger
canvas. However, what that project might be remained obscure.

Gruen had wanted to design the stage Americans lived their lives on.
Like other European modernists, he had attempted to reform people's
daily lives by controlling their physical environments. Based on his
retail successes, Gruen had supreme confidence in his ability to shape
people's experiences. However, in Gruen's drive to increase the scale of
his projects—from a single store to a single city—he had finally run into
a dead end. He wanted to exert his will over larger and larger sweeps of
space. Finding a client with the capital to set Gruen loose on an entire
metropolis from downtown to suburbia seemed impossible. He had
reached the outer limits of scale.

Even with his bitter critiques, Gruen did not completely give up on
architecture. With his new firm, Victor Gruen International, he undertook a diversity of projects. He designed a modernized Tehran for the
shah of Iran, a future university in Louvrain, Switzerland, renewal plans
for the Duomo area of Venice, and a pedestrian mall and parking garage
for central Vienna.[18] However, in Europe as earlier in America, Gruen

had one concept that people wanted to pay handsomely for: the shopping center. Even as Gruen complained that Americans had "bastardized" his shopping center ideals for private profit and fled their downtowns for the suburbs, he began repeating the same formula in Europe. He designed suburban shopping centers for the outskirts of Vienna (1966), for Printemps around Paris (Tête Défense in La Défense, 1968), along the French Riviera (CAP 3000 shopping mall, 1969), and for Glatt in Zurich (1971). He literally exported the form of the shopping center that he had perfected in suburban America to Europe's new suburbs. "Gruen's ideas," one journalist reported, "are, no doubt, the best things a native son ever brought home from America."[19] Once again, Gruen promised that the shopping center could improve the city. He said he could correct the mistakes he had made in his American shopping centers. "Europeans," Gruen wrote to a colleague in 1966, "do not necessarily have to repeat everything which was done in the United States." He chose to emphasize that as "magnets of attraction for other activities," European shopping centers could spur the development of new downtowns.[20] As earlier, Gruen was imagining retail to be the motor driving the creation of an improved metropolitan life. As Gruen had fled Vienna in 1938 and then looked back longingly across the Atlantic for inspiration, so upon returning to Vienna Gruen drew on his American experience. Ironically, he reversed his own equation and began an Americanization of Europe.

Gruen happened upon one client who perhaps could realize his modernizing dreams for reshaping a city, determining people's movements, and making their lives beautiful and efficient. He was hired by the shah of Iran to redesign the capital city, Tehran. Beginning in 1961, the shah had initiated a series of land reforms and a program of countrywide modernization dubbed the "White Revolution." The shah's pursuit of efficiency and Westernization led him to the United States for technological and economic support. Also seeking expertise to rearrange his new secular cities, the shah called on Gruen.

Gruen eagerly began replanning Tehran. The shah was the client that Gruen had long wanted—in this case, a dictator capable of giving Gruen the land, power, and means to control every facet of the environment: houses, stores, highways, lakes, and parks. Perhaps Gruen saw the shah as Hudson's without their desire for real estate profits or J. B. Thomas without the defeats from the Texas legislature. But Gruen did not reckon on the will of the Iranian people. Just as he had called on "the public" to rein in shopping center development in the United States, Iranians

FIGURE 41. Master plan of Tehran prepared for the shah of Iran, c. 1967. From Victor Gruen Associates, "Comprehensive Plan for Tehran," c. 1968. American Heritage Center, Victor Gruen Collection.

dealt him an unexpected blow. Staging mass protests in 1978 and over-throwing the shah in 1979, the Iranian people rebelled against the shah's program of Westernization and secularization. Whatever dream city Gruen had planned for Tehran was soon lost in the collapse of the shah's regime and Gruen's own failing health.[21]

The following year Victor Gruen passed away. In America his death elicited few notices. Just the same, Gruen had convinced a few observers with his recasting of his career. One journalist, writing in the *Washington Post*, mourned Gruen's passing and celebrated his contributions to American cities. Wolf Von Eckhardt focused on Gruen's commitment to cities. He knighted Gruen an "urban liberator." "Among the most important architect-planners of our time," he called Gruen. Von Eckhardt applauded Gruen for leading "the fight to liberate the American city from the tyranny of the automobile." The obituary looked glancingly at Gruen's shopping centers, simply saying that Gruen had attempted to re-create the Greek agora for Americans. Gruen's most influential and pervasive idea—the covered shopping mall—had become so ubiquitous that there was no need to explain its impact. Instead, the journalist chose to portray Gruen as the last friend of cities. "Largely because of Gruen and his insistence on separating 'human flesh from combustion engines,' the hearts of our cities are beating more strongly," the obituary noted.[22] Gruen would have been pleased with the verdict.

The Gruen Effect, as the 1997 Mall of America conference participants opined, was the bedazzlement by goods and the power of their presentation to provoke more purchases. This was the trick that elevated purchasing places into realms of wonder. Gruen had built his name and career on this effect. But underneath it was another that he could not have anticipated—one that betrayed the tensions within his career. In his work Gruen continually swerved between extremes: hating the car but always catering to it; bringing Main Street to the suburbs and yet lamenting the destruction of downtowns; expressing concern about shopping centers being devoted to retailing yet always working as a commercial architect; wanting to build spaces for the people but building larger and larger spaces for private corporations. In America, Victor Gruen had found his greatest expressions within the commercial sphere. The realm that fused profits and the public, merchants and the masses, was what gave Gruen the freedom to build his architectural creations and attempt to reform the American metropolis. Within that realm, he continually struck a balance that produced new forms and spaces for public life. Thus, in Gruen's successes as well as his failures, he redefined how Americans thought of themselves, their relationship to others, and their lives within the public realm. If at his life's end he found little solace in his career, then his critique fell on deaf ears. Americans—as developers, merchants, and consumers—would continue to build on Gruen's creations and elevate shopping into a central place in American life.

Notes

Introduction: The Gruen Effect

Notes to epigraphs: Victor Gruen, "What to Look for in Shopping Centers," *Chain Store Age* (July 1948), Library of Congress Victor Gruen Collection (hereafter LoCVGC) (92081474), OV 15 and American Heritage Center Victor Gruen Collection (hereafter AHCVGC) (5809-84-09-10), box 11; Richard G. Hubler, "A Cure for Sick Cities," *Los Angeles Times*, December 20, 1964, LoCVGC, OV 43.

1. Thomas Gifford, "That's Mall There Is, Folks," *Minneapolis Telegraph-Herald*, December 4, 1997, Opinion, A4. See also Kelly Whitman, "The Mauling of America," *Minneapolis City Pages* 18, no. 886 (November 26, 1997); Linda Mack, "Designers Hope You'll Lose Yourself in Shopping," *Minneapolis Star-Tribune*, November 24, 1997, Metro, B3.

2. Walter Guzzardi, Jr., "An Architect of Environments," *Fortune* (January 1962): 78. Biographical information on Gruen has been pieced together from a variety of sources. These include *Current Biography* (March 1959): 14; Victor Gruen, "Biography of the Founder," 1–7, LoCVGC, box 21; Victor Gruen, untitled, c. 1977, LoCVGC, box 20. For the little written on Gruen, the best is Howard Gillette, "The Evolution of the Planned Shopping Center in Suburb and City," *Journal of the American Planning Association* 5, no. 4 (1985): 449–60; see also David Hill, "Sustainability, Victor Gruen, and the Cellular Metropolis," *Journal of the American Planning Association* 58, no. 3 (summer 1992): 312–26; Diane Cohen, "Victor Gruen and the Regional Shopping Center," master's thesis, Columbia University, 1982; Guzzardi, "Architect of Environments," 77–80, 134–38; and Wolf Von Eckardt, "The Urban Liberator: Victor Gruen and the Pedestrian Oasis" (obituary), *Washington Post*, February 23, 1980, Style, Cityscape, B1.

3. The following are the best historical treatments of postwar cities and suburbia: Kenneth Jackson, *Crabgrass Frontier: The Suburbanization of the United States* (New York: Oxford University Press, 1985); Evan McKenzie, *Privatopia: Homeowner Associations and the Rise of Residential Private Government* (New Haven, Conn.: Yale University Press, 1994); Dolores Hayden, *Redesigning the American Dream: The Future of Housing, Work, and Family Life* (New York: Norton, 1984); William Sharpe and Leonard Wallock, "Bold New City or Built-Up 'Burb? Redefining Contemporary Suburbia," *American Quarterly* 46, no. 1 (March 1994): 1–30; Robert Fishman, *Bourgeois Utopias: The Rise and Fall of Suburbia* (New York: Basic Books, 1987). For contemporary descriptions of the suburbs see Auguste C. Spectorsky, *The Exurbanites* (New York: Lippincott, 1955); John Keats, *The Crack in the Picture Window* (Boston: Houghton Mifflin, 1956); Edward Higbee, *The Squeeze: Cities Without Space* (New York: William Morrow, 1960); and Herbert J. Gans, *The Levittowners: Ways of Life and Politics in a New Suburban Community* (New York: Pantheon, 1967).

4. See Juliet B. Schor, *The Overspent American: Upscaling, Downshifting, and the New Consumer* (New York: Basic Books, 1998), 72–74.

5. LoCVGC, box 20, folder 22.

6. Guzzardi, "Architect of Environments," 77–80, 134–38.

7. Victor Gruen, *The Heart of Our Cities: The Urban Crisis, Diagnosis and Cure* (New York: Simon and Schuster, 1964), 342.

8. Quoted in Von Eckardt, "Urban Liberator," B1.

9. "It was total environment we were after," another partner explained. "The Partners Talk About Victor Gruen Associates (for Biographical Notes)"; quotes are from Edgardo Contini and Karl Van Leuven, c. 1970, LoCVGC, box 78.

10. Victor Gruen and Larry Smith, *Shopping Towns USA: The Planning of Shopping Centers*, Progressive Architecture Library (New York: Reinhold, 1960); Gruen, *Heart of Our Cities*; Gruen, *Centers for the Urban Environment: Survival of the Cities* (New York: Van Nostrand Reinhold, 1973). See Robert B. Harmon, *Victor Gruen, Architectural Pioneer of Shopping Centers: A Selected Bibliography* (Monticello, Ill.: Vance Bibliographies, 1980) and Dale E. Casper, *Victor Gruen's Architectural Projects, 1957–1987* (Monticello, Ill.: Vance Bibliographies, 1988). As the building of shopping centers slows, the literature analyzing them grows quickly. See Jon Goss, "The 'Magic of the Mall': An Analysis of Form, Function, and Meaning in the Contemporary Retail Built Environment," *Annals of the Association of American Geographers* 83, no. 1 (March 1993); Margaret Crawford, "The World in a Shopping Mall," in Michael Sorkin, ed., *Variations on a Theme Park: The New American City and the End of Public Space* (New York: Noonday Press, 1992), 3–30; Lizabeth Cohen, "From Town Center to Shopping Center: The Reconfiguration of Community Marketplaces in Postwar America," *American Historical Review* 101, no. 4 (October 1996): 1050–81; Thomas W. Hanchett, "U.S. Tax Policy and the Shopping-Center Boom of the 1950s and 1960s," *American Historical Review* 101, no. 4 (October 1996): 1082–1110; Kenneth Jackson, "All the World's a Mall: Reflections on the Social and Economic Consequences of the American Shopping Center," *American Historical Review* 101, no. 4 (October 1996): 1111–21; Neil Harris, "The City That Shops: Chicago's Retailing Landscape," in John Zukowsky, ed., *Chicago Architecture and Design, 1923–1993* (Chicago: Art Institute of Chicago and Prestel, 1993), 178–99; Harris, "Spaced Out at the Shopping Center," in *Cultural Excursions: Marketing Appetites and Cultural Tastes in Modern America* (Chicago: University of Chicago Press, 1990), 278–88; William Kowinski, *The Malling of America* (New York: William Morrow, 1985); Witold Rybczynski, "The New Downtowns: Shopping Malls," *Atlantic Monthly* 271, no. 5 (May 1993).

11. Gruen was born Victor Gruenbaum; he legally changed his name to Victor David Gruen in 1941 when he applied for U.S. citizenship.

12. Victor Gruen and Larry Smith, "Shopping Centers: The New Building Type," *Progressive Architecture* (June 1952), AHCVGC, box 11.

Chapter 1. Escaping from Vienna to Fifth Avenue

Notes to epigraphs: Gruen, "The Case of Displayman Versus Store-Designer," *Display World* 39 (September 1941) 3, LoCVGC, OV 11; L-O-F [Libbey-Owens-Ford Company, New York] *Glassic* 3 (July 1941): 1.

1. Victor Gruen and Elsie Krummeck, "Face to Face," *Apparel Arts* (June 1940): 52–55, LoCVGC, OV 11; Gruen, "Case of Displayman," 3.

2. Gruen, untitled, c. 1977, LoCVGC, box 20. This manuscript contains Gruen's initial notes for an autobiography. They were organized and transcribed by someone else, which resulted in the awkward use of the third-person pronoun for Gruen's personal

memories. These papers also consistently use the letter z instead of y, which I have corrected. Hereafter, I will refer to these papers as "Reminiscences."

3. Gruen, "General Book Plan," LoCVGC, box 77, folder 2; Gruen, "Reminiscences."

4. The most informative sources on Gruen's years in Vienna, 1903–1938, are George E. Berkley, *Vienna and Its Jews: The Tragedy of Success, 1880s-1980s* (Cambridge, Mass.: ABT Books, 1988); Harriet Pass Freidenreich, *Jewish Politics in Vienna, 1918–1938* (Bloomington: Indiana University Press, 1991); Steven Beller, *Vienna and the Jews, 1867–1938: A Cultural History* (Cambridge: Cambridge University Press, 1989); Helmut Gruber, *Red Vienna: Experiment in Working-Class Culture, 1919–1934* (New York: Oxford University Press, 1991); Marsha L. Rozenblit, *The Jews of Vienna, 1867–1914: Assimilation and Identity* (Albany: State University of New York Press, 1983); Bruce Pauley, *From Prejudice to Persecution: A History of Austrian Anti-Semitism* (Chapel Hill: University of North Carolina Press, 1992); Peter Gay, *Freud: A Life for Our Time* (New York: W.W. Norton, 1988); and the memoir of Stephen S. Kalmar, *Goodbye, Vienna!* (San Francisco: Strawberry Hill Press, 1987). For other contemporary accounts of the situation in Vienna, see Oswald Dutch, *Thus Died Austria* (London: Edward Arnold, 1938) and G. E. R. Gedye, *Fallen Bastions* (London: Victor Gollancz, 1939).

5. Gruen, "General Book Plan," 3; Gruen, *Centers for the Urban Environment: Survival of the Cities* (New York: Van Nostrand Reinhold, 1973), 173.

6. See Rozenblit, *Jews of Vienna*, chap. 5, "Education, Mobility, and Assimilation: The Role of the *Gymnasium*," 99–125.

7. During these dire times, Gruen had his first contact with America. Sixty years later, he vividly remembered how the U.S. government had distributed food to starving Austrians in the state park and provided supplies for summer youth camps. Gruen recalled this interaction as his first of many encounters with "American generosity"; see "Reminiscences."

8. Quoted in Walter Guzzardi, Jr., "An Architect of Environments," *Fortune* (January 1962): 79.

9. Gruen, "General Book Plan, chapter 3: Theater or Architecture," 4.

10. Quoted in Guzzardi, "Architect of Environments," 79.

11. See Gruber, *Red Vienna*, 33, 40–41.

12. Gruen, "Reminiscences."

13. Gruen's family had lived in Central District 1, in the heart of Vienna. By one estimate Jews had once made up 46 percent of all gymnasium students in Vienna's first and ninth districts; see Beller, *Vienna and the Jews*, 53. This percentage is calculated for 1870–1910 for Central Districts 1, 2, and 9. See also Rozenblit, *Jews of Vienna*, 99–125. Gruen's quote appeared in "Reminiscences."

14. Author interview with Cesar Pelli, New Haven, Conn., March 5 1998.

15. Gruen, untitled, LoCVGC, box 20 and box 77 folder 11; the historian quoted is Freidenreich, *Jewish Politics*, 87. See also Walter Simon, "The Jewish Vote in Austria," *Leo Beck Institute Yearbook* 16 (1971): 108 and Walter Simon, "The Jewish Vote in Vienna," *Jewish Social Studies* 23, no. 1 (1961): 38–48.

16. Gruen, "Reminiscences," 1; see also Gruber, *Red Vienna*, 166. These scouts may have been the Kinderfreunde, which was organized for children ages six to ten, although Gruen would have been a little older than this group; the red scarf detail suggests that these scouts may have been a predecessor of the Rote Falken (Red Falcons), famous for their red scarves, which was the Socialist Party's adaptation of the German folkloric Wandervogel and Soviet Russian Pioneers.

17. Lizzie (Alice) Kardos, letter to Victor Gruen, August 7 1977, LoCVGC, box 77, folder 3.

18. George Clare, *Last Waltz in Vienna: The Destruction of a Family, 1842–1949* (New York: Holt, Rhinehart and Winston, 1982), 105.

19. Beller, *Vienna and the Jews*, 65. Beller writes eloquently about the philosophy underlying the Austro-Marxist housing program: "To provide the all-important environment in which the worker family would be socialized so as to become ordentlich and be educated by an emerging party culture in the direction of neue Menschen" (63).

20. Talbot Hamlin, "Some Restaurants and Recent Shops," *Pencil Points* 20 (August 1939): 485–505; "Initials in the Decorative Scheme," *Display* (August 1935): 233; "From Darkness to Delight," *Display* (December 31 1935): 2001. All three of these articles are found in Gruen's scrapbook, LoCVGC, OV 11. These Viennese stores were the Deutsch Herrenmoden, Lowenfeld, Bristol's Parfumerie, Depot de Guerlain, Park-Confiserie Bonbons, Singer, and Stoll & Riener men's wear.

21. Gruen, "General Book Plan, Chapter 1: The Fire," 2; see also Gruen, *Ein Realistischer Traumer: Ruckblicke, Einblicke, Ausblicke*, December 1979, LoCVGC, box 77, folder 4. He burned "Notizen, Manuskripte, Propgrammhefte, Fotografien, Zeitungsartiken, Buhenbild-und Kostumentwurfe," all connected with the Politisches Kabarett.

22. Freidenreich, *Jewish Politics*, 206–7.

23. Kalmar, *Goodbye, Vienna!* 104; Gay, *Freud*, 629.

24. Gruen, "Reminiscences."

25. Martin Gumpert, *Autobiography* (New York: Duell, Sloan, and Pearce, 1941), 222–23, as quoted in Helmut F. Pfanner, *Exile in New York: German and Austrian Writers After 1933* (Detroit: Wayne State University Press, 1983) 36; Gumpert was describing his 1936 trip. See also Gumpert, *First Papers*, trans. Heinz Norden and Ruth Norden (New York: Duell Sloane, 1941); and Erich Maria Remarque, *Shadows in Paradise*, trans. Ralph Manheim (New York: Harcourt Brace, 1971).

26. Gruen, "General Book Plan, Chapter 5: On the High Sea," 3; and Lizzie Gruen, letter to Victor Gruen, August 7 1977, 2.

27. Lizzie Gruen, letter to Victor Gruen, August 7 1977, 2. Ruth Yorke, born in New York, trained as an actress in Vienna with Max Reinhardt's theater seminar. She also married a member of the Viennese Refugee Artists' Group. See Sylvia Regan, "Who's Who in the Cast," *New York Morning Star*, April 20 1940, LoCVGC, OV 59. Yorke's friend Paul Goodman of Socony Oil signed as Gruen's sponsor for emigration. Yorke went on to use her Viennese training in American radio soap operas.

28. For descriptions of Jewish émigrés' arrivals in New York City, see Klaus Mann, *The Turning Point: Thirty Five Years in This Century* (New York: L.B. Fischer, 1942); Anna Rauschning, *No Retreat* (New York: Bobbs-Merrill, 1942); Gumpert, *Autobiography*; Bella Fromm, *Blood and Banquets: A Berlin Social Diary* (New York: Harper and Bros., 1942); and Remarque, *Shadows*. An evocative scholarly account of this experience is given by Pfanner, *Exile in New York*.

29. Gruen, "Reminiscences."

30. Author interview with Cesar Pelli.

31. Gruen, "Reminiscences."

32. Population figures taken from Kenneth Jackson, ed., *The Encyclopedia of New York City* (New Haven, Conn.: Yale University Press, 1995), 921, and Pauley, *From Prejudice to Persecution*, 208.

33. Gruen, "Reminiscences," May 17 1974; quoting a statement of Elsie Krummeck Crawford, Gruen's later architectural partner and second wife.

34. See the excellent article by Daniel Horowitz, "The Emigre as Celebrant of American Consumer Culture: George Katona and Ernest Dichter," in Charlie McGovern, Susan Strasser, and Matthias Judt, eds., *Getting and Spending: European and American Consumer Societies in the Twentieth Century* (New York: Cambridge University Press, 1998), 149-66. See also Lewis Coser, *Refugee Scholars in America: Their Impact and Their Experiences* (New Haven, Conn.: Yale University Press, 1984), 3-15; Anthony Helibut, *Exiled in Paradise: German Refugee Artists and Intellectuals in America from the 1930s to the Present* (New York: Viking Press, 1983).

35. F. Scott Fitzgerald, *The Great Gatsby* (New York: Charles Scribner's Sons, 1925). On the 1939 World's Fair see Roland Marchand, *Creating the Corporate Soul: The Rise of Public Relations and Corporate Imagery in American Big Business* (Berkeley: University of California Press, 1998), 291-311; Terry Smith, *Making the Modern: Industry, Art, and Design in America* (Chicago: University of Chicago Press, 1993), 405-21; Robert Caro, *The Powerbroker: Robert Moses and the Fall of New York* (New York: Knopf, 1974), 1082-85. For two memoirs about the fair see Morris Lapidus, *Too Much Is Never Enough: An Autobiography* (New York: Rizzoli, 1996), 115-22; Robert Moses, *Public Works: A Dangerous Trade* (New York: McGraw-Hill, 1970), 536-41.

36. *New York Times*, March 16, 1937, 25; Grover Whalen as quoted in Smith, *Making the Modern*, 405.

37. Jeffrey A. Kroessler, "World's Fairs," in Jackson, *Encyclopedia of New York City*, 1276. See also David Nye, *American Technological Sublime* (Cambridge, Mass.: MIT Press, 1994), 210.

38. Gruen, "General Book Plan," 5.

39. See Gruber, *Red Vienna*, 60-70; Gruber points out that even in the most modern socialist housing projects in Vienna indoor plumbing was communal and the seven-story buildings were difficult to get up and down without elevators.

40. Lewis Mumford, "Introduction: A Backward Glance," in Mumford, ed., *Roots of Contemporary American Architecture*, 2nd ed. (1952; New York: Grove Press, 1959; reprint, New York: Dover, 1972), 16; Fiske Kimball and George Edgell, *A History of Architecture*, 2nd ed. (New York: Harper and Bros., 1918), 565; see also Ralph Adams Cram, *My Life in Architecture* (Boston: Little, Brown, 1935). In addition, a group of Viennese architects (Paul T. Frankl, Joseph Urban, Frederick Keisler, Kim Weber, and Richard Neutra) had moved to America after World War I. While Neutra and Weber affected design in Los Angeles, overall their impact was much less dramatic than the 1930s modernists, perhaps because they were more eclectic and mixed commercial work with popular treatises. See Robert Reed Cole, *Joseph Urban: Architecture, Theater, Opera, Film* (New York: Abbeville Press, 1992); see also Paul T. Frankl, *New Dimensions: The Decorative Arts of Today in Words and Pictures* (New York: Payson and Clarke, 1928); Frankl, *Form and Re-Form: A Practical Handbook of Modern Interiors* (New York: Harper and Bros., 1930); and Frankl, *Space for Living* (New York: Doubleday, Doran, 1938).

41. Still the best synthesis on European modernist architects' emigratiion to the United States remains William H. Jordy, "The Aftermath of the Bauhaus in America: Gropius, Mies, and Breuer," in Donald Fleming and Bernard Bailyn, eds., *The Intellectual Migration: Europe and America, 1930-1960* (Cambridge, Mass.: Harvard University Press, 1969), 485-543.

42. This avoidance of retail design was especially true for East Coast architects in New York and Boston, while architects in Chicago engaged in commercial designs with a little more frequency. See Robert Bruegmann's comprehensive work, *The Architects and*

the City: Holabird and Roche of Chicago, 1880–1918 (Chicago: University of Chicago Press, 1997); for an overview of the architectural profession at the time, see Alan Gowans, *Styles and Types of North American Architecture: Social Function and Cultural Expression* (New York: HarperCollins, 1992), 210–69.

43. Morris Ketchum, Jr., *Shops and Stores*, Progressive Architects Library (New York: Reinhold, 1948), 9. See also Jose Fernandez, "Modernized Store Fronts," *Paint Logic* (October 1947): 14, 64, LoCVGC, OV 14. Fernandez notes that "in the early twenties, the contractor . . . usually designed the front as well as built it . . . and superficially installed a 'modernistic' front." This is the text of a speech that Fernandez gave at the landmark Store Modernization Show in New York, 1947.

44. Morris Lapidus, *An Architecture of Joy* (Miami: E.A. Seemann, 1979), 73.

45. Gruen, "Correction and Amplification," letter, *Architectural Forum* 86, no. 1 (January 1947): 42, 46. Gruen was responding to a review of a mid-1940s Hollywood Grayson's store on Hollywood Boulevard.

46. Roberto Schezen, Kenneth Frampton, and Joseph Rosa, *Adolf Loos, Architect, 1903–1932* (New York: Monacelli Press, 1996), 70–77. Loos designed Knize men's shops in Vienna (1913), Berlin (1924), and Paris (1927).

47. Morris Lapidus, "Store Design: A Merchandising Problem," *Architectural Record* 89 (February 1941): 113–36.

48. Lapidus, *Architecture of Joy*, 17–53.

49. The Columbia architecture faculty and students embraced Greek and Roman classicism as late as the 1930s; Professor Talbot Hamlin was working on his magnum opus on American classicism while Lapidus attended Columbia. See Talbot Hamlin, *Greek Revival Architecture in America* (London: Oxford University Press, 1944).

50. For further descriptions of artists and architects turning their attentions to the bustling New York City scene for inspiration, see Ann Douglas, *Terrible Honesty: Mongrel Manhattan in the 1920s* (New York: Knopf, 1995); and Elisabeth Sussman, ed., *City of Ambition: Artists and New York* (New York: Whitney Museum of American Art in association with Flammarion, 1996).

51. Lapidus, *Architecture of Joy*, 31, 61–69.

52. Flyer from New Citizens' Educational Center, Volkshochschule "Volksheim" New York City, c. 1940, LoCVGC, OV 11; the flyer lists under miscellaneous activities for new immigrants "Architectural League (Victor Gruen)"; "Reunion in New York for the Benefit of the Jersey City Refugee Aid Committee," *Playbill*, June 25 1940, LoCVGC, OV 59.

53. See Samuel L. Leiter, *The Encyclopedia of the New York Stage, 1930–1940* (Westport, Conn.: Greenwood Press, 1989), 256–57, 670; Peter Bauland, *The Hooded Eagle: Modern German Drama on the New York Stage* (Syracuse, N.Y.: Syracuse University Press, 1968), 145–46; and Morgan Yale Himelstein, *Drama Was a Weapon: The Left-Wing Theater in New York, 1929–1941* (New Brunswick, N.J.: Rutgers University Press, 1963).

54. Sophie Steinbach, "From Jobless Refugee to Stage Manager," *Christian Science Monitor*, May 10, 1940; "Goings on About Town," *New Yorker*, March 2, 1940; Richard Watts, Jr., "The Theaters," *New York Herald Tribune*, February 22, 1940; George Ross, "Reunion in New York Has Viennese Flavor," *New York World-Telegram*, February 22, 1940; "Reunion in New York Is the Second Revue by the Kleinkunstbuehne from Vienna," *New York Times*, February 22, 1940. All are in Gruen's scrapbooks, LoCVGC, OV 59, OV 11.

55. "And Now 'From Vienna,'" *New York Times*, 1939, LoCVGC, OV 11.

56. Albert Einstein to Gruen, September 28, 1938, LoCVGC, box 71, folder 4. Einstein

also vouched for Gruen's reputation, saying that he knew him "personally" and had "complete trust in the ability and trustworthiness of Mr. Gruen."

57. Steinbach, "From Jobless Refugee to Stage Manager," unidentified newspaper, LoCVGC, OV 11.

58. "Vienna Exiles Find Broadway More to Liking," *New York Herald Tribune*, February 18, 1940; cartoon, *New York Times*, February 18, 1940; George Ross, "Reunion in New York Has Viennese Flavor," *New York World-Telegram*, February 22, 1940; "Reunion in New York Is the Second Revue."

59. See Robert A. M. Stern, Gregory Gilmartin, and Thomas Mellins, *New York 1930: Architecture and Urbanism Between the Two World Wars* (New York: Rizzoli, 1987); personal communication with Charles Blau, Lederer owner, on 613 Madison Avenue, April 6, 1998. "'Sets' Star in New Accessories," *Women's Wear Daily*, June 9, 1939, LoCVGC, OV 11. Lederer de Paris in New York was the first American unit of a projected chain of six stores with twenty-five stores abroad.

60. See "The New House of 194X," *Architectural Forum* 77, no. 3 (March 1942): 92 for Ketchum's biographical materials.

61. Only nine years later, after his brief collaboration with Gruen, Ketchum would go on to author a comprehensive review of contemporary retail designs, *Shops and Stores*.

62. This information is gleaned from Stern et al., *New York 1930*; Norval White and Elliot Willensky, *Guide to New York City* (New York: American Institute of Architects, 1968); and Federal Writers' Project of the Works Progress Administration, *New York City Guide* (New York: Random House, 1939).

63. Robert Angell, "Everything Money Can Buy," *Holiday*, 1949 as reprinted in Alexander Klein, ed., *The Empire City: A Treasury of New York* (New York: Rinehart, 1955), 111, 116–17.

64. "Stores," *Architectural Forum* (December 1939): 429.

65. Gruen had used Carrara marble for a men's shop in Vienna, so the glass facsimile made a nice substitute.

66. Hamlin, "Restaurants and Recent Shops," 495. Interestingly, Talbot Hamlin was the son of A. D. F. Hamlin, director of Columbia University's architecture program. The younger Hamlin's acknowledgment of retail architecture suggests the beginnings of the changing attitude toward commercial design as it became part of the accepted realm of professionally trained architects.

67. Lederer de Paris and Ciro of Bond Street were located on the east side of Fifth Avenue at 55th Street, Steckler Haberdashery was at Broadway and 72nd, and Paris Decorators was on the Grand Concourse in the Bronx. See Marshall Berman, *All That Is Solid Melts into Air: The Experience of Modernity* (New York: Simon and Schuster, 1982), 287–348; Berman writes that for his parents the Grand Concourse's buildings, like Gruen's Paris Decorators shop, "represented a pinnacle of modernity" (295).

68. Lewis Mumford, "The Skyline: New Faces on the Avenue," *New Yorker*, Talk of the Town, September 15, 1939 (one of his "Skyline" articles that ran in 1931–40); "Lederer Front Is New Departure," *Women's Wear Daily*, June 16, 1939; "Store of the Month," *Store of Greater New York* (November 1939), LoCVGC, OV 11; John McAndrew, *Guide to Modern Architecture: Northeast States* (New York: Museum of Modern Art, 1940), 77–83. See also "Symphony in Stores: Two Inspirations Within the Reach of New York," *Store of Greater New York* (August 1939), LoCVGC, OV 11.

69. Mumford, "The Skyline: New Faces," 62–64; Hamlin, "Restaurants and Recent Shops," 498; "Stores," 427; McAndrew, *Guide to Modern Architecture*, 77; see also Stern et al., *New York 1930*, 312.

70. On arcades, see Walter Benjamin, *The Arcades Project*, trans. Howard Eiland and Kevin McLaughlin based on German volume edited by Rolf Tiedemann (Cambridge, Mass.: Harvard University Press, 1999); Walter Benjamin, *Charles Baudelaire: A Lyric Poet in the Era of High Capitalism*, trans. Harry Zohn (London: Verso, 1983); Susan Buck-Morris, *The Dialectics of Seeing: Walter Benjamin and the Arcades Project* (Cambridge, Mass.: MIT Press, 1989); Johann Friedrich, *Arcade: The History of a Building Type* (Cambridge, Mass.: MIT Press, 1983); Michael J. Bednar, *Interior Pedestrian Places: Arcades, Galerias, Marketplaces, Atria, Winter Gardens, Skyways, and Concourses* (New York: Whitney Library of Design, 1989). The term *arcade* has a long, complicated history. Originally, the word had been used in English in seventeenth-century descriptions of Italian arcades: it did not then have a distinctly commercial connotation and was used to describe covered walkways, trellises, niches, and connected arches. However, the term soon assumed a commercial meaning, as John Evelyn in his 1655 *Diary of Italy* wrote, "In the aracdo . . . stand 24 statues of great price." An 1830 English *Dictionary of Architecture* complained that "the use of this word is very very vague and indefinite" (*Oxford English Dictionary*, 1961), 429. Throughout the nineteenth century, in Europe, England, and the Americas, developers purposely applied "arcade" to large, covered urban retail structures in an attempt to conjure up the European aura of the Italian arcade. Of course, the most famous arcades were the ones in Paris that Benjamin later analyzed (some with open sides, like Rue de Rivoli, Palais Royal, and Old Place Royal, some completely covered, like Passages des Panoramas, Jouffroy, and de Princes). *The American Encyclopaedia Britannica* of 1875 (9th ed.) noted that all these arcades were "more or less lined with elegant shops" (Boston: Little Brown, 1875), 325–26. In America the form of a retail arcade, similar to Parisian arcades, was used in the Arcade of Cleveland of 1910. The use of the term as applied to a single store in the 1930s implied simply a covered area off the sidewalk where goods were displayed. The term, of course, still conjured up the grand feeling of nineteenth-century commercialism. The Museum of Modern Art made this connection clear by observing that Lederer de Paris's design was "a fresh and trim version of the XIX shopping arcade" (McAndrew, *Guide to Modern Architecture*, 78).

71. "Lederer de Paris Front Is New Departure," *Women's Wear Daily*, June 16, 1939, LoCVGC, OV 11.

72. See Kew, "Glamour in Glass," *Men's Wear*, November 8, 1939, 24–25. The article was talking about the Steckler shop on Broadway at 72nd Street.

73. Gruen and Krummeck, "Face to Face," June 1940. In his autobiography Morris Ketchum later described collaborating with Gruen on the arcades and "abolishing a building-line storefront in order to create a recessed outdoor shopping lobby with three times as many display possibilities as a conventional storefront." Morris Ketchum, Jr., *Blazing a Trail* (New York: Vantage Press, 1982), 3. Ketchum also credited these arcade storefronts with inspiring the creation of "a grander shopping lobby," or the suburban shopping mall, of which his 1951 Shopper's World, in Framingham, Massachusetts, was one of the largest centers for its time. See also "Stores" and Lapidus, "Store Design," 115.

74. Ketchum, *Shops and Stores*, 148–49; Lapidus, *An Architecture of Joy*, 80.

75. Morris Lapidus, "Store Design," *Chain Store Age* (April 1944).

76. Gruen and Krummeck, "Face to Face," June 1940.

77. For one of the best treatments on store display and retailing see William Leach, *Land of Desire: Merchants, Power, and the Rise of a New American Culture* (New York: Pantheon, 1993), 55–70.

78. "Recent Work by Gruen, Krummeck, & Auer," *Architectural Forum* (September 1941): 191.

79. R. G. Walters, John W. Wingate, and Edward J. Rowse, *Retail Merchandising* (Cincinnati, Ohio: South-western Publishing, 1943), 262–63.

80. John Paver, *Window Display: Circulation and Market Coverage, How to Select— How to Verify* (Cambridge, Mass.: Advertising Research Foundation, 1937). The report went on to call the sparse display method "a merchandise impression type of window display associated with department stores, apparel or variety stores."

81. J. Gordon Lippincott, *Design for Business* (Chicago: Paul Theobald, 1947), 156.

82. Author interview with Charles Blau, Lederer owner, April 6, 1998.

83. Gruen, speech, "Notes on City Planning in 2000," LoCVGC; reprinted as "Store Design Report in the Year 2000," *Women's Wear Daily*, February 15, 1950.

84. "Store of the Month," *Store of Greater New York.*

85. A glass company reiterated this theory and claimed that glass allowed "a uniform decorative treatment inside and out, further eliminating any visual barrier between merchandise and passing traffic." See L-O-F advertisement, "Look What You Can Do with a VISUAL FRONT," front endpaper, *Modern Stores Produce Bigger Home Goods Profits* (Chicago: National Retail Furniture Association, 1945).

86. "Lederer," *Women's Wear Daily.*

87. See Hamlin, "Restaurants and Recent Shops," 495.

88. "De Luxe Modernization," *Chain Store Age* (April 1946): 26.

89. At 184 square feet the Steckler lobby totaled almost a third of the store's entire sales area, "Stores," *Architectural Forum*, 429; "Commercial Portfolio: 2. Shoe Store," *Architectural Forum* 82 (May 1945): 116.

90. Lapidus, "Store Design," 114–28; emphasis in original.

91. Gruen and Elsie Krummeck, "Face to Face," *Apparel Arts* (June 1940): 52–55. LoCVGC, OV 11.

92. Mumford, "The Skyline: New Faces."

93. Lewis Mumford, "The Skyline: New Facades," *New Yorker*, November 20, 1937, 90.

94. Mumford in his "Skyline" articles; see also Daniel Miller, *Lewis Mumford: A Life* (New York: Weidenfeld and Nicolson, 1989), 170–91, 375–37; and Robert Wojtowicz, ed., *Sidewalk Critic: Lewis Mumford's Writings on New York* (New York: Princeton Architectural Press, 1998).

95. Hamlin, "Restaurants and Recent Shops," 496.

96. Gruen, interoffice communication to partners, 27 December 1961, AHCVGC, box 36.

97. Gruen, "Displayman Versus Store-Designer," 3.

98. Altman & Kuhne Invitation, December 1939, LoCVGC, OV 11. "Altman & Kuhne formerly of Vienna Confectioners . . . opens on Fifth Avenue," their opening invitation announced.

99. Front page, *New York Times*, December 3, 1939, LoCVGC, OV 11. See also "Candy Shop for Altman and Kuhne, New York City," *Architectural Forum* 75, no. 2 (February 1940): 89–92, LoCVGC, OV 11.

100. "Gossip Department," *New York World-Telegram*, December 15, 1939; Hugh Ferriss, Chairman, Architectural League of New York, to Victor Gruen, both in LoCVGC, OV 11.

101. See Stern et al., *New York 1930*; the authors compare the gridded interior of the Altman & Kuhne confectionery to the German expressionist inspired designs of Kim

Weber in Los Angeles; Gruen and Krummeck, "Face to Face"; "Gossip Department," *New York World-Telegram*, 15 December 1939; "Fifth Avenue Candy Shop Very Sweet," *Store of Greater New York* (1939), LoCVGC, OV 11; Fernandez, "Modernized Store Fronts," 14 (Fernandez gave all credit for the invention of this storefront to Gruen, Krummeck, Lapidus, and Ketchum). See also "Candy Shop for Altman & Kuhne" and Lapidus, *Too Much Is Never Enough*, 100. See also McAndrew, *Guide to Modern Architecture*, 77 where he marvels at how the "whole shop becomes display."

102. Ketchum, *Shops and Stores*, 152; Gruen and Krummeck, "Face to Face," 55. "The *entire store* rather than just the show windows becomes a medium for display or advertising," Fernandez explained about Gruen and Krummeck's design. "In the open front," he added, "the whole front becomes alive with the activity in the store." See Fernandez, "Modernized Store Fronts," 14, 64.

103. Walters et al., *Retail Merchandising*, 265.

104. Emrich Nicholson, *Contemporary Shops in the United States* (New York: Architectural Book Publishing, 1945), 45.

105. "The Time to Stop Shoplifting Is Before It Happens," *Chain Store Age* (March 1940): 72. See also Marchand, *Creating the Corporate Soul*, 301–10; Marchand points out that mechanical exhibitions with plenty of moving parts also gained popularity at the New York World's Fair.

106. Frederick Kiesler, *Contemporary Art Applied to the Store and Its Display* (New York: Brentano's, 1930), 79–84.

107. "Store Designers Don't Suffer from Tradition Fixations–Thank God," Walter Gropius, "Jewelry Shop," Jose Fernandez, "Jewelry Store," and Pietro Belluschi, "Shoes and Leather Goods," *Pencil Points* (August 1944): 40–57.

108. See Coser, who stresses the potential for refugees to make an immediate impact on American ideas (*Intellectuals*, 10).

109. McAndrew, *Guide to Modern Architecture*, 81; Guzzardi, "Architect of Environments," 80; Nicholson, *Contemporary Shops*, 52; "Recent Work of Gruen, Krummeck & Auer," 192; "How a Small Chain Grew," *Chain Store Age* (March 1952): 253; "We're in Our 50's," *Barton's Bonbonniere Sweet News* 2, no. 1, April 25, 1952, 1, LoCVGC, OV 19. Barton's also hired Morris Lapidus for their store designs; see "To Be Unveiled: Impulse Sales Catcher," *Chain Store Age* (November 1947).

110. Gruen, "Store Designing for the 'Feminine Touch': Famed Store Designer Tells Interior Secrets," *West Coast Feminine Wear*, April 29, 1947, 12, LoCVGC, OV 14; Gruen, "The Case for the Flexible Ceiling," *Electrical West* (September 1949).

111. See Louis Parnes, *Planning Stores That Pay*, An Architectural Record Book (New York: F.W. Dodge, 1948).

112. "Special Packages and Design in Relation to Impulse Buying Urged," *New York Times*, March 1, 1940, 4; "Window Display," *Fortune*, 15, no. 1 (January 1937): 91–100; Ketchum, *Shops and Stores*, 12–13. See also Lippincott, *Design for Business*, 161; his motto was "shopping means impulse sales."

113. Parnes, *Planning Stores That Pay*, 231; *Architectural Record* 89 (March 1941): 64. The article was speaking specifically about three Morris Ketchum stores, one which was Ciro's of London.

114. Paver, *Window Display*; see also Walters et al., *Retail Merchandising*.

115. Robert and Helen Lynd, *Middletown in Transition: A Study in Cultural Conflicts* (New York: Harcourt, Brace, 1937), 17.

116. Quoted in Chester Whitney Wright, *Economic History of America*, 2nd ed. (New York: McGraw-Hill, 1949), 220.

117. Simon Patten, "Reconstruction of Economic Theory," 1912, reprinted in *Essays in Economic Theory, by Simon Nelson Patten*, ed. Rexford Tugwell (New York: Knopf, 1924), as quoted in Leach, *Land of Desire*, 238. Leach provides a full and valuable treatment of Patten's glorification of the market and consumers. See also Daniel Fox, *Discovery of Abundance: Simon N. Patten and the Transformation of Social Theory* (Ithaca, N.Y.: Cornell University Press, 1968); James Livingston, *Pragmatism and the Political Economy of Cultural Revolution* (Chapel Hill: University of North Carolina Press, 1994).

118. Christine Frederick, *Selling Mrs. Consumer* (New York: Business House, 1929) 4–5, as cited in Rita Barnard, *The Great Depression and the Culture of Abundance: Kenneth Fearing, Nathanael West, and Mass Culture in the 1930s* (New York: Cambridge University Press, 1995), 24; Lewis Mumford, *The Culture of Cities* (New York: Harcourt, Brace, 1938), 462. Mumford was discussing what he called a biotechnic economy or one that relied on continual technological innovation.

119. See "Store Modernization," *New York Times*, June 28, 1940, 7.

120. See Jeffrey L. Meikle, *Twentieth Century Limited: Industrial Design in America, 1925–1939* (Philadelphia: Temple University Press, 1979), 4. According to Meikle's perceptive anaylsis, "Products redesigned in the new style would stimulate the economy by attracting customers. Underconsumption, considered by most businessmen the nation's major economic problem, would be ended." See also Meikle, *American Plastic: A Cultural History* (New Brunswick, N.J.: Rutgers University Press, 1995), 106; and Roland Marchand, *Advertising the American Dream: Making Way for Modernity, 1920–1940* (Berkeley: University of California Press, 1985), 120–27.

121. Gruen quoted in "Recent Work by Gruen, Krummeck & Auer."

122. Lapidus, "Store Design," 113–36.

123. Leach, *Land of Desire*, 71–111.

124. Morris Ketchum, "Services for Sale," *Architectural Record* 90 (July 1941): 85.

125. "Window Display," *Fortune* 15, no. 1 (January 1937): 91; Leach, *Land of Desire*, 55; Paver, *Window Display*, 2–3.

126. John Steinbeck, *New York Times Magazine*, 1953, as reprinted in Klein, ed., *The Empire City*, 472–73.

127. See Walter Benjamin, *Reflections: Essays, Aphorisms, Autobiographical Writings*, trans. Edmund Jephcott, ed. Peter Demetz (New York: Schocken Books, 1986), 100, 102. See also Wolfgang Schivelbush, *The Railway Journey: The Industrialization of Time and Space in the Nineteenth Century* (Berkeley: University of California Press, 1986), 45–51 and *Disenchanted Night: The Industrialization of Light in the Nineteenth Century* (Berkeley: University of California Press, 1988), 143–54.

128. Lapidus, "Store Design," 97.

129. Gruen, speech to L. S. Ayres & Company, Indianapolis, "Draft: Branches for Department Stores," October 20, 1955, 8, AHCVGC, box 53; "Recent Work by Gruen, Krummeck & Auer." See also Gruen, "Some Notes on Modern Store Design," *Architect and Engineer* (February 1942), LoCVGC, OV 12.

130. Gruen and Krummeck, "Face to Face." Later Gruen applied the theater metaphor to shopping centers: "compared to the high drama of the big shopping center, these neighborhood groups are 'little theater,' with the star performer a food market or a variety store instead of a big department store. The audience is smaller, too, but it gets just as enthusiastic about the show." See "Two 'Pocket' Shopping Centers," *Architectural Forum* (January 1956): 140–43, LoCVGC, OV 24. See also Ketchum, *Shops and Stores*, 150 where he calls show windows "miniature theater sets."

131. Of course, store windows could also become the focus for people's protests over

their economic situation; see Jack Conroy, *The Disinherited* (1933; reprint Columbia: University of Missouri Press, 1991). Rather than focusing on the rich display of goods, Conroy wrote of "the ubiquitous spiders" who "were at work filming the edges of the window and the spaces between shelves." For Conroy, the show window's display was a blatant metaphor for capitalism's destructive powers: a fat cat knocked around a helpless mouse while unemployed men gathered and gawked (223). See also Don Langan, "Consumers Arise!" *Americana* 2 (November 1933): 15, quoted in Warren Susman, ed., *Culture and Commitment, 1929-1945* (New York: George Braziller, 1973), 143-46. In this story, Langan has an activist organization called "Consumers" breaking show windows on Broadway. The windows made one too many false promises to the consumers, Langan claimed.

132. Gruen, *Shopping Towns USA: The Planning of Shopping Centers*, Progressive Architecture Library (New York: Reinhold, 1960), 147. See David Harvey, *The Urban Experience* (Baltimore: Johns Hopkins University Press, 1989), 168-80. Harvey perceptively suggests that America became obsessed with "a way of life in which speed and rush to overcome space was of the essence" (179). These store designs were also a reaction to this frenetic living; the stores attempted to offer a respite from speed by offering people a relaxed, slow atmosphere in which people could linger and shop.

133. Gruen, "Problems of Store Design," *Southwest Builder and Contractor* (January 23, 1948). The article was excerpted from a speech given at the California AIA convention; the speech was also very similar to the address given to the Store Modernization Show in New York City which appeared as "Modernize Your Store," *Foundation Garment Review* (January 1948): 51-52, 85.

134. Kew, "Glamour in Glass," 24; "Initials in the Decorative Scheme," *Display* (August 1935): 233; "From Darkness to Delight," *Display* (December 31, 1935): 2001, LoCVGC, OV 11.

135. Paver, *Window Display*; Mumford, "New Faces on the Avenue," 63.

136. Pittsburgh Plate Glass Company advertisement in *Modern Stores* (New York: National Retail Furniture Association, 1945). Of course, the glass industry already had close ties to retail through the selling of plate glass windows, but the industry greatly expanded its architectural product line for the retail trade throughout the 1930s.

137. "Landscape of glass" is borrowed from Leach, *Land of Desire*, 55.

138. Libbey-Owens-Ford, "It Pays to Be Open Minded," advertisement, *Chain Store Age* (May 1946): 67; or Libbey-Owens-Ford, "How to Open Your Business to New Sales and Profit," advertisement, *Chain Store Age* (January 1944): 43.

139. *LOF Glassic* 3 (July 1941); Lippincott, *Design for Business*, 162. See also Raymond McGrath, *Glass in Architecture and Decoration* (London: Architectural Press, 1937).

140. United States Tariff Commission, *Plate Glass*, Report no. 110, 2nd ser. (Washington, D.C.: U.S. Government Printing Office, 1936), 2.

141. Total losses are given as $421,880.30 for the first half of 1938. Letter from President John Biggers, *Income and Expense Statement, for six months ended June 30 1938* (Toledo, Ohio: L-O-F Glass Company, 1938), n.p.

142. Kawneer Company, "Machines for Selling!" advertisement, *Modern Stores*, back cover. An informative pamphlet on structural glass storefronts has been published by the U.S. Department of the Interior; see Gregory Kendrick, ed., *The Preservation of Historic Pigmented Structural Glass (Vitrolite and Carrara Glass)*, Preservation Briefs 12 (Washington, D.C.: U.S. Department of the Interior, 1984); see also H. Ward Jandl, *Rehabilitating Historic Storefronts*, Preservation Briefs 11 (Washington, D.C.: U.S. Department of the Interior, 1982).

143. "Store Fronts Advertisement," *Chain Store Age,* General Merchandise ed. (May 5, 1930): 58. The advertisement featured a Holabird and Root design for a Walden Book Shop in Chicago.

144. Letter from President John Biggers, *Income and Expense Statement, for nine months ended Sept. 30 1939* (Toledo, Ohio: L-O-F Glass Company, 1939; L-O-F, "Look What You Can Do with a VISUAL FRONT"; L-O-F, "Designed for Selling," advertisement, *Interior Design & Decoration* (March 1942), LoCVGC, OV 12.

145. As cited in Kendrick, ed., "The Preservation of Historic Pigmented Structural Glass," 2.

146. See Meikle, *Twentieth Century Limited,* 117-25 for a brief but excellent description of industrial designers' storefront work, especially the commissions of Walter Dorwin Teague and Raymond Loewy; "Modernize Main Street," *Architectural Record* (October 1935): 209-66. See also Robert Caro, *The Powerbroker* (New York: Knopf, 1974), 368-72; Caro describes architects begging Robert Moses to work on his public works projects designing bathhouses and bridges because private construction had virtually dried up.

147. National Retail Dry Goods Association, *Planning the Store of Tomorrow* (New York: National Retail Dry Goods Association, 1945), 38-39, 48.

148. Cover, *Pencil Points/Progressive Architecture* 25 (August 1944), LoCVGC, OV 12; "Men's Store Modernization," *Daily News Record,* December 30, 1946, 2, LoCVGC, OV 13.

149. Gruen, "What About 'Modernized' Store Fronts," *Glass Digest: National Magazine of the Flat Glass Industry* (October 1947): 13-14, 40-41. For Ketchum see *Modern Furniture Store*; National Retail Dry Goods Association, *Planning the Store of Tomorrow,* 38-39, 48; Pittsburgh Plate Glass Company, "Give the job to Glass," advertisement, *Architectural Record* 87 (June 1940): 127. See also "The Shoe Store with EYE-Appeal" (about Shiff's of Los Angeles), *Boot and Shoe Recorder* (15 April 1947) 299; "If You Sell Style Dress the Part," United States Plywood Corporation, Retail Management, September 1947 (Hastings Shoe Store in basement of St. Francis Hotel, San Francisco); "Plexiglass" (J. Magnin, Palo Alto staircase), Rohm & Haas, October 1947; "Saftee Subjects," Saftee Glass (Grayson-Robinson dressing rooms), October-November 1947, LoCVGC, OV 14; "Creating the Spectacular, Kurt Versen Focal Lighting" (Grayson shop, Los Angeles), 1947; "Light with Distinction . . . Comfort . . . Utility," Pittsburgh Reflector Company (Joseph Magnin, Sacramento), *Chain Store Age* (November 1947)—all in LoCVGC, OV 14.

150. Pittsburgh Plate Glass Company, "How EYE-APPEAL INSIDE and OUT Increases Retail Sales," advertisement, 1945, LoCVGC, OV 12; *Architectural Record* 87 (June 1940): 127.

151. Personal communication from D. B. Garvan, curator, New Hampshire Historical Society. Her father was a ceramic tile installer in New Hampshire who began installing glass tiles on storefronts during the 1940s; he also used leftover tiles to modernize the family's kitchen and bathroom.

152. Pittsburgh Plate Glass Company advertisement (using Lederer's store design, 1945, LoCVGC, OV 12. See also Pittsburgh Plate Glass Company, "How Eye Appeal Inside and Out Increases Retail Sales," 2-3.

153. Pittsburgh Plate Glass Company, "78," *Pittsburgh Plate Products* 48, no. 1 (January-February 1939): back cover. By September-October the number was up to 81: see Pittsburgh Plate Glass Company, "81," *Pittsburgh Plate Products* 48, no. 5 (September-October 1939): back cover.

Chapter 2. How Main Street Stole Fifth Avenue's Glitter

Note to epigraph: Victor Gruen, untitled, in "Modernized Store Layout" panel at New York Store Modernization Show, July 8, 1947, 5, in *Speeches of Victor Gruen*, vol. A, 1943–56, LoCVGC, 81. This speech was reprinted as Victor Gruen, "Problems of Store Design," *Southwest Builder and Contractor* (January 23, 1948) and Victor Gruen, "Modernize Your Store," *Foundation Garment Review* (January 1948): 51–52, 85, both in LoCVGC, OV 15.

1. "Recent Work of Gruen, Krummeck & Auer," *Architectural Forum* (September 1941): 191, LoCVGC, OV 11.

2. The women's apparel shops were Janet's of Oklahoma City, the Canterbury Shop in White Plains, and Grayson's in Seattle. Gruen also completed designs for two New York City candy shops, Barton's Bonbonniere and Henny Wyle. See Victor Gruen and Elsie Krummeck, "Job Listings," February 22, 1951, LoCVGC, OV 11.

3. Victor Gruen, untitled, May 17, 1974, LoCVGC, box 20, folder 18.

4. Gruen and Krummeck designed or remodeled Grayson's stores in Santa Monica (1414 Third Avenue, 1940), Seattle (1514 Third Avenue, 1940), Buffalo (Robinson's at 448–450 Main Street, 1941), Pasadena (635 South Broadway, 1941), Los Angeles (Crenshaw Boulevard, 1941), Inglewood (1942), San Diego (1038 Fifth Avenue, 1942), San Francisco (renovation, 1944), El Paso (Mesa Avenue and Texas Street, 1945), Philadelphia (Market Street, 1946), Hollywood (1946), and Salt Lake City (1947). All these stores are found in Gruen's scrapbooks, LoCVGC, OV 12–14. Grayson's also appears to have opened a New York City shop, although Gruen and Krummeck did not design the store, see "Grayson Shops Leases Space NYC," *New York Times*, July 18, 1944, 2.

5. Grayson-Robinson stores, New York, *Annual Report for Year Ended September 30, 1945,* LoCVGC, OV 12. The company operated seventeen Robinson's stores, twenty-five Grayson's stores, and an S. Klein department store on Union Square in Manhattan. See also Grayson-Robinson Stores, *Annual Report for Year Ended September 30, 1946*, 5, LoCVGC, OV 14; the company operated forty-six stores by 1946.

6. See Godfrey Lebhar, *Chain Stores in America, 1859–1950* (New York: Chain Store Publishing, 1952), 338. The sales figures were taken from Lebhar's use of a ranking of the 100 Largest U.S. Retail Organizations for all department, specialty, and apparel stores compiled by the National City Bank of New York; the list excluded retail companies that did not report their sales publicly for 1950.

7. Gruen, "Reminiscences," box 22.

8. Gruen, "Reminiscences," box 20.

9. Gruen, "Reminiscences," box 22. See also Gruen, "Address to Victor Gruen Associates," Los Angeles, February 13, 1962, audiotape, AHCVGC, Box 62.

10. Grayson's work totaled $600,000 which was 89 percent of the firm's total projects. This figure is based on the firm's Job Listings for the approximate costs of all projects from 1939 to 1951, February 22, 1951, LoCVGC.

11. J. Magnin is often confused with the San Francisco I. Magnin department store; the stores were owned by the same family. J. Magnin was a women's specialty store that made a name for itself by offering trendy, New York-inspired clothing for the growing upper-middle-class suburbs of Northern California.

12. Foristall, "Grayson's Growth"; "S. Klein on the Square Bought for $3,000,000," *Women's Wear Daily*, February 5, 1946, 1, both in LoCVGC, OV 13.

13. Alice Kessler-Harris, *Out to Work: A History of Wage-Earning Women in the United States* (New York: Oxford University Press, 1982), 276–77. Kessler-Harris thor-

oughly disassembles this number and gives a more realistic one, saying that 3.7 million new workers entered jobs between 1940 and 1945. On working women and their increasing disposable incomes during the war, see Elaine Tyler May, *Homeward Bound: American Families in the Cold War Era* (New York: Basic Books, 1988), 73; May claims that 6.5 million working women acquired $8 billion more to spend during the war years.

14. Numbers from "Boom Towns in Wartime," *Chain Store Age* (1943). Another report claimed that San Diego increased by 43.7 percent or had 164,985 new white residents from 1940 to 1944; see Lowell Carr and James Sterner, *Willow Run: A Study of Industrialization and Cultural Inadequacy* (New York: Harper and Bros., 1952), 356; and Carl Abbott, *The Metropolitan Frontier: Cities in the Modern American West* (Tucson: University of Arizona Press, 1993), 12–13. Abbott describes San Diego as the fastest growing city in America from April 1940 to October 1941. See also "Seattle: A Boom Comes Back," *Business Week*, June 20, 1942, 26.

15. See "Small Chains Lead in Sales Gains, Harvard Survey Shows," *Chain Store Age* (September 1944): 94. The Harvard survey cited was titled "Expenses and Profits of Limited Price Variety Stores in 1943."

16. Lebhar, *Chain Stores*, 64. See also Cole, Hoisington & Co., *Consumer's Purchasing Power and Mass Distribution*, December 1944, 12–13, Hagley Museum and Library, Pamphlet Collection, Wilmington, Delaware. These analysts reported that one department store saw a sales increase of 4.2 percent in women's ready-to-wear between 1939 and 1943 due to working women. Also Merrill Lynch, Pierce, Fenner and Beane, *Chain Stores–1944* (New York: Merrill Lynch, 1944), Hagley Museum and Library, Pamphlet Collection.

17. Thomas M. Foristall, "The Inquiring Investor: Grayson's Growth," *Wall Street Journal*, April 17, 1946, LoCVGC, OV 13. On the importance of the women's clothing market during the War, see Michael Denning's discussion of Elizabeth Hawes's works in *The Cultural Front: The Laboring of American Culture in the Twentieth Century* (New York: Verso, 1996), 146–51, 455–58. See also Richard Polenberg, *One Nation Divisible: Class, Race, and Ethnicity in the United States Since 1938* (New York: Penguin, 1980), 46–85.

18. "Where Smart Women Buy Smart Clothes for Less," Grayson's advertisement, *San Francisco Examiner*, 1942, LoCVGC, OV 12.

19. For the Kresge store numbers, see Robert Hendrickson, *The Grand Emporiums: The Illustrated History of America's Great Department Stores* (New York: Stein and Day, 1979), 195. While some department stores had been consolidating into their own national chains (Macy's, which purchased Lasalle's of Ohio, Davidson's of Atlanta, and Bamberger's of New Jersey and Federated, which owned Filene's of Boston, Bloomingdale's of New York, Abraham & Strauss of Brooklyn, and F. R. Lazarus of Cincinnati), the majority of department stores remained locally and independently owned. On the growth of Macy's and Federated, see Hendrickson, 69, 258.

20. See Susan Strasser, *Satisfaction Guaranteed: The Making of the American Mass Market* (New York: Pantheon, 1989).

21. Wright Patman, *The Robinson-Patman Act: What You Can and Cannot Do Under This Law* (New York: Ronald Press, 1938), 3, 35–36. See also Lewis Atherton, *Main Street on the Middle Border* (Bloomington: Indiana University Press, 1954; paperback 1966), 240–42. Atherton relates that Midwest merchants printed and distributed anti-chain-store journals with such provocative names as *Chained*, *Chain Store Menace*, and *The Booster*.

22. *Chain Store Age* (May 1940) contains the full congressional testimony of President Earl Sams of J. C. Penney.

23. Lebhar, *Chain Stores*, 63. According to Lebhar, of 1.7 million stores across America only 105,000 were defined as chains, which meant that the parent companies were operating a minimum of four stores.

24. "What Makes a 1940 Store Obsolete?" *Architectural Forum* (August 1950): 2, LoCVGC, OV 17, AHCVGC, box 11.

25. Atherton, *Main Street*, 240. Atherton dedicated his book about small Midwestern towns to two relatives' independent stores in Bosworth, Missouri, which eventually went out of business in the face of chain-store competition.

26. *Merchant's Record and Show Window* (April 1935): 76.

27. Lebhar, *Chain Stores*, 63.

28. Kresge and McCrory's were located across Market Street from Grayson's. W. T. Grant's was two doors down from Grayson's. Gimbel's Department Store was down the block and across the street from Strawbridge and Clothier Department Store. See *Philadelphia Address and Telephone Directory*, Spring 1950; *Franklin's Business Occupancy Map of Central Philadelphia*, 1946; and *Nirenstein's Real Estate Atlas: States of Pennsylvania, Virginia, and West Virginia, 1950* (Springfield, Mass.: Nirenstein's, 1950).

29. See Lebhar, *Chain Stores*, 74–76. See also Grayson's "Most Unique Store in America Opens Here Tomorrow!" *Evening Outlook*, Santa Monica, California, November 29, 1940, 17, LoCVGC, OV 11; see also "Latest Store Architecture Embodied in Grayson Units," *Los Angeles Times*, 1942, Realty Section, 3, LoCVGC, OV 12.

30. Robinson advertisement, "Tomorrow Buffalo Is Invited Shopping at America's Newest and Most Beautiful Store," *Buffalo Evening News*, September 5, 1941; "Robinson's to Open Unit in Buffalo," *Women's Wear Daily*, July 16, 1941, both in LoCVGC, OV 11.

31. "Designed for Dominance," *Chain Store Age* (June 1946): LoCVGC, OV 13.

32. Jose Fernandez, *The Specialty Shop (A Guide)* (New York: Architectural Book Publishing, 1950), 32.

33. Robinson advertisement, "Tomorrow Buffalo" (ellipsis in original); Morris Lapidus, "Store Design: A Merchandising Problem," *Architectural Record* 89 (February 1941): 113, LoCVGC, OV 11; Victor Gruen, *Ein realisticher Traumer: Ruckblicke, Einblicke, Ausblicke*, December 1979, 129, LoCVGC, box 77, folder 4.

34. Victor Gruen, "The California Look in Store Design," *California Men's Stylist* (April 1945): 80–81; see also "This Month," *Progressive Architecture/Pencil Points* (July 1946): 14, LoCVGC, OV 13; "New Stores Bring Metropolitan Beauty to Smaller Communities," *Chain Store Age* (February 1941): 85.

35. Lapidus, "Store Design," 94. See also Robert Lynd and Helen Lynd, *Middletown in Transition: A Study in Cultural Conflicts* (New York: Harcourt, Brace, 1937), 379. The Lynds were writing specifically about news, fashion, and entertainment, which the retail trade was becoming a part of in many ways, and observed that there was a "closer binding of Main Street to Fifth Avenue."

36. *Chain Store Age* (November 1946): 41, LoCVGC, OV 13.

37. Gruen, "Application for Certificate of Arrival"; and "Preliminary Form for Petition for Naturalization," Los Angeles, December 16, 1941, LoCVGC, box 22; see Gruen, "Some Notes on Modern Store Design," *Architect and Engineer* (February 1942), LoCVGC, OV 12; and Gruen and Krummeck, "Shopping Center," *Architectural Forum* (May 1943): 101–3, both in LoCVGC, OV 12.

38. Interview with Peggy Gruen, March 16, 1998, Amherst, Mass.; interview with Michael Gruen, New York City, April 6, 1998.

39. "New Stores Opened by Ingenious Use of Substitute Materials," *Chain Store Age* (January 1944): 24, LoCVGC, OV 12.

40. Gruen, "Application for Certificate of Arrival," Gruen to Attorney General Francis Biddle, January 30, 1942, LoCVGC, box 22.

41. Gruen, "Reminiscences," box 22; Victor Gruen, report card, University of California, Berkeley, LoCVGC, box 22, Folder 6. Gruen took Mechanical Perspective (November 1942) and Production Illustration (February 1943), receiving Bs in both classes; see also Gruen, "Reminiscences," box 22.

42. "Timely Trims," *Chain Store Age* (January 1943): 42; "Government War Drives," *Chain Store Age* (October 1943): 50–51, which shows illustrations of War Bond windows and the hosiery salvage campaign; "New York City Stores Plan Ad Campaign to Aid Victory Loan Drive," *New York Times*, November 12, 1945, 6. Grayson's pursuit of customers through exaggerated patriotism was quite common. In a similar vein, after Pearl Harbor the Strawbridge and Clothier department store of Philadelphia decided to make a "jumbo sign" for its main sales floor reading "Join the War Against Waste to Help Win the War Against Aggressors"; the store also used the slogan in its "general publicity." See Special Operating Board Meeting, December 5, 1941 with emendations December 27, 1941, Hagley Museum, Strawbridge and Clothier Collection, box 8, vol. 1939–44.

43. "New Lights Will Be Extinguished," *Inglewood Daily News*, Inglewood, Calif., August 20, 1942, 7, LoCVGC, OV 12; "Substitute Materials"; "Chain Apparel Shop," *Architectural Forum* 81 (October 1944): 89–91, both in LoCVGC, OV 12. Strawbridge and Clothier hosted War Bond rallies inside its store: see Operating Board Meeting, December 29, 1943, Hagley Museum, Strawbridge and Clothier Collection, box 9, vol. 1939–44.

44. Taped interview with Inez Sauer, conducted and transcribed by Lorraine McConaghy, February 26, 1985, Museum of History and Industry, Historical Society of Seattle and King County, Homefront Exhibit Box. The changing of stock was not necessarily done to curry favor with the patrons; Inez Sauer remembered that one store put away its white opera gloves when Boeing workers arrived to shop.

45. "Substitute Materials." For an article on the San Francisco store, see "Commercial Remodeling," *Architectural Forum* 81 (October 1944): 81–99, and advertisement for Grayson's "Victory Store" at 875 Market Street, *San Francisco Chronicle*, c. 1944, LoCVGC, OV 12.

46. Gruen, "Reminiscences," LoCVGC, box 22.

47. "Commercial Remodeling"; "Substitute Materials."

48. See Donald Albrecht, ed., *World War II and the American Dream: How Wartime Building Changed a Nation* (Cambridge, Mass.: MIT Press and National Building Museum, 1995); Polenberg, *One Nation Divisible*, 46–85; John Morton Blum, *V Was for Victory: Politics and American Culture During World War II* (New York: Harcourt Brace, 1976); Joseph Horowitz, *Understanding Toscanini: A Social History of American Concert Life* (Berkeley: University of California Press, 1987), 177–80; Barbara McLean Ward, ed., *Produce & Conserve, Share & Play Square: The Grocer & the Consumer on the Homefront Battlefield During World War II* (Portsmouth, N.H.: Strawberry Banke Museum, 1994).

49. Paul H. Nystrom, "The Retailer's Part in Winning the War," *Chain Store Age* (January 1942): 34. Nystrom also served as the President of the Limited Price Variety Stores Association.

50. For a description of the importance of central buying organizations for women's apparel stores, see William R. Davidson and Alton F. Doody, *Retailing Management*, 3rd ed. (1951; New York: Ronald Press, 1966), 530, 547.

51. Robinson advertisement, "Tomorrow Buffalo"; "New Stores Bring Metropolitan Beauty," 85, LoCVGC, OV 11.

52. Polenberg, *One Nation Divisible*, 54–55. Sociologist William H. Whyte, Jr., would later label this generation "the Transients" and trace their uprooted nature to their wartime experience; see Whyte, *The Organization Man* (New York: Simon and Schuster, 1956; reprint Philadelphia: University of Pennsylvania Press, 2002), 267–80; as he acutely observed, "The man who leaves home is not the exception in American society but the key to it."

53. One of the most compelling explorations of abstract political commitment to World War II being forged through personal experiences of popular culture, or "living theory," is Robert Westbrook, "'I Want a Girl, Just like the Girl That Married Harry James': American Women and the Problem of Political Obligation in World War II," *American Quarterly* 42, no. 4 (December 1990): 587–614. See also Lizabeth Cohen, *Making a New Deal: Industrial Workers in Chicago, 1919–1939* (Cambridge: Cambridge University Press, 1990), 99–158; Cohen has argued that Chicago workers' identities and political affiliations were forged through their encounter with mass culture: "workers increasingly were shopping at the same chain stores, buying the same brand goods, going to the same chain theaters, and listening to the same radio programs on chain networks. Ethnic workers began to have more in common with their co-workers of different ethnicity and race and with their own children . . . they were beginning to share a cultural life with workers elsewhere in the country" (157).

54. Gruen, "New Trends in Branch Store Design," speech delivered at the National Retail Dry Goods Association, New York, c. 1950, in *Speeches of Victor Gruen*, vol. A, *1943–56*, LoCVGC, box 81.

55. Gruen's comments are in "What Makes a 1940 Store Obsolete?" *Architectural Forum* (August 1950): 3, LoCVGC, OV 17, AHCVGC, box 11.

56. "Grayson's Launches Three-Day Grand-Opening Event," *Inglewood Daily News*, Inglewood, Calif., August 20, 1942, 7, LoCVGC, OV 12.

57. Gerald Wendt, *Science for the World of Tomorrow* (New York: W.W. Norton, 1939), 100–101.

58. Carl Feiss, "Shopping Centers," *House and Garden* 76, no. 6 (December 1939): 48–66. Feiss, professor of planning at the University of Colorado, wrote about the lack of urban aesthetics in public and private housing developments, which echoed his call for the shopping center. See Blake McKelvey, *The Emergence of Metropolitan America, 1915–1966* (New Brunswick, N.J.: Rutgers University Press, 1968), 121, 130. Likewise, city planner Harland Bartholomew maintained that real estate speculation in taxpayers "has invited and produced blighting of large stretches of property along our main thoroughfares" as quoted in Clarence S. Stein and Catherine Bauer, "Store Buildings and Neighborhood Shopping Centers," *Architectural Record* 75 (February 1934): 187. For more on Bartholomew's influential views about commercial strips, see Harland Bartholomew, *Urban Land Uses* (Cambridge, Mass.: Harvard University Press, 1932) and *Land Uses in American Cities* (Cambridge, Mass: Harvard University Press, 1955). Bartholomew maintained in 1955 that "the strip along each major thoroughfare, the corners of every busy street intersection, and a large zone centering on the hub of the city were seen as choice business sites. This overexploitation was fostered by numerous individuals and groups interested in quick turnovers and high returns" (*Land Uses*, 46). I

benefited greatly from conversations with Marina Moskowitz about Bartholomew's work.

59. On the development of Los Angeles automobile strips and commercial architecture there is no better or more thorough source than Richard Longstreth's work; see his *City Center to Regional Mall: Architecture, the Automobile, and Retailing in Los Angeles, 1920–1950* (Cambridge, Mass.: MIT Press, 1997) and *The Drive-In, the Supermarket, and the Transformation of Commercial Space in Los Angeles, 1914–1941* (Cambridge, Mass.: MIT Press, 1999).

60. "Novel Design Proves to Have Customer Pulling Power," *Women's Wear Daily*, February 24, 1941, LoCVGC, OV 11; "Designed for Dominance," *Chain Store Age* (June 1946) LoCVGC, OV 13; "Trade," *Architectural Forum* (October 1946): 132–33, LoCVGC, OV 13; "Grayson's Launches Three-Day Grand-Opening Event," *Inglewood Daily News*; "Modern Store Is Roadside Display Case," *Chain Store Age* (October 1947): 212, LoCVGC, OV 14. See also "Store Designed to Draw Attention of Auto Traffic," *Southwest Builder and Contractor* (June 27, 1947): 24; and "Furniture Store in Los Angeles Is Designed for Motorist Attention and Minimum Cost," *Architectural Forum* (April 1947): 88–89, both in LoCVGC, OV 14.

61. Lucius S. Flint, "How Chain Stores Are Selecting Locations," *Chain Store Age* (March 1946): 11; "Facade with a Flourish," *Business Week*, September 14, 1946, both in LoCVGC, OV 13.

62. "Retail Stores Go Heavy on Light," *Women's Wear Daily*, February 25, 1948, 70, LoCVGC, OV 15.

63. Victor Gruen and Larry Smith, *Shopping Towns USA: The Planning of Shopping Centers*, Progressive Architecture Library (New York: Reinhold, 1960), 159. On the importance of lighting in retail, see William Leach, *Land of Desire: Merchants, Power, and the Rise of a New American Culture* (New York: Pantheon, 1993), 47–48, 144–45. See also Wolfgang Schivelbush, *The Railway Journey: The Industrialization of Time and Space in the 19th Century* (Berkeley: University of California Press, 1986), 45–51; and Wolfgang Schivelbush, *Disenchanted Night: The Industrialization of Light in the Nineteenth Century* (Berkeley: University of California Press, 1988), 146–54.

64. Gruen, "Architects and Lighting Engineers Use Similar Approach to the Problem of Suitable Lighting," *Southwest Builder and Contractor* (April 28, 1950): 11, 50, LoCVGC, OV 52; this article was based on a speech Gruen gave to a joint meeting of the Southern California chapters of A.I.A. and the Illuminating Engineering Society in Los Angeles. The descriptions "awe-filled" to "sweet romance" are from Gruen, "Lighting and Architectural Design," *Architect and Engineer* (April 1949): 33, 35, 38, 43, LoCVGC, OV 16; this article was adapted from a speech Gruen gave to the South Pacific Coast Regional Conference of the Illuminating Engineering Society in San Francisco, March 3, 1949. This second article also appeared as Victor Gruen, "The Case for the Flexible Ceiling," *Electrical West* (September 1949), LoCVGC, OV 60.

65. Gruen, "Lighting and Architectural Design," 35. The Hobby Horse store is illustrated in "Stores," *Architectural Forum*. See also *Magazine of Light* (published by Lamp Department, General Electric Company) no. 1 (1946), both in LoCVGC, OV 13.

66. "De Luxe Modernization," *Chain Store Age* (April 1946): 26, LoCVGC, OV 13; Fernandez, *Specialty Shop*, 49; *Magazine of Light*.

67. Miralumes advertisement, *Modernizing Furniture Stores*, 1945, backcover.

68. J. Gordon Lippincott, *Design for Business* (Chicago: Paul Theobald, 1947), 180. This Chicago store designer described the ideal store lighting as "high overall intensity of lighting throughout [and] concentrated direct light where needed to spotlight specific merchandise for greater interest" (183).

69. Morris Ketchum, Jr., *Shops and Stores*, Progressive Architecture Library (New York: Reinhold, 1948), 70. Sylvania Company advertisement, in and advice manual by its Commercial Engineering Department, "Better Light Fewer Mistakes Better Production with Miralumes," *Fluorescent Lighting Handbook* (Salem, Mass., 1942), back endpaper.

70. Ketchum, *Shops and Stores*, 63.

71. "Ask Our Architect," *Chain Store Age* (August 1946): 62, LoCVGC, OV 13; Victor Gruen, "Lighting Today's Interior," speech to New York A.I.A. and publishers of *Lighting & Lamps*, January 21, 1953, 4–5, LoCVGC, box 81, folder 3, *Speeches of Victor Gruen*, Vol. A, *1943–56*.

72. Louis Parnes, *Planning Stores That Pay*, An Architectural Record Book (New York: F.W. Dodge, 1948), 231. See also Gruen, "Lighting Today's Interior" and Gruen, "Some Notes on Modern Store Design."

73. Lapidus, "Store Design," 99.

74. R. G. Walters, John W. Wingate, and Edward J. Rowse, *Retail Merchandising* (Cincinnati: South-western Publishing, 1943), 87. See also Nelson A. Miller, Harvey W. Hugey, et al., *Grocery Store* (Washington, D.C.: U.S. Government Printing Office, 1945), 6–7, 27–28, 40–44, as cited in Roland Marchand, "Suspended in Time: Mom-and-Pop Groceries, Chain Stores, and National Advertising During the World War II Interlude," in Ward, ed., *Produce and Conserve*, 117–39.

75. Wendt, *Science*, 175. For a quirky history of the acceptance of fluorescent lighting, see Wiebe E. Bijker, *Of Bicycles, Bakelites, and Bulbs: Toward a Theory of Sociotechnical Change* (Cambridge, Mass.: MIT Press, 1995), 199–267. Bijker suggests that fluorescents were first valued for their soft, colored lighting effect and only came to be valued for their white light a little later. See also David Nye, *American Technological Sublime* (Cambridge, Mass.: MIT Press, 1994). Morris Lapidus would later recall that fluorescent lighting appeared in stores after its introduction at the New York World's Fair: see John W. Cook, *Conversations with Architects* (New York: Praeger, 1973), 151. On the significance of lighting at the World's Fair, see Helen Harrison, "The Fair Perceived: Color and Light as Elements in Design and Planning," in Helen Harrison ed., *Dawn of a New Day: The New York World's Fair, 1939/40* (New York: Queens Museum and New York University Press, 1980), 43–55.

76. Parnes, *Planning Stores*, 239.

77. The Sylvania Lighting Company explained, "The change from the small, almost point light source of the incandescent lamp to the fluorescent lamp means that the concentrated brilliance of the former has been spread out into a long, comparatively glareless tube of light in the latter" (Sylvania, *Fluorescent Lighting Handbook*).

78. Charles L. Amick, *Fluorescent Lighting Manual* (New York: McGraw-Hill, 1942), vii, sales figures on 2; see Bijker, *Bicycles, Bakelites, and Bulbs*, 226; Amick, 163.

79. "Store of the Month," *Store of Greater New York* (November 1939), LoCVGC, OV 11.

80. Victor Gruen, "Some Words on Lighting and the Relativity of Light," July 27, 1950, speech, 1–4, AHCVGC, Box 27. This strategic approach to lighting was also employed at the 1939 New York World's Fair where parts of the Fair were left in the dark to highlight words, logos, murals, or statues at night; see Nye, *American Technological Sublime*, 200.

81. Amick, *Fluorescent Lighting Manual*, 240; Parnes, *Planning Stores*, 232. And see Walters et al., *Retail Merchandising*, 88–89, which provides a useful comparison of the "old type and new type" of drugstores, illustrating the difference between incandescent

and fluorescent lighting; see also "Trade," *Architectural Forum* (October 1946), LoCVGC, OV 13.

82. "Novel Design Proves to Have Customer Pulling Power," *Women's Wear Daily*, February 24, 1941; "Robinson's to Open Unit in Buffalo," *Women's Wear Daily*, July 16, 1941, both in LoCVGC, OV 11. The first article described Grayson's Santa Monica store.

83. Lippincott, *Design for Business*, 165; flyer from Associated Lighting Service, San Francisco, formerly Associated Theatrical Service, showing Gruen's lighting designs for C. H. Baker shoe stores in Oakland and San Francisco, J. Magnin and Hastings in Oakland, 1948, LoCVGC, OV 15.

84. Walters et al., *Retail Merchandising*, 265.

85. Gruen, "The Case for the Flexible Ceiling," *Electrical West* (September 1949), LoCVGC, OV 60; see also Parnes, *Planning Stores*, 132–41; Ketchum, *Shops and Stores*, 137–39. Ketchum gave Gruen and Krummeck credit for devising and perfecting what he called the flexible ceiling in their 1944 interior design work on Macy's San Francisco store.

86. "New Stores Opened by Ingenious Use of Substitute Materials," *Chain Store Age* (January 1944): 24, LoCVGC, OV 12.

87. O. P. Cleaver [of Westinghouse Electric and Manufacturing Company, Commercial Engineering Department], internal memorandum dated April 25, 1940, in Committee on Patents, *Hearings before the Committee on Patents, U.S. Senate, 77th Cong., 2nd Sess. on S.2303 and S.2491, pt. 9, August 18–21, 1942: 4753–5032* (Washington, D.C.: U.S. Government Printing Office, 1942), 4855–4957; 4955, as quoted in Bijker, *Bicycles, Bakelites, and Bulbs*, 233.

88. Sylvania, *Fluorescent Lighting*, 60.

89. General Electric, *Magazine of Light*, 1946; the stores were Altman & Kuhne (10), Steckler Shop (18), Seattle Grayson's (19), Pasadena Grayson's (20). See also Ketchum, *Shops and Stores*, 71, for a good description of the lighting methods used in the Altman & Kuhne store.

90. See Karl Van Leuven to Gruen, November 6, 1945; Van Leuven to Gruen, December 7, 1945 both in LoCVGC, OV 12. Karl Van Leuven worked for Raphael G. Wolff Studios, Hollywood, and would later become a partner with Gruen.

91. Gruen, "Modernized Store Layout," Store Modernization Show, speech, July 8, 1947, 1–4; "Biggest News for Retailers in 50 Years!" Store Modernization Show flyer, July 1947, both in LoCVGC, OV 14.

92. One of the most interesting works on the significance of "pleasure" in the rise of modern consumption is Colin Campbell, *The Romantic Ethic and the Spirit of Modern Consumerism* (London: Blackwell, 1987). Campbell writes about this new attitude: "The primary object is to squeeze as much of the quality of pleasure as one can from all these sensations which one actually experiences during the course of the process of living. All acts are potential 'pleasure' if only they can be approached or undertaken in the right manner" (69, 92).

93. Gruen, "Architect Bites Client," *Architectural Forum* (February 1948), LoCVGC, OV 15.

Chapter 3. Wartime Planning for Postwar Prosperity

Note to epigraph: Gruen, "Controlling Factors in the Establishment of Regional Shopping Centers," speech at Regional Conference on the Effect of Current War Conditions on Real Estate Market and Valuation Problems, 1943, in *Speeches of Victor Gruen*, vol. A, 1943–56, LoCVGC, box 81.

1. Morris Lapidus, "Planning Today for the Store of Tomorrow," *Chain Store Age* (April 1944): 24–30.

2. "New Buildings for 194X," *Architectural Forum* 78 (May 1943): 69–189, AHCVGC, box 23, 2, and 54, LoCVGC, OV 12. One of the best treatments of World War II planning for the postwar city remains Mell Scott, *American City Planning Since 1890* (Berkeley: University of California Press, 1969), 368–471; the two quotes are cited by Scott, 370 and 404. See also Robert Beauregard, *Voices of Decline: The Postwar Fate of US Cities* (Cambridge, Mass.: Blackwell, 1993), 108–57. For an anti-urban screed and argument for decentralization written during the war, see Elmer Peterson, ed., *Cities Are Abnormal!* (Norman: University of Oklahoma Press, 1946).

3. "The New House of 194X," *Architectural Forum* 77, no. 3 (March 1942): 65–152; Gardner Dailey and Joseph Esherick, "House De-2, Magic Carpet Series," in "New House of 194X," 132–35.

4. Howard Meyers, "Confidential Copy for May 1943 Forum Advertisers," February 1943, AHCVGC, box 54; "New Buildings for 194X," 69.

5. William Lescaze, "Service Station," 132–33; Oscar Stonorov and Louis Kahn, "Hotel," 74–79; Mies van der Rohe, "Museum," 84–85; Charles Eames, "City Hall," 88–90; and Victor Gruen and Elsie Krummeck, "Shopping Center," 101–3, all in "New Buildings for 194X."

6. "Stores," *Architectural Forum* 74, no. 12 (December 1939): 427–45; "Candy Shop for Altman & Kuhne, New York City," *Architectural Forum* 75, no. 2 (February 1940): 89–92, both in LoCVGC, OV 11; "Recent Work of Gruenbaum, Krummeck & Auer," *Architectural Forum* 76, no. 9 (September 1941): 191–200, LoCVGC, OV 11, AHCVGC, box 2.

7. Talbot Hamlin, "Some Restaurants and Recent Shops," *Pencil Points* 20 (August 1939): 498.

8. "New Buildings for 194X," 69–70.

9. "New Buildings for 194X," 70. For more on wartime worries about declining downtowns, see Beauregard, *Voices of Decline*, 74–105; and Thomas J. Sugrue, *Origins of the Urban Crisis: Race and Inequality in Postwar Detroit* (Princeton, N.J.: Princeton University Press, 1996), 139–40.

10. On Country Club Plaza of Kansas City, see Richard Longstreth, "J. C. Nichols, the Country Club Plaza, and Notions of Modernity," *Harvard Architecture Review* (1986): 120–35; William S. Worley, *J. C. Nichols and the Shaping of Kansas City* (Columbia: University of Missouri Press, 1990), chap. 8; Alexander Garvin, *The American City: What Works and What Doesn't* (New York: McGraw-Hill, 1996), 108–10; and William S. Worley, *The Plaza, First and Always* (Lenexa, Kan.: Addax Publishing, 1997); and Dory DeAngelo, *The Plaza* (Prairie Village, Kan.: Country Club Plaza, 1989).

11. "Buildings for 194X," 70.

12. In a strange mutation from representing a respected member of the body politic, by the 1920s "taxpayer" had become a derogatory term for excessive real estate speculation. The *Oxford English Dictionary* (1971) cites the first reference to "taxpayer" as a real estate term in 1921, reflecting the rampant speculation in commercial properties at the time (123): B. Matthews, *Essays on Engineering* (1921), 134: "A resplendent electric sign on top a two-story taxpayer." On "taxpayers" or "strips," see Richard Longstreth, *City Center to Regional Mall: Architecture, the Automobile, and Retailing in Los Angeles, 1920–1950* (Cambridge, Mass.: MIT Press, 1997), 62–71; and Chester Liebs, *Main Street to Miracle Mile: American Roadside Architecture* (Boston: Little, Brown, 1985), 10–37.

13. See Catherine Gudis, "The Road to Consumption: Advertising and the American cultural Landscape, 1917–1965," Ph.D. dissertation, Yale University, 1998. Gudis discusses the way billboards were used as speculative investments on the commercial strip. I am grateful for all the conversations with Cathy about automobile strips and commercial development.

14. J. C. Nichols, "Planned Shopping Centers," *National Real Estate Journal* (March 22, 1926): 47; J. C. Nichols, "Developing Outlying Shopping Centers," *American City* 41, no. 1 (July 1929): 98.

15. Bartholomew is quoted by Catherine Bauer and Clarence Stein, "Store Buildings," *Architectural Record* (1934): 187. For more of Bartholomew's influential views on commercial zoning of land, see Harland Bartholomew, *Urban Land Uses* (Cambridge, Mass.: Harvard University Press, 1932) and Harland Bartholomew, *Land Uses in American Cities* (Cambridge, Mass.: Harvard University Press, 1955). Bartholomew maintained in 1955 that "the strip along each major thoroughfare, the corners of every busy street intersection, and a large zone centering on the hub of the city were seen as choice business sites. This over-exploitation of land was fostered by numerous individuals and groups interested in quick turnovers and high returns" (46).

16. Bauer and Stein, "Store Buildings," 174, 177–78, 185. See also Geoffrey Baker and Bruno Funaro, *Shopping Centers: Design and Operation* (New York: Reinhold, 1951), 23. The two architects reminded the prospective shopping center developer that zoning "may actually be of advantage . . . by denying sites to his prospective competitors."

17. All the Gruen and Krummeck correspondence with *Architectural Forum* is in AHCVGC, box 54. The file contains a note from Hortense Hockett—Gruen's personal secretary throughout the 1960s—to Claudia Moholy-Nagy, director of the Victor Gruen Foundation for Environmental Planning, suggesting that Gruen saw the 194X shopping center project as a landmark in his career. "Claudia: For the pages of history—Victor's original outline & sketches for 1943 for *Forum*. HH"

18. Ruth Goodhue, telegram to Gruenbaum and Krummeck, February 10, 1942; Victor Gruenbaum to Miss Goodhue of *Architectural Forum*, February 16, 1943, both in AHCVGC, box 54.

19. Advertisement, ". . . Next Month New Buildings for 194X," *Architectural Forum* 78, no. 4 (April 1943): 145. See also Baker and Funaro, *Shopping Centers*, 10; they equate new suburban shopping centers with "existing downtown shopping centers." And see Lowell Carr and James Sterner, *Willow Run: A Study of Industrialization and Cultural Inadequacy* (New York: Harper & Brothers, 1952), 57; they refer to downtown Ypsilanti, Michigan, as a "shopping center."

20. Victor Gruenbaum to *Architectural Forum*, February 26, 1943, AHCVGC, box 54.

21. Gruen, "Stores—Communal," c. March 1943, AHCVGC, box 54.

22. Gruen to *Architectural Forum*, March 1943, AHCVGC, box 54.

23. Howard Meyers to Gentlemen, February 16, 1943, AHCVGC, box 54.

24. Gruen to *Architectural Forum*, February 26, 1943, AHCVGC, box 54.

25. Gruen to *Architectural Forum*, February 26, 1943.

26. Morris Ketchum, Jr., "Store Block," *Architectural Forum* 73, no. 3 (October 1940): 294–95. When Ketchum received a large commission for designing a shopping center during the postwar, it would be nearly opposite from this 1940 proposal. Eleven years later Ketchum and his partners planned Shopper's World in Framingham, Massachusetts. When opened it was not a mixed office and retail center downtown but a suburban center devoted to retail with a large central courtyard. See Morris Ketchum, "Grass on Main

Street, Rye, New York," *Architectural Forum* 85, no. 8 (August 1946): cover and 76–79; and "Withering Grass," *Architectural Forum* 85, no. 12 (December 1946): 12, 14.

27. For the best analysis of Los Angeles retail at this time, see Longstreth, *City Center to Regional Mall*; and Richard Longstreth, *The Drive-In, the Supermarket, and the Transformation of Commercial Space in Los Angeles, 1914–1941* (Cambridge, Mass.: MIT Press, 1999).

28. George Nelson to Victor Gruenbaum, March 3, 1948, 1–2, AHCVGC, box 54.

29. Victor Gruen and Elsie Krummeck, "Project for a Small Post-war Shopping Center," c. April 1943, AHCVGC, box 54; Lewis Mumford, "The Sky Line: New Facades," *New Yorker*, November 20, 1937, 90.

30. Victor Gruen and Elsie Krummeck, "I. Building Plan," c. April 1938, AHCVGC, box 54.

31. Gruen and Krummeck, "Project for a Small Post-War Shopping Center."

32. Feiss, "Shopping Centers," 66.

33. Baker and Funaro, *Shopping Centers*, 69; Victor Gruen, "What to Look For in Shopping Centers," *Chain Store Age* (July 1948), AHCVGC, box 9, LoCVGC, OV 15.

34. See William Leach, *Land of Desire: Merchants, Power, and the Rise of a New American Culture* (New York: Pantheon, 1993).

35. Victor Gruen and Larry Smith, "Shopping Centers: A New Building Type," *Progressive Architecture* (June 1952): 68, AHCVGC, box 11.

36. For instance, the circular supermarket, by J. Gordon Carr, employed a system of merchandise slips and conveyor belts that allowed people to shop more efficiently with no parcels in their arms, "Supermarket, Buildings for 194X," 98–100. Gruen and Krummeck modestly sought to "improve shopping conditions."

37. Charles Eames, "City Hall," 88–90; Jedd S. Reisner and J. Stanley Sharp, "Hardware Store," 106–7; Pietro Belluschi, "Office Building," 108–12, all in "Buildings for 194X."

38. Whitney Smith, "No Cars on Main Street," *Better Homes and Gardens* (January 1945): 21. On Linda Vista see "'Grass on Main Street' Becomes a Reality; Shopping Center, Linda Vista, California," *Architectural Forum* 81 (September 1944); and Longstreth, *City Center to Regional Mall*, 295–98.

39. Baker and Funaro, *Shopping Centers*, 236.

40. Morris Lapidus, "Shopping Facilities in Wartime," *Architectural Record* 92 (October 1942): 64; see also Baker and Funaro, *Shopping Centers*, 128.

41. Lapidus, "Wartime," 63; Ketchum, *Shops and Stores*, 271. See also Lapidus, "Wartime," 68.

42. Ketchum, *Shops and Stores*, 271–72.

43. Baker and Funaro, *Shopping Centers*, 242–43; see also Lapidus, "Wartime," 63–78.

44. "Community Shopping Centers," *Architectural Record* 87 (1941): 119–20. The article described a shopping center in Chevy Chase, Maryland, designed by architect James Hogan.

45. Baker and Funaro, *Shopping Centers*, 5.

46. Baker and Funaro, *Shopping Centers*, 60–63.

47. See Morris Ketchum, Jr., *Blazing A Trail* (New York: Vantage Press, 1982), 3.

48. Gruen and Krummeck, "Project for a Small Post-War Shopping Center."

49. Victor Gruen, "Notes for a Regional Conference on the Effect of Current War Conditions on Real Estate Market and Valuation Problems," 1943, LoCVGC, box 81. In the 1940s, decentralization of residences, retail, and industry was seen as one of the meth-

ods by which to improve cities; for an example of this rhetoric, see the collected essays in Peterson, ed., *Cities Are Abnormal!* One Gruen-designed shopping center, Randhurst, outside Chicago, actually used the bomb shelter idea and placed it next to its delivery tunnels.

Chapter 4. Seducing the Suburban Autoist

Note to epigraph: Gruen, "What to Look for in Shopping Centers," *Chain Store Age* (July 1948), LoCVGC, OV 15 and AHCVGC, box 11.

1. The J. Magnin stores were in Palo Alto (1946), Sacramento (1946), Oakland (1948), San Mateo (1950), Lake Tahoe (1950), and again in Sacramento (1950). See Barbara Bancroft, "Joseph Magnin Store in Palo Alto like Home," *San Francisco Bulletin*, June 25, 1946, 5; and "50,000 'Partners' for Sacramento Store," *Fashion Trades*, September 20, 1946, LoCVGC, both in OV 13; "JM 'Shops Around Court' Keyed for Shopping Ease," *Oakland Tribune*, November 25, 1948, LoCVGC, OV 15.

2. Gruen, "Reminiscences," box 22.

3. Gruen, "What's Wrong with Store Design?" *Women's Wear Daily*, October 18, 1949, 62, LoCVGC, OV 16.

4. The first Gruen-Krummeck commission in the Los Angeles area was for Grayson's in Santa Monica, which opened in 1940. See "Grayson's 'Most Unique Store in America' Opens Here Tomorrow!" *Santa Monica Evening Outlook*, November 29, 1940, 17, LoCVGC, OV 11.

5. See Greg Hise, *Magnetic Los Angeles: Planning the Twentieth Century Metropolis* (Baltimore: Johns Hopkins University Press, 1997). Hise goes a long way to refute the prevailing interpretation that wartime and postwar suburbs in Los Angeles were unplanned and decentralization, later derided as sprawl, was uncontrolled. Instead, he convincingly argues that developers coherently planned large tracts of land according to industrial, commercial, and residential zoning that had been prescribed by the government. See also Mike Davis, *City of Quartz: Excavating the Future in Los Angeles* (New York: Verso, 1990), 375–440, on Kaiser Steel's wartime development of Fontana. The story of the development of the Westchester tract becomes quite confusing. Greg Hise states that the land was owned by Security-First National Bank, who then sold three thousand acres to four builders; Security also held on to a percentage of the commercial area along Sepulveda Boulevard, Hise, *Magnetic Los Angeles*, 143. An article written in 1949 claims that there were three owners of the commercial property: Superior Oil, Security National Bank, and the Los Angeles Extension Company, with Frank H. Ayers & Son acting as the developer, "Something New in Stores," *Architectural Forum* 90, no. 6 (June 1949): 105. See also Richard Longstreth, *City Center to Regional Mall: Architecture, the Automobile, and Retailing in Los Angeles, 1920–1950* (Cambridge, Mass.: MIT Press, 1997), 241–46.

6. Geoffrey Baker and Bruno Funaro, *Shopping Centers: Design and Operation* (New York: Reinhold, 1951), 6.

7. Milliron's brochure, "Presenting Milliron's Beautifully Restyled Third Floor of Fashions," July 1947, LoCVGC, OV 14.

8. J. W. Milliron to Victor Gruen, February 28, 1947, LoCVGC, OV 14.

9. Baker and Funaro, *Shopping Centers*, 6. Victor Gruenbaum to Ms. Goodhue, February 26, 1943, 2, AHCVGC, box 54.

10. See Gruen, *The Heart of Our Cities: The Urban Crisis: Diagnosis and Cure*, (NY:

Simon and Schuster, 1964), 81. Gruen also described Los Angeles during the 1930s as being a "famous Miracle Mile." Since he did not move there until 1941, perhaps he was remembering the city when he first arrived.

11. O.G., "Department Store of Tomorrow: Milliron's Emporium Could Be the Model," *Interiors* 109, no. 5 (October 1949): 112–19, AHCVGC, box 11.

12. Abbot Kinney, "Shape of Suburban Department Store Buildings," *Women's Wear Daily*, July 30, 1947, LoCVGC, OV 14; O.G., "Department Store," 112.

13. "In a central business district which is failing to keep up with general prosperity because of a parking shortage, immediate action may be the first need," two experts recommended. Geoffrey Baker and Bruno Funaro, *Parking* (New York: Reinhold, 1958), 98. See also Geoffrey Baker and Bruno Funaro, "Shopping Centers: Building Types Study Number 152," *Architectural Record* 106, no. 2 (August 1949).

14. "Evanston Store," February 25, 1947, 1, 5, Wieboldt Department Store Collection, Chicago Historical Society, box 6; Gruen, "What's Wrong with Store Design?" *Women's Wear Daily*, October 18, 1949, 62. "Completed Scale Model Reveals Features of Milliron's Westchester Suburban Store," *Westchester News-Advertiser*, November 13, 1947, front page, LoCVGC, OV 14. See also "Future Westchester Development of Milliron's Department Store to Feature Roof Parking," *Southwest Builder and Contractor* (May 23, 1947): 16–17, LoCVGC, OV 14.

15. Milliron's was not the first suburban department store to employ rooftop parking. The design for Milliron's parking lot was most certainly influenced by a Los Angeles Sears, Roebuck store at West and Pico Boulevards, which had opened nine years earlier. *Architectural Forum* had explained that Sears needed parking to survive commercially and that this ingenious scheme had been arrived at through an "intense concentration on 'merchandising' rather than 'architecture.'" The *Forum* glowed that the parking was executed in "a highly dramatic fashion." In the same issue, Gruen and Krummeck had some of their New York retail work illustrated; see "Store Building for Sears Roebuck," "Candy Shop for Altman & Kuhne, New York City," both in *Architectural Forum* 73, no. 10 (February 1940): 70–76, 89–92, LoCVGC, OV 11. Rooftop parking had also been proposed by Gruen's former partner Morris Ketchum in his ideas for a downtown store/office block. Ketchum proposed escalators to bring shoppers from the roof into the heart of the store which was similar to the Milliron's design. See Morris Ketchum, Jr., "Store Block," *Architectural Forum* 73, no. 3 (October 1940): 294–95. Gruen and Krummeck would undoubtedly have been familiar with these earlier proposals.

16. O.G., "Department Store," 114; Baker and Funaro, *Parking*, 121.

17. "Something New in Stores," *Architectural Forum* 90, no. 6 (June 1949): 105, LoCVGC, OV 16.

18. Gruen, "Problems of Store Design," *Southwest Builder and Contractor* (January 23, 1948), LoCVGC, OV 15; the article contained excerpts from a speech Gruen gave at the California AIA Convention, Catalina Island, October 23, 1947. See also Kinney, "Shape of Buildings." Kinney went on to observe that the Milliron's designers were "telescoping a typical multiple-story department store operation into one efficient, radially laidout floor."

19. Reynar Banham, *Los Angeles: The Architecture of Four Ecologies* (New York: Harper and Row, 1971), 153.

20. Geoffrey Baker and Bruno Funaro, "Shopping Centers: Building Types Study Number 152," *Architectural Record* 106, no. 2 (August 1949): 130–31; see also Baker and Funaro, *Shopping Centers*, 77, 168–70.

21. Baker and Funaro, *Shopping Centers*, 77.

22. See William Leach, *Land of Desire: Merchants, Power, and the Rise of a New American Culture* (New York: Pantheon Books, 1993).

23. O.G., "Department Store," 116.

24. Gruen and Larry Smith, *Shopping Towns USA: The Planning of Shopping Centers*, Progressive Architecture Library (New York: Reinhold, 1960), 48.

25. "Civic Leaders Hail Announcement of Milliron's Store Auditorium," *Westchester News-Advertiser*, June 12, 1947, 1–2; "Milliron's Reveals Plans for Store at Sepulveda, La Tijera Blvds.," *California Apparel News*, June 20, 1947, 2, both in LoCVGC, OV 14.

26. O.G., "Department Store," 112–19.

27. The practice of building freestanding branch department stores did not completely disappear with the rise of the shopping center. For instance, as late as the 1960s Straw-bridge and Clothier of Philadelphia chose not to build a shopping center with James Rouse as developer and Victor Gruen as architect. Instead, after three years of intense planning and debate, they went with a much less expensive single department store in Springfield, New Jersey with the exterior designed by Gruen and the interior designed by Welton Becket. See HMSCC Series 1: Corporate records, box 8, two volumes on Delaware County project.

28. "Suburban Retail Districts," *Architectural Forum* 93 (August 1950): 107.

29. Gruen, "Talk on Public Relations," AIA Meeting, August 9, 1949, 1–3, AHCVGC, box 27; Victor Gruen, "Triple Target for Economy," *Chain Store Age* (July 1949); Victor Gruen, "Architect's Complete Control of Design and Furnishings Effects Large Savings for Owner," *Southwest Builder and Contractor* (April 22, 1949): 8–12, both in LoCVGC, OV 52.

30. Gruen, speech to the Western Savings and Mortgage Conference of the American Bankers Association, Los Angeles, February 9, 1953, *Speeches of Victor Gruen*, vol. A, 1943–56, LoCVGC, box 81; see Victor Gruen, "Basic Planning Concepts of Correlated Shopping Center Expounded to Bankers," *Southwest Builder and Contractor* (March 27, 1953): 2.

31. Gruen, "What to Look for in Shopping Centers," *Chain Store Age* (July 1948), LoCVGC, OV 17.

32. Gruen, "Reminiscences," box 20.

33. Gruen, "What to Look for in Shopping Centers."

34. "Big New Shopping District Planned," *Los Angeles Times*, September 22, 1950, pt. 1, 8, LoCVGC, OV 17. Plan caption: "SHOPPING CIRCLE—Bird's-eye view of proposed Olympic Shopping Circle looking from Whittier Blvd. towards Olympic Blvd. In upper right-hand corner is the movie theater and lower and toward the middle a large department store."

35. "Big New Shopping District Planned."

36. Gruen, "Work in Progress," 1951, 2, LoCVGC. Gruen received $6,112.95 for his work on "preliminaries for the Olympic Shopping Circle" from an unnamed client. When Gruen made up this sheet in 1951, he did not anticipate any further income from the job.

37. Gruen, "What's Wrong with Store Design?" See also Victor Gruen, "The Decentralization Plan of the J. L. Hudson Company for the Metropolitan Area of Detroit," c. 1951, AHCVGC.

38. "How Stores Can Modernize," *Department Store Economist* (August 1949), LoCVGC, OV 16; "Wins Store Modernization Award," *Building News*, July 7, 1949, LoCVGC, OV 16.

39. Jose Fernandez, "Modernized Store Fronts," *Paint Logic* (October 1947): 14, 64;

Victor Gruen, "Shun Skin-Deep Beauty," speech at New York Store Modernization Show, 1947, Published in *Men's Wear*, August 22, 1947, 65–67; and "How to Cook a Store Front," *Hardware and Metal & Electrical Dealer*, August 23, 1947, all in LoCVGC, OV 14.

40. "Opposes Modernizing Store Fronts Alone," *New York Times*, July 10, 1947, front page. See also "Trend to Full-Store View Through Windows Gains," *New York Herald Tribune*, July 10, 1947; and Earl A. Dash, "Stores Urged Not to Change Fronts Only," *Women's Wear Daily*, July 10, 1947, all in LoCVGC, OV 14.

41. Much of this tale is taken from Victor Gruen, "The Northland Story," c. 1968, LoCVGC, and Gruen, *Centers for the Urban Environment: Survival of the Cities* (New York: Van Nostrand Reinhold, 1973). The broad points of this story are also corroborated in other accounts of planning Northland, Eastland, and Westland, for example in Jeanne Lowe's *Saturday Evening Post* article about Southdale and Northland, c. May 1959. In a letter to Gruen dated May 18, 1959, Lowe wrote that, "in my story I said that you spent two weeks behind closed doors at Hudson's drawing their first center, you emerged with plans for not one, but four, and a thirty year decentralization program." This story is also corroborated or at least repeated in Eugene J. Kelley, *Shopping Centers: Locating Controlled Regional Shopping Centers* (Saugatuck, Conn.: Eno Foundation for Highway Traffic Control, 1956), Chapter XV, "Northland Center, Detroit, Michigan," 139–50.

42. Unfortunately, this letter does not survive in the Dayton-Hudson's archives or in either of the Victor Gruen collections. The quotes are from Gruen's retelling of the story in his c. 1968 "Northland Story."

43. Gruen, "Northland Story."

44. Gruen, "Northland Story," 4.

45. Gruen, "Oscar Webber," c. 1968, 2, LoCVGC.

46. Gruen, "Northland Story," 2.

47. Gruen, "The Decentralization Plan of the J. L. Hudson Company for the Metropolitan Area of Detroit," c. 1953, AHCVGC. Their proposal was quite bold for the time; for instance in 1950 the New York developer William Zeckendorf said, "I see the regional center as a minimum of 20 acres and a maximum of 50 acres." He thought that large centers would generate horrific traffic jams and subsequently fail. As quoted in "Suburban Retail Districts," *Architectural Forum* (August 1950): 108.

48. Acreage numbers vary in different accounts. These numbers are from Gruen, "Decentralization Plan."

49. See Gruen, "Oscar Webber." See also "Suburban Retail Districts," *Architectural Forum* (August 1950): 107, where a Hudson's executive claimed that "the best salesman we have is the U.S. Census Bureau."

50. Gruen, "Decentralization Plan."

51. "Suburban Retail Districts," 107.

52. Gruen, "Circular Store for Traffic Flow," *Chain Store Age* (July 1951), AHCVGC, box 22.

53. "Hudson's to Build 102-Acre Suburban Shopping Center," *Detroit News*, June 4, 1950, LoCVGC, OV 20.

54. "Hudson's No. 1, 2, 3, 4 in Detroit," *Detroit Free Press*, 1954, LoCVGC, OV 20; Earl Wegmann, "J. L. Hudson to Build Huge Shopping Center," *Detroit Free Press*, June 4, 1950, 1.

55. Clarence Stein and Catherine Bauer, "Store Buildings and Neighborhood Shopping Centers," *Architectural Record* 75 (February 1934): 185. See also Clarence Stein, "Store-Building to Meet the Need," *American City* 49 (1934): 71.

56. "'Grass on Main Street' Becomes a Reality; Shopping Center, Linda Vista, Califor-

nia," *Architectural Forum* 81, no. 9 (September 1944): 83; Whitney Smith, "No Cars on Main Street," *Better Homes and Gardens* 23, no. 5 (January 1945): 20.

57. Gruen, "What to Look for in Shopping Centers."

58. Public Relations Department, "To All Hudsonians," April 23, 1951, J. L. Hudson Company Archives, Northland Shopping Center; Gruen, "Oscar Webber," c. 1968, 2.

59. Gruen, "Memorandum Concerning the Retail Trade Opportunities at Montclair in Suburban Houston," c. 1950, 5. See also Victor Gruen, "Montclair," rough outline of report, both in AHCVGC, box 47.

60. "$12,000,000 Montclair Center Will Be Houston," *Houston Chronicle*, December 17, 1950; "Brasco in Your Design for Shopping keeps Customers Coming," "Brasco Safety-Set Store Fronts advertisement for their Dor-o-matic," *Chain Store Age* (April 1952): 12; photo caption: "One of the largest stores in the southwest. The new Weingarten Super Market in Houston with Concealed Door Control," c. 1952, last two in LoCVGC, OV 19.

61. Gruen, "Memorandum," 18.

62. "109-Store Houston Shopping Center of 1952 to Feature Pedestrian Mall," *Women's Wear Daily*, January 3, 1951; "First Part of $12 Million Shopping Center Is Started," *Houston Post*, December 17, 1950, sec. 3, 10, both in AHCVGC, box 47.

63. "Texas Beauty," *Chain Store Age* (March 1952), LoCVGC, OV 19.

64. *Houston Post*, "First Part of $12 Million Shopping Center"; "Suburban Retail Districts," *Architectural Forum* (August 1950); see also "Montclair Center Will Get Large Weingarten Store," *Houston Chronicle*, c. January 1951, LoCVGC, OV 18.

65. See Gruen and Smith, *Shopping Towns USA*, 90.

66. The Montclair shopping center that was eventually built copied a popular Houston model from the 1920s, the River Oaks shopping center.

67. Gruen and Larry Smith, "Shopping Centers: The New Building Type," *Progressive Architecture* (June 1952): 90, LoCVGC, OV 19. Unfortunately, the magazine editors misread the site plan and suggested that the bisecting avenue would be routed over the shopping center to serve the rooftop parking lots, rather than underneath it.

68. Gruen also began seeking speaking engagements with financial experts; see Gruen, speech to the Western Savings and Mortgage Conference; Gruen, "Basic Planning Concepts of Correlated Shopping Center Expounded to Bankers," 2.

69. Victor Gruen, "Commercial Structures and the Architect," speech to Southern California Chapter of the AIA, August 14, 1956, 2–3, in *Speeches of Victor Gruen*, vol. A, 1943–56, LoCVGC, box 81.

70. "The Ten Steps Preceding Shopping Center Construction," *Women's Wear Daily*, July 2, 1952, LoCVGC, OV 19, quoting from Gruen and Smith, "Shopping Centers."

71. Gruen to G. Stockton Strawbridge, president of Strawbridge and Clothier, December 21, 1961, HMSCC.

72. Gruen, "How to Get More Than You Pay For in Dealing with Architects on Store Modernization," *Building Supply News* (September 1948): 69, LoCVGC, OV 15.

Chapter 5. A "Shoppers' Paradise" for Suburbia

Note to epigraph: Victor Gruen, "Commercial Structures and the Architect," talk to Southern California Chapter of the AIA, August 14, 1956, in *Speeches of Victor Gruen*, vol. A, 1943–56, LoCVGC, box 81 and AHCVGC, box 27. One hundred-and-eighty people turned for Gruen's speech; see "August Meeting," *Bulletin, Southern California Chapter of AIA* 20, no. 8 (August 1956), LoCVGC, OV 25.

1. J. M. Baskin, "Carson's New Branch Will Open Next Fall," *Women's Wear Daily*, December 10, 1953, LoCVGC, OV 20; "Carson's Woodmar Store to Open Doors Monday," *Hammond Times*, October 31, 1954, LoCVGC, OV 21.

2. "The Store That Cars Built," *Architectural Forum* (May 1952): 132–35, AHCVGC, box 22.

3. Gruen and Larry Smith, "Shopping Centers: The New Building Type," *Progressive Architecture* (June 1952), AHCVGC, box 11, LoCVGC, OV 11. See also "The Ten Steps Preceding Shopping Center Construction," *Women's Wear Daily*, July 2, 1952, LoCVGC, OV 11.

4. *Progressive Architecture* (July 1954): 74–77, LoCVGC, OV 1; see also "Shopping Centers of Tomorrow," *Arts and Architecture* (January 1954), AHCVGC, box 33; Victor Gruen, Listing of Projects, "Shopping Centers of Tomorrow Exhibition," c. 1956, AHCVGC, box 23.

5. Richard Neutra quoted in exhibition press release, 1953, LoCVGC, OV 1.

6. Victor Gruen Associates, *Shopping Centers of Tomorrow*, American Federation of Arts, 1953, AHCVGC, box 33 and LoCVGC, OV 1; Victor Gruen, untitled, draft of *Shopping Center of Tomorrow* text, c. 1953, AHCVGC, box 33.

7. "Too Many Shopping Centers?" *Business Week*, November 17, 1956, LoCVGC, OV 25. See also Arthur Rubloff, "Are Shopping Centers Failing?" *Super Market Merchandising* 19 (February 1954): 67–68, LoCVGC, OV 21. The question was answered with an unambiguous yes; with thousands of retail facilities on the drawing boards, economic failure was unavoidable.

8. Robert Fitzsimmons, "Shopping Center Boom Poses Problems," *Journal of Commerce and Commercial*, October 1, 1954, LoCVGC, OV 21. The realtor quoted was Arthur Rubloff of Chicago.

9. Joseph F. Dinneen, "Huge Crowds at Opening of Fabulous Shoppers World," *Boston Daily Globe*, October 5, 1951, 1, as cited in Kathleen Kelly Broomer, "Shoppers World and the Regional Shopping Center in Greater Boston," *Society of Commercial Archeology: News Journal* 13, no. 1 (Fall–Winter 1994–95): 2–9.

10. "Caution Is Urged on Store Centers," *Detroit Fee Press*, June 26, 1954, LoCVGC, OV 21; Ernest Fuller, "Rubloff Rips Unwarranted Shop Centers," *Chicago Tribune*, June 26, 1954, LoCVGC, OV 21.

11. Gruen, "Commercial Structures and the Architect," 2.

12. Victor Gruen, "A Shopping Center Is More Than a Collection of Stores," *Practical Builder, Chicago* 3 (October 1953): 67. The same article appeared as "Planned Shopping Center," *Dun's Review* (May 1953): 37–38, 113–14, both in LoCVGC, OV 20; see also Victor Gruen, "Basic Planning Concepts of Correlated Shopping Center Expounded to Bankers," *Southwest Builder and Contractor* (March 27, 1953): 2–6, which was an address delivered at the Western Savings and Mortgage Conference of the American Bankers Association, Los Angeles, February 9, 1953, in *Speeches of Victor Gruen*, vol. A, 1943–56, LoCVGC, box 81.

13. See G. Stockton Strawbridge, Minutes of Executive Committee Meeting, HMSCC, box 8. Strawbridge's executives always bemoaned the annual loan of $1,000,000 that they took to pay operating expenses; by the mid-1950s the loan had increased to $2,000,000.

14. In one instance, Strawbridge and Clothier of Philadelphia spent $12,500 for an "architectural and site plan and interior traffic study." The deal eventually fell apart, and they lost their investment. Strawbridge and Clothier Executive Committee Meeting, June 2, 1959, HMSCC, box 8.

15. One precarious financing scheme, employed by a Philadelphia department store,

was to sell off its flagship store to an insurance agency for cash. The department store then leased the store back and used the cash for its suburban expansion. One complicated manifestation of this strategy was for department stores to contemplate selling stores even before they had been constructed. For instance, Strawbridge planned to build a branch at the Cherry Hill Shopping Center and then immediately sell the store to the Equitable Life Assurance Society for cash; Strawbridge would then "leaseback" the property. See Minutes of Executive Committee Meeting, "Terms of Proposed Sale and Leaseback of the Cherry Hill Store," April 3, 1959 and April 17, 1959, HMSCC, Executive Committee Minutes, box 8. See also G. Stockton Strawbridge to James Rouse, "Cherry Hill Shopping Center," August 14, 1959. Stockton explained to Rouse the sale of the proposed building to Equitable: "the purpose of such sale and leaseback is to enable us to finance the cost of such improvements" that were "proposed to be constructed by us." Executive Committee Minutes, HMSCC, box 8. In 1947 the Wieboldt Department Store of Chicago contemplated a similar financial deal of building a new store in Evanston, selling the store to an insurance company, and then leasing the store back from the new owner. See "Evanston Store," February 25, 1947, 5, Wieboldt Department Store Collection, Chicago Historical Society, box 6.

16. Larry Smith and Company, *Bay-Fair Progress Report*, sec. 2: "Mortgage Financing," January 18, 1954, 4, AHCVGC, box 7.

17. See "Property Settlement Agreement Between Elsie Krummeck and Victor Gruen," July 20, 1951, LoCVGC, box 45 and LoCVGC, box 77; Victor Gruen, "Historic Development," notes on firm, LoCVGC, box 22; Mary Morris, "How Miss Van Houten Became Mrs. Gruen," *Detroit News*, February 15, 1954, LoCVGC, OV 21; and Lazette Van Houten obituary, *Home Furnishings Daily*, July 17, 1962, LoCVGC, box 22.

18. Karl Van Leuven to Gruen, c. June 1973, LoCVGC, box 22.

19. Memorandum, on previews, February 12, 1954, J. L. Hudson's Department Store Archives, NSC; Horace Carpenter, Jr., Vice President, "Subject: Opening Arrangements and Publicity," c. March 1, 1954, NSC.

20. Horace Carpenter, Jr., "Welcome to this Press Preview of Northland Center," March 15, 1954, NSC. See "Shopping Center Near a Defense Cluster," *Progressive Architecture* (1954), AHCVGC, box 14; "20th Century Bazaar," *Life*, August 30, 1954, AHCVGC, box 35; and "Detroit," *Industrial Design* (October 1955), AHCVGC, box 22.

21. "Northland: A New Yardstick for Shopping Center Planning," *Architectural Forum* (June 1954): 102–19, AHCVGC, box 35 and 12, LoCVGC, OV 21; Lloyd B. Reid, "Cars and People at Northland in April 1959," July 8, 1959, LoCVGC, box 45. Reid's counts: "People: Tuesday 36,081, Wed 44,356, Th 63,203, Fri 62,272, Sat 89,949, Total 329,062." Dorothy Thompson, "Commercialism Takes—and Wears—a New Look," *Ladies' Home Journal* (June 1954), AHCVGC, box 22.

22. Frederick Lewis Allen, "The Big Change in Suburbia," *Perspectives USA* 9 (Autumn 1954): 60–81; and "The Big Change in Suburbia, Part 1," *Harper's* (June 1954): 72, LoCVGC, OV 21.

23. Eugene Kelley, *Shopping Centers: Locating Controlled Regional Shopping Centers* (Saugatuck, Conn.: Eno Foundation for Highway Traffic Control, 1956).

24. "Northland."

25. Kelley, *Shopping Centers*, 200.

26. "Population, Wealth, and Northland," *Detroit Free Press*, c. March 1954, NSC.

27. "Golden-Haired Child," *Detroit Free Press*, c. March 1954, NSC; the average home in Oakland County was evaluated at $8,282, according to the Census Bureau, see "Characteristics of Eastland Shopping Center," 1955, NSC.

28. Victor Gruen, "Victor Gruen's Speech at Press Preview, Northland," March 15, 1954, AHCVGC, box 27.

29. C. B. Palmer, "The Shopping Center Goes to the Shopper," *New York Times Magazine*, November 29, 1953, 15, 38–44, LoCVGC, OV 20.

30. Gruen, "Speech at Press Preview."

31. Gruen and Larry Smith, *Shopping Towns USA: The Planning of Shopping Centers*, Progressive Architecture Library (New York: Reinhold, 1960), 125–27; "Huge New Shopping Center Sets Detroiters Buzzing," *Automobile Facts* (Automobile Manufacturers Association) 12, no. 9 (December 1953): 4–5; "The Store That Cars Built," *Architectural Forum* (May 1952): 132, the last two in AHCVGC, box 22.

32. Victor Gruen Associates, *A Revitalization Plan for the City Core of Cincinnati* (Los Angeles: Victor Gruen Associates, June 1962), 13, AHCVGC, box 58B; Victor Gruen to Editor, *Detroit Free Press*, January 22, 1960, AHCVGC, box 36.

33. "'Grass on Main Street' Becomes a Reality; Shopping Center, Linda Vista, California," *Architectural Forum* 81, no. 9 (September 1944): 83. See also Richard Longstreth, *City Center to Regional Mall: Architecture, the Automobile, and Retailing in Los Angeles, 1920–1950* (Cambridge, Mass.: MIT Press, 1997).

34. See Meredith L. Claussen, "Northgate Regional Shopping Center—Paradigm from the Provinces," *Journal of the Society of Architectural Historians* 43 (May 1984): 144–61.

35. Gruen and Smith, *Shopping Towns USA*, 24, 147; Victor Gruen, "The Urban Crisis," speech sponsored by the Oakland Chamber of Commerce and the Oakland City Planning Commission, October 19, 1956, 1–7, in *Speeches of Victor Gruen*, vol. A, 1943–56, LoCVGC, box 81 and AHCVGC, box 27; Edgardo Contini, "Anatomy of the Mall," *AIA Journal* (February 1969), AHCVGC, box 14.

36. Thompson, "Commercialism"; see also "Northland," *Architectural Forum*, where the shopping center is compared to medieval European market centers.

37. Barbara Flanagan, "He Brought Charm to Southdale," *Minneapolis Sunday Tribune*, October 7, 1956, 26.

38. Author interview with Peggy Gruen, Amherst, Mass., March 16, 1998.

39. Untitled film, c. 1966, AHCVGC, box 62. See also Victor Gruen to his children, October 1979, LoCVGC, box 22; Walter Guzzardi, Jr., "An Architect of Environments," *Fortune* (January 1962): 80; Author interview with Cesar Pelli, New Haven, Conn., March 5, 1998. See also Daniel Horowitz, "The Émigré as Celebrant of American Consumer Culture: George Katona and Ernest Dichter," in Charlie McGovern, Susan Strasser, and Matthias Judt, eds., *Getting and Spending: European and American Consumer Societies in the Twentieth Century* (London: Cambridge University Press, 1998), 149–66.

40. Gruen, *Centers for the Urban Environment: Survival of the Cities* (New York: Van Nostrand Reinhold, 1973), 173; Author interview with Peggy Gruen. Historian Harriet Freidenreich has characterized postwar Viennese Jews' relationship with their city as one based entirely on "nostalgia." "Some Viennese Jews," she writes, "can still nostalgically recall the 'good old days' before the war when they felt at home in Vienna and its vibrant cultural life." Harriet Pass Freidenreich, *Jewish Politics in Vienna, 1918–1938* (Bloomington: Indiana University Press, 1991), 208–9.

41. Gruen's tourist visa to return to Vienna was issued July 31, 1948 and remained valid until August 9, 1948, LoCVGC, box 21.

42. Author interview with Peggy Gruen.

43. Gruen and Smith, *Shopping Towns USA*, 24, 80, 147. See also "At Southdale, They

Were Having a Ball," *Minneapolis Star*, April 25, 1960; "School in a Shopping Center," *Minnesota Journal of Education* (October 1961), LoCVGC, OV 5.

44. Gruen, "Urban Crisis" (speech), 3, LoCVGC, box 81.

45. Gruen and Lazette Van Houten, "Remarks by Mr. & Mrs. Gruen," National Home Fashions League, Southern California Chapter, Biltmore Bowl, Los Angeles, July 11, 1956, 6, in *Speeches of Victor Gruen*, vol. A, 1943–56, LoCVGC, box 81.

46. Victor Gruen, "Role of the Architect in Stimulating Better Urban Planning," speech to AIA San Fernando Valley chapter, 1964, AHCVGC, box 62.

47. Gruen, *Heart of Our Cities*, 24, 28, 152.

48. Gruen and Smith, "Shopping Centers: The New Building Type," 67, AHCVGC, box 11; see also Gruen and Smith, *Shopping Towns USA*, 24 and "The Ten Steps Preceding Shopping Center Construction," *Women's Wear Daily*, July 2, 1952, LoCVGC, OV 19.

49. Victor Gruen, "Planning for Shopping," speech to Boston Conference on Distribution, Boston, Mass., October 18, 1955, in *Speeches of Victor Gruen*, vol. A, 1943–56, LoCVGC, box 81. As one of Gruen's associates wrote about Northland in 1953: "The services go beyond the commercial. The regional center can and does provide a cultural, social, and civic focus for the entire trade area." Karl O. Van Leuven, "From Joe's Hot Dog Stand To a Regional Shopping Center," *American City* (April 1953): 98–99, AHCVGC, Box 14.

50. Gruen and Smith, "Shopping Centers: The New Building Type," 67, AHCVGC, box 11; and Gruen and Smith, *Shopping Towns USA*, 24; Rouse is quoted in Gruen and Smith, *Shopping Towns USA*, 258.

51. Donald L. Curtiss, *Operation Shopping Centers: Guidebook to Effective Management and Promotion* (Washington, D.C.: Urban Land Institute, 1961), 24.

52. Gruen, "Commercial Structures and the Architect" speech, August 14, 1956, 1, 5; Gruen and Smith, *Shopping Towns USA*, 21–23.

53. Gruen and Smith, *Shopping Towns USA*, 153; Thompson, "Commercialism"; "20th Century Bazaar," *Life*, August 30, 1954, AHCVGC, box 35.

54. Quoted in Gruen, "Dynamic Planning for Retail Areas," *Harvard Business Review* 32, no. 6 (November–December 1954): 53–62, AHCVGC, boxes 11, 23; Gruen and Smith, *Shopping Towns USA*, 148, 153, 157.

55. Thompson, "Commercialism."

56. Author interview with Peggy Gruen; Victor Gruen, untitled preliminary draft of text for shopping center exhibition, 1952, 1, AHCVGC, box 33.

57. Chris Claussen, "L.A. Beats Decentralization Blight, Architect Declares," *Los Angeles Examiner*, March 27, 1955, 23, LoCVGC, OV 22.

58. Gruen, *Heart of Our Cities*, 342.

59. Gruen, "Urban Renewal," speech before Lambda Alpha in Los Angeles, in *Appraisal Journal* (American Institute of Real Estate Appraisers), January 1956, AHCVGC, box 17.

60. Gruen, "Speech at Memorial Art Galleries, Rochester, New York," September 30, 1950, in *Speeches of Victor Gruen*, vol. A, 1943–56, LoCVGC, box 81.; he delivered nearly the same speech eight years later: "Arts, Architecture, and the Man-Made Environment," speech before the Architectural League of New York, September 4, 1958, 1–12, AHCVGC, box 27.

61. Gruen, "Arts, Architecture," speech, September 4, 1958, 2. Ironically, this type of commercial ballyhoo, which Gruen so passionately critiqued, was exactly the kind of design upon which he had built his retail reputation in the 1930s and 1940s.

62. Gruen, *Heart of Our Cities*, 45; Victor Gruen, "The City in the Automobile Age," *Perspectives USA* no. 16 (Summer 1956): 45–54, AHCVGC, box 2.

63. Sam Gottesfeld, "A Bright New Future for Retailing," *Women's Wear Daily*, December 26, 1956, LoCVGC, OV 25.

Chapter 6. Planning the New "Suburbscape"

Note to epigraph: "Southdale Center Presents New Design, Decor Approach," *Women's Wear Daily*, October 9, 1956, LoCVGC, OV 4.

1. "Dayton's Edina Center Brings Staff Shifts," *Minneapolis Morning Tribune*, June 18, 1952, 1, 15, LoCVGC, OV 4.

2. Flyer, Dayton's, "The New Southdale Center," 1952, LoCVGC, OV 04; "New Zoning Approved for Dayton Unit," July 7, 1952, *Retailing Daily*, LoCVGC, OV 4.

3. The one big exception to this would be Columbia, Maryland, planned by Gruen's sometime collaborator James Rouse.

4. "The Splashiest Shopping Center in the U.S.," *Life*, December 10, 1956, 16; "Retail Trade: Pleasure-Domes with Parking," *Time*, October 15, 1956, 96–98; Theodore Irwin, "Suburbia's Growing Market Place," *Steelways* (February 1956): 16–18; "For Diner's Delight," *Institutions Magazine* 42, no. 2 (February 1958): n.p., all in AHCVGC, box 22.

5. Harold L. Klefsaos to S. K. Widdess, "Southdale Publicity Memorandum," January 26, 1962, Dayton-Hudson's Archive, Minneapolis, Minn., hereafter cited as D-HA.

6. "Work Begins on 10 Million Dollar Southdale Shopping Center," *Minneapolis Star*, October 29, 1954, 52, D-HA.

7. "July Heat for January Shoppers," *Business Week*, January 26, 1957; "Design For a Better Outdoors Indoors," *Architectural Record* (June 1962); "Southdale Is 11th of Its Kind in Nation," *Minneapolis Sunday Tribune*, October 7, 1956, 5, all in D-HA.

8. "A Break-Through for Two-Level Shopping Centers: Two-Level Southdale," *Architectural Forum* (December 1956), D-HA; Arthur Herzog, November 18, 1962, 110; Victor Gruen, "The Future of the Planned Shopping Center," in *Advanced Retail Management: Tobe Lecture Series* (Cambridge, Mass.: Harvard Graduate School of Business Administration and New York: Fairchild, 1957), 102, AHCVGC, box 5.

9. "Southdale Shopping Center," *Architectural Forum* (April 1957), AHCVGC, box 35.

10. "Splashiest Shopping Center in the U.S.," 61–66.

11. Martin Meyerson, *Face of the Metropolis*, film, 1963, AHCVGC, box 62; "Pleasure-Domes with Parking," 97; Victor Gruen, *Centers for the Urban Environment: Survival of the Cities* (New York: Van Nostrand Reinhold, 1973), 36–37.

12. "Brisk Business for a Bright Shopping Center," *Fortune* (February 1957): 141; *Architectural Forum* "Southdale Shopping Center"; Gruen, "Planning for Shopping," speech, October 18, 1955, 1 in *Speeches of Victor Gruen*, vol. B, 1957–58, LoCVGC, OV 82.

13. *Time*, "Pleasure-Domes with Parking," 96; "Southdale Center Presents New Design, Decor Approach," *Women's Wear Daily*, October 9, 1956, LoCVGC, OV 4; Victor Gruen, "The Will, the Ways, and the Means," talk to be delivered at the N.R.D.G.A. National Convention's General Merchandising Session, "Reversing the Down Trend of 'Downtown' Volume," January 8, 1957, in *Speeches of Victor Gruen*, vol. B, 1957–58, LoCVGC, OV 82; "Southdale Center," *Shopping Centers Today* (May 1991) 47, D-HA.

14. See "L. S. Donaldson Joins Dayton's in New Center," *Women's Wear Daily*, October 26, 1953; "Donaldson's and Dayton's Merge Shopping Center in $15,000,000 South-

dale Project," October 25, 1953, *Mineapolis Sunday Tribune*; and "Donaldson's Had Planned Another Suburban Center," *Minneapolis Sunday Tribune*, October 7, 1956, 5, all in LoCVGC, OV 4.

15. Author interview with Rod Kirkland, Seattle, November 12, 1998.

16. Neil Harris suggests that the form of Southdale was quickly imitated across the country. While this observation is true on a gross level, the size of Southdale's court is not replicated in that many other shopping centers, just the interior mall idea. See Neil Harris, "Spaced Out at the Shopping Center," *Cultural Excursions: Marketing Appetites and Cultural Tastes in Modern America* (Chicago: University of Chicago Press, 1990), 278–88.

17. "Minneapolis Crucified by Architect," *Rapid City (S.D.) Journal*, November 29, 1956, LoCVGC, OV 4.

18. Gruen, *Centers for the Urban Environment*, 36–37; "A Break-Through for Two-Level Shopping Centers," *Architectural Forum*, The *Forum* also maintained that "Southdale uncannily conveys the feeling of a metropolitan downtown."

19. "For Diner's Delight," *Institutions Magazine*. Another new phenomenon—the television sitcom—also romanticized the close, ethnic urban experience for exurbanites. Popular shows like *The Honeymooners* and *I Love Lucy* portrayed idealized urban memories for new suburbanites.

20. Calkins & Holden, Inc., "Southdale Opening Plan," April 17, 1956, 2, D-HA.

21. "Dayton's Edina Center Brings Staff Shifts," *Minneapolis Morning Tribune*, June 18, 1952, 15. See also Donald Dayton as quoted in Peg Meier, "The Shopping Center That Spawned a Community," *Minneapolis/Saint Paul Magazine* (August 1981): 67.

22. Larry Smith and Co., "Randhurst Market Analysis, Revised," August 24, 1960, 9, Randhurst Shopping Center Archives, Mount Prospect Historical Society, Mount Prospect, Ill.; J. M. Baskin, "Carson's New Branch Will Open Next Fall," *Women's Wear Daily*, December 10, 1953. Baskin quotes Carson's president.

23. "Three Successful Shopping Centers," *Architectural Forum* (October 1957): 112.

24. Victor Gruen and Larry Smith, *Shopping Towns USA: The Planning of Shopping Centers*, Progressive Architecture Library (New York: Reinhold, 1960) 55.

25. Farnham's advertisement, "Adding to the Farnham Picture"; Juvenile shoe stores advertisement, "Now 4 Convenient Locations'; see also Flagg Bros. Shoes advertisement, "Another One for Minneapolis," all in *Minneapolis Sunday Tribune*, October 7, 1956, 34, 14, 26, respectively.

26. Gruen, *Heart of Our Cities*, 56; Gruen quoted in Claussen, "L.A. Beats Decentralization Blight," *Los Angeles Examiner*, March 27, 1955, 23.

27. Arthur B. Gallion, *The Urban Pattern: City Planning and Design* (New York: Van Nostrand, 1950), 170.

28. Gruen, "Urban Renewal," *Appraisal Journal* (American Institute of Real Estate Appraisers) (January 1956): n.p.

29. Donald Dayton in Meier, "Shopping Center That Spawned a Community," 67.

30. "Work Begins on 10 Million Dollar Southdale Shopping Center," *Minneapolis Star*, October 29, 1954, 52; Donald C. Dayton, memo to employees, June 17, 1952, D-HA.

31. Gruen, December 17, 1953, rev. June 24, 1954; see also "Southdale Realty Master Plan Southdale Area, Sept. 1955"; and "Proposed Medical Center, Proposed Zoning drawn by RP 8-30-55." Victor Gruen, "Southdale Development Master Plan-Street Improvement," Minnesota Historical Society, Southdale Collection, box 9.

32. Gruen, "Urban Renewal."

33. Gruen, *Heart of Our Cities*, 32, 39.

34. Gruen, "Cities for Warm Bodies," phonotape of staff meeting of the Center for the Study of Democratic Institutions, Santa Barbara, Calif., c. 1969, AHCVGC, box 62.

35. Karl O. Van Leuven, "New Commercial Areas," *Planning 1952* (Chicago: American Society of Planning Officials, 1952), 31.

36. "Facts on Southdale," 5, D-HA; "Home Building Spurts Near Southdale," *Minneapolis Sunday Tribune*, October 7, 1956, 31; Thorpe Brothers, "Southdale Homesites," flyer, 1953, LoCVGC, OV 4.

37. Jane Jacobs to Victor Gruen, 1; Victor Gruen, "Role of the Architect in Stimulating Better Urban Planning," A.I.A. speech to San Fernando Valley chapter, 1964, AHCVGC, box 62.

38. G. Stockton Strawbridge to Larry Smith, May 4, 1962, 1–2, HMSCC.

39. Gruen to Joseph L. Hudson of J. L. Hudson Company, July 30, 1965, AHCVGC.

40. Gruen, "The Northland Story," 1968, AHCVGC, box 79; Victor Gruen to Bruce Dayton, January 23, 1967, 1, LoCVGC, box 77.

41. In many ways, Gruen was here advocating what would be dubbed "edge cities" by the 1990s. However, observers of edge cities—a dense growth of commercial buildings and offices in suburbia—saw them as being built only by developers without the help of architects. While this may have become true by the 1980s, in the 1950s architects like Gruen clearly had a hand in shaping the edge-city developments. For the best analysis of edge cities see Joel Garreau, *Edge Cities: Life on the New Frontier* (New York: Doubleday, 1991); Robert Fishman, *Bourgeois Utopias: The Rise and Fall of Suburbia* (New York: Basic Books, 1987); and Alexander Garvin, *The American City: What Works, What Doesn't* (New York: McGraw-Hill, 1995).

42. Examples of Gruen's many speeches and press coverage of them include Victor Gruen, untitled speech to San Francisco Planning and Housing Commission, January 31, 1956 at Commercial Club San Francisco, 1–18, LoCVGC, OV 24; see newspaper coverage, "Expert Warns Against Urban Renewal Haste," *San Francisco Examiner*, February 1, 1956, "S.F. Master Plan or 'Suburbia,'" *San Francisco Examiner*, February 2, 1956; Victor Gruen, "City Planning for the Year 2000," An Address by Victor Gruen at Cooper Union, 1 September 1956, LoCVGC, 81; Victor Gruen, untitled, speech to California Council of Landscape Architects, Santa Barbara, California, October 13, 1956, LoCVGC, 81; Victor Gruen, "The Urban Crisis," speech sponsored by the Oakland Chamber of Commerce and the Oakland City Planning Commission, October 19, 1956, 1–7, LoCVGC, 81.

43. "Tishmans Start West Coast Job," *New York Times*, April 22, 1956, LoCVGC, OV 24; "$10,000,000 Apartments Set for Wilshire," *Los Angeles Times*, August 29, 1956, LoCVGC, OV 25.

44. "City Housing Units Ready," *Los Angeles Examiner*, Real Estate and Building, sec. 3, October 9, 1955, LoCVGC, OV 23.

45. "La Canada Tract Previewed Today," *Pasadena Star News*, March 18, 1956; "Kitchen Items Prove Popular at Project," *Los Angeles Times*, January 15, 1956; "Sunset Hills Home Setting," *Los Angeles Examiner*, April 15, 1956, all in LoCVGC, OV 24.

46. "Splashiest Shopping Center in the U.S.," 61; "Pleasure-Domes with Parking"; "What's New . . . in Your Future," *Glamour* (January 1956), LoCVGC, OV 24; "New City," *New Yorker*, March 17, 1956, LoCVGC, OV 24.

47. William Percival, "'We Can Build a Better City': This Is How It Could Be," *World Telegram and Sun Saturday Magazine*, March 10, 1956, 10, 12.

48. Gruen, untitled speech given on the occasion of the Fourth Annual Awards of *Pro-*

gressive Architecture, New Orleans, La., January 19, 1957, 5, in *Speeches of Victor Gruen*, vol. B, 1957–58, LoCVGC, OV 82.

49. Gruen, "Where Is Modern Architecture Taking Us?," speech delivered to the Economic Club of Detroit, November 12, 1956, in *Speeches of Victor Gruen*, vol. A, 1943–56, LoCVGC, OV 81.

50. Gruen, speech to *Progressive Architecture* awards, 3–7.

Chapter 7. Saving Our Cities

Note to epigraph: Gruen, "Planning for Shopping," speech at the Boston Conference on Distribution, October 18, 1955, in *Speeches of Victor Gruen*, vol. A, 1943–56, LoCVGC, OV 81.

1. Hal Burton, *The City Fights Back* (New York: Citadel Press, 1954). See also Miles Colean, *Renewing Our Cities* (New York: Twentieth Century Fund, 1953), 3.

2. Gruen, "Dynamic Planning for Retail Areas," *Harvard Business Review* 32, no. 6 (November–December 1954): 53–62, AHCVGC, boxes 11, 23. See also Victor Gruen, "Urban Renewal," *Appraisal Journal* (American Institute of Real Estate Appraisers) (January 1956), LoCVGC, OV 24.

3. All above quotes from Gruen, "Dynamic Planning," 53–62.

4. "Northland: A New Yardstick for Shopping Center Planning," *Architectural Forum* 100, no. 6 (June 1954): 102–19, AHCVGC, box 54; Lois Balcom, "The Best Hope for Our Big Cities," *Reporter*, October 3, 1957, AHCVGC, box 22.

5. "Retailer's Problem: Reviving a Sick Old 'Downtown,'" *Business Week*, January 15, 1955, 42–50; "Dynamic Planning Can Modernize Retail Shopping Districts," *Des Moines Tribune*, January 24, 1955; Bernard Newer, "Downtown Stores Gird for Battle," *Syracuse Post Standard*, January 23, 1955; Ed Morse, "Shopping Center Riding High, But Main Street May Retailate," *Providence Rhode Island Journal*, March 13, 1955 (Associated Press story carried in at least 35 papers across the nation); see also Herbert Koshetz, "The Merchant's Point of View," *New York Times*, January 16, 1955; all in LoCVGC, OV 22.

6. Bernard J. Frieden and Lynne B. Sagalyn, *Downtown, Inc.: How America Rebuilds Cities* (Cambridge, Mass.: MIT Press, 1989), 17.

7. Gruen, "The Emerging Urban Pattern," *Progressive Architecture* (July 1959): 162, AHCVGC, box 16.

8. Gruen, "Dynamic Planning." Thomas's interest in Gruen's article is described in "Master Plan for Revitalizing Ft. Worth's Central Core," *Business Week*, March 17, 1956, 70, AHCVGC, box 22. Gruen quoted in "Downtown Needs a Lesson from the Suburbs," *Business Week*, October 22, 1955, 64–66, AHCVGC, box 11.

9. Victor Gruen Associates, *A Greater Fort Worth Tomorrow* (Los Angeles: Victor Gruen Associates, 1956), AHCVGC, box 58B. W. Dwayne Jones generously allowed me to read his paper about Fort Worth urban renewal and shared his Fort Worth research files with me: see "A Greater Fort Worth Tomorrow" (Texas Historical Commission, Austin, 1997, photocopy). See also "Fort Worth, Texas," *Architectural Digest* (October 1956): 314–31, AHCVGC, box 22; "Typical Downtown Transformed," *Architectural Forum* (May 1956), AHCVGC, box 22; Grady Clay, "Metropolis Regained," *Horizon* 1 (July 1959): 8–9, AHCVGC, box 41.

10. Gruen, "Cityscape and Landscape," *Arts and Architecture* (September 1955). The article was an excerpted version of Gruen's speech given at the International Conference of Design in Aspen, Colorado, in June 1955, in *Speeches of Victor Gruen*, vol. A, 1943–56, LoCVGC, box 81.

11. "Downtown Needs a Lesson," *Business Week*; "Master Plan for Revitalizing Ft. Worth's Central Core," *Business Week*.

12. Thomas Creighton, ed., "What Can a Public Relations Counsel Do?" *Progressive Architecture* (February 1955): 75–76, LoCVGC, OV 22.

13. Both quotes from Harley Pershing, "Daring Plan for City Has Roots in Old World," *Fort Worth Star-Telegram*, March 11, 1956, sec. 1, 10.

14. Gruen Associates, *Greater Fort Worth Tomorrow*.

15. "City Leaders Throw Solid Support Behind Futuristic Municipal Plan," *Fort Worth Star-Telegram*, March 11, 1956, 12.

16. "Statement by Mr. J. B. Thomas, President of Texas Electric Service Company for Opening the Meeting of Civic Leaders for Presentation of the Gruen Plan on March 10, 1956," manuscript, City of Fort Worth Resource Library.

17. "City Leaders Throw Support"; "Plan for 'City of Tomorrow' Outlined to Civic Leaders," *Fort Worth Star-Telegram*, March 11, 1956, 12; Pershing, "Daring Plan."

18. "More About Design for Future City," *Fort Worth Star-Telegram*, March 11, 1956.

19. "City Leaders Throw Support"; "Plan for 'City of Tomorrow.'"

20. "City Leaders Throw Support"; "The Gruen Plan: Tomorrow's Greater Fort Worth . . . a Bold, Aggressive Future," *Fort Worth Press*, March 11, 1956, 9.

21. Chamber of Commerce quoted in "Gruen Plan: Tomorrow's Greater Fort Worth," 9.

22. "Thomas 'Outstanding Citizen,'" *Fort Worth Press*, February 22, 1961.

23. "What's New . . . in Your Future," *Glamour* (January 1956), LoCVGC, OV 24.

24. James Rouse, speech to the Conference of Mayors, 1960, cited in Victor Gruen Associates, "Planning," *Victor Gruen Associates* (Los Angeles: Victor Gruen Associates, c. 1966), AHCVGC, box 51.

25. "Plan for Fort Worth," *Dallas Morning News*, March 13, 1956.

26. W.R.H., the Home Towner, "Look into the Future," *Fort Worth Press*, March 11, 1956; "Presenting Your Fort Worth of Tomorrow," *Fort Worth Press*, March 11, 1956, AHCVGC, box 14.

27. W.R.H., "Look into the Future"; "Statement by Mr. J. B. Thomas."

28. In 1940, the city's population was 177,662; the county's was 225,521. By 1960 the numbers had increased to 356,268 and 538,495 respectively. *Fifteenth Census of the U.S. Population*, vols. 1–3 (Washington, D.C.: U.S. Government Printing Office, 1960).

29. "Statement by Mr. J. B. Thomas."

30. "Every 'Big Business' Draws Honor from Thomas' Efforts in Water Conservation," *Fort Worth Press*, May 5, 1950, 11. See also "J. B. Thomas Inscribes Name in Fort Worth Golden Deeds Book," *Fort Worth Star-Telegram*, April 25, 1961.

31. Chamber of Commerce quoted in "Gruen Plan: Tomorrow's Greater Fort Worth"; Thomas quoted in "How Plan Got Start," *Fort Worth Star-Telegram*, March 11, 1956, 1.

32. Victor Gruen, untitled, c. 1967, 1–3, AHCVGC, box 31.

33. All the above quotes are from Gruen Associates, *Greater Fort Worth Tomorrow*.

34. "New City," Talk of the Town, *New Yorker*, March 17, 1956, LoCVGC, OV 24.

35. "Merchants Lose Downtown Blues," *New York Times*, February 27, 1955, LoCVGC, OV 22.

36. Harley Pershing, "Merchants Will Have Big Stake in Development of City of Tomorrow," *Fort Worth Star-Telegram*, April 2, 1956.

37. Gruen Associates, *Greater Fort Worth Tomorrow*.

38. Pershing, "Merchants Will Have Big Stake."

39. Jane Jacobs, "Downtown Is for People," in Editors of Fortune, *The Exploding*

Metropolis (Garden City, N.Y.: Doubleday, 1958), 157–84; Jane Jacobs to J. B. Thomas, forwarded by Jacobs to Gruen, July 31, 1959, LoCVGC.

40. Gruen, "The City in the Automobile Age," *Perspectives USA* 16 (Summer 1956): 45–54, AHCVGC. See also Richard Lawrence Nelson and Frederick T. Aschman, *Conservation and Rehabilitation of Major Shopping Districts* (Washington, D.C.: Urban Land Institute, 1954): "The older districts . . . suffer both from inadequate parking and from the type of major street congestion that makes shopping a chore" (7).

41. Richard Kluger, "Less Rural, More Wistful America," *Harper's* (January 1965), LoCVGC, OV 43; author interview with Cesar Pelli, New Haven, Conn., March 5, 1998.

42. Gruen, "City in the Automobile Age"; Victor Gruen, *The Heart of Our Cities: The Urban Crisis, Diagnosis and Cure* (New York: Simon and Schuster, 1964), 45. See also Victor Gruen, "Renewing Cities for the Automobile Age," speech to the Potomac Chapter of the National Housing and Redevelopment Officials at the National Housing Center, Washington, D.C., January 3, 1957, in *Speeches of Victor Gruen*, vol. B, 1957–58, LoCVGC, box 82, and Victor Gruen, "Retailing and the Automobile," *Architectural Record* (March 1960): 191–214.

43. Gruen, *Heart of Our Cities*, 69.

44. "Revolution in Retail Selling," *U.S. News & World Report*, June 20, 1958, 48–58, LoCVGC, OV 9; Pershing, "Daring Plan." See also "Gay, Handsome Streets of Future," *Fort Worth Press*, March 11, 1956, 19A, AHCVGC, box 14; and Arthur McVoy, "Pedestrian-Way Business," *American City* (March 1957): 136–38, 171–77, LoCVGC, OV 9.

45. Andrew Drysdale, "Downtown Is Treated as Big Shop Center," *Dayton (Ohio) Journal-Herald*, Dayton, Ohio, January 27, 1958, LoCVGC, OV 9; "What's New . . . in Your Future."

46. Pershing, "Daring Plan."

47. Gruen, "City in the Automobile Age." See also Victor Gruen, "Renewing Cities for the Automobile Age," speech to the Los Angeles chapter of the Institute of Real Estate Management, February 27, 1957, 1–14, AHCVGC, box 30.

48. Witherspoon and Associates Public Relations, "Information on the Gruen Plan," March 11, 1956, 14. See also Pershing, "Daring Plan": "This tantalizing dish for future growth is based on the knowledge and experience . . . gained in their work on Northland." See also "Topics of the Times," *New York Times*, November 5, 1956, LoCVGC, OV 25; the article emphasized that Gruen was the "philosopher of the shopping center."

49. "Architect Says Suburb Center Can Aid Loop," *Minneapolis Morning Tribune*, June 18, 1952, 12, LoCGVC, OV 19; Victor Gruen and Larry Smith, *Shopping Towns USA: The Planning of Shopping Centers* (New York: Reinhold Progressive Architecture Library, 1960), 271. See also "Topics of the Times," where the *New York Times* presents Northland and Southdale as models for his downtown work.

50. "Merchandise Sold by Trees, Benches," *Fort Worth Press*, March 11, 1956, 20A, AHCVGC, box 14; "Gay, Handsome Streets of Future."

51. Harold Monroe, "Shopping Center Near Detroit Operates on Gruen Principle," *Fort Worth Star-Telegram*, September 23, 1956.

52. "Gruen Hopes Plan Will Shock People," *Fort Worth Star-Telegram*, March 11, 1956, 21A.

53. "Future on File," WEVD radio, New York, New York, 11:00 P.M., February 26, 1952. Full text of Victor Gruen interview by Tom Morgan prepared by Radio Reports, New York, LoCVGC, OV 20.

54. Victor Gruen, "The Emerging Urban Pattern," *Progressive Architecture* (July 1959): 118, 162.

55. Victor Gruen, "1976: Rough Outline of Ideas," August 5, 1955, AHCVGC, box 15.

56. Chamber of Commerce statement quoted in "Two Aims," *Fort Worth Star-Telegram*, March 30, 1956. See also Irv Farman, "Gruen Pains: A Downtown Fort Worth Master Planner Is Finally Remembered for the Right Reasons," *Once Over Lightly* (Fort Worth, Texas: n.d.).

57. W.R.H., "Look into the Future."

58. "What's It All About," *Fort Worth Press*, March 11, 1956, 18A.

59. Pattern for "Vigorous City Growth," *Fort Worth Star-Telegram*, March 16, 1956, 20.

60. "Citizens Sound Off on City's Future Improvement Needs," *Fort Worth Press*, March 2, 1958, 2.

61. "Here's What They're Thinking," *Fort Worth Press*, March 2, 1958, 1; "The Pattern of the Future," *Newsweek*, September 2, 1957, 64.

62. "State Funds Denied for Gruen Plan," *Fort Worth Star-Telegram*, March 10, 1956.

63. John Ohendalski, "Gruen Plan Backers Await Legislation," *Fort Worth Press*, January 9, 1957.

64. Sam Kinch, "Revival Sought for Gruen Bill," *Fort Worth Star-Telegram*, April 9, 1957, 2; "Gruen Bill Defeat Laid to Lack of Understanding," *Fort Worth Star-Telegram*, April 9, 1957, 2; "Urban Renewal Bill Goes to House," *Fort Worth Star-Telegram*, March 12, 1957.

65. "Thompson to Resign from Gruen Group," *Fort Worth Star-Telegram*, March 5, 1957, 1; "Gruen Parking Bill Dies; Slum Plan Given Boost," *Fort Worth Star-Telegram*, April 30, 1957; "Texas Senate Kills Parking Garage Bill," *Fort Worth Star-Telegram*, April 30, 1957.

66. Walter Humphrey, "Let's Try Being *FOR* Something! An Editorial Letter to All Fort Worthers," *Fort Worth Press*, June 22, 1958, LoCVGC, OV 9.

67. Victor Gruen, "City Planning for the Year 2000," address at Cooper Union, September 1, 1956, AHCVGC, box 62 and in *Speeches of Victor Gruen*, vol. A, 1943–56, LoCVGC, box 81.

68. Frederic Sherman, "On the Future of Our Cities," LoCVGC, OV 25.

69. Victor Gruen, Letter to the Editor, *The Gazette*, Charleston, W. Va., October 30, 1959. Gruen wrote about an October 8, 1959, article by Thomas Stafford, AHCVGC, box 36.

Chapter 8. The Suburbanization of Downtown

Note to epigraph: Victor Gruen, *The Heart of Our Cities: The Urban Crisis, Diagnosis and Cure* (New York: Simon and Schuster, 1964), 173.

1. "Contract for Downtown Study Signed," *Kalamazoo Gazette*, April 18, 1957; "Downtown Revitalization," editorial, *Kalamazoo Gazette*, April 22, 1957, both in LoCVGC, OV 51.

2. Hayden Bradford, "Start Made on Research into What's Needed for Downtown Revitalization," *Kalamazoo Gazette*, May 16, 1957, LoCVGC, OV 51.

3. Raymond Dykema as quoted in Clarence Schlaver, "Downtown Perks Up But Will Our Dealers Stay?" *Office Appliances* (April 1960): 4; "New Greenery: Money and Mall," *Kalamazoo Times Herald*, August 20, 1959; Bradford, "Just a Year Old, How It's Grown," August 14, 1960, AHCVGC, box 15.

4. "Downtown Gets Uplift," *Life*, October 1959, 115–17, AHCVGC, box 41; "Plan New

Kalamazoo Exhibit: City Chosen for Display in Germany," *Kalamazoo Gazette*, March 20, 1958, AHCVGC, box 15.

5. "Early Verdict on Burdick Mall: It's a Big Success," *Kalamazoo Gazette*, August 20, 1959, LoCVGC, OV 51; "Will Downtown Malls Work?" *Chain Store Age* (October 1959): 1–6.

6. "Mayor Offers Idea for Mall," *Bridgeport (Conn.) Post*, August 16, 1959, LoCVGC, OV 51; Bradford, "Just a Year Old, How It's Grown."

7. "Mayor Offers Idea for Mall"; Eugene Segal, "No Place for Malls, Says Planning Chief," *Cleveland Plain Dealer*, August 31, 1959; Sam Gottesfeld, "Malls Held Last Step in Downtown Revival," *Women's Wear Daily*, August 25, 1959, 1, 6, all in LoCVGC, OV 51.

8. "Malls Tried in 55 Cities: But Gruen Warns They're Not Just Gimmicks," *Bridgeport Herald*, December 20, 1959. See also "How Leading Chains View Downtown Malls," *Chain Store Age* (December 1959), AHCVGC, OV 15; and Laurence Alexander, "Some Second Thoughts on Downtown Malls," *Stores* (October 1959), both in AHCVGC, box 15.

9. Wolf Von Eckardt, Review of *The Heart of Our Cities: The Urban Crisis: Diagnosis and Cure*, *New Republic*, January 1965, 18–19, AHCVGC, box 16.

10. "Permanent Mall Huge Success," *Fort Worth Star-Telegram*, September 20, 1959; John Ohendalski, "Was Gruen Plan Born Too Soon in Fort Worth?" *Fort Worth Press*, September 20, 1959, LoCVGC, OV 9.

11. Jeanne Lowe, "What's Happened in Fort Worth?" *Architectural Forum* (May 1959): 136–139, AHCVGC, box 41. See also Jeanne Lowe, *Cities in a Race with Time: Progress and Poverty in America's Renewing Cities* (New York: Random House, 1967).

12. "Downtown Core Is Revived," *Shopping Center Age* 1, no. 8 (August 1962): 18–19, 29–31; Victor Gruen, "The Will, the Ways, and the Means," speech delivered at the N.R.D.G.A. National Convention's General Merchandising Session, "Reversing the Down Trend of Downtown Volume," January 8, 1957, 3, in *Speeches of Victor Gruen*, vol. B, 1957–58, LoCVGC, box 82.

13. Gruen, *Heart of Our Cities*, 300–320.

14. Gruen, "The Urban Crisis," speech sponsored by the Oakland Chamber of Commerce and the Oakland City Planning Commission, October 19, 1956, 1–7, AHCVGC, box 27 and in *Speeches of Victor Gruen*, vol. A, 1943–56, LoCVGC, box 81.

15. Robert Lewis, "A New Downtown," *Washington Star Sunday Magazine*, November 3, 1963, 12, AHCVGC, box 35; Ogden Tanner, "Renaissance on the Genesee," *Architectural Forum* (July 1959): 105, AHCVGC, box 41.

16. Gruen to partners, Venice, October 5, 1960, 2, AHCVGC, box 8.

17. Tanner, "Renaissance on the Genesee," 104–9; Lewis, "A New Downtown," 12.

18. Tanner, "Renaissance on the Genesee," 105; John Crosby, *New York Herald Tribune*, April 6 1962, AHCVGC, box 12; Lewis, "A New Downtown," 12.

19. Personal communication from Prof. David Ames of the University of Delaware, who worked for the Worcester Redevelopment Agency.

20. U.S. Congress, *Small Business Problems in Urban Areas, vol. 3, pursuant to House Resolution 13* (Washington, D.C.: U.S. Government Printing Office, 1965), 359; *World Book Encyclopedia, 1962 Year Book* (New York: World Book, 1962) AHCVGC, box 14.

21. Lewis, "A New Downtown," 12; Gruen, *Heart of Our Cities*, 299.

22. Gruen, "The Suburban Regional Shopping Center and the Urban Core Area," *American Review* 2, no. 2 (May 1962), AHCVGC, box 17.

23. "Midtown Plaza: The Rochester, NY Demonstration of Downtown Renewal," *Urban Land* 21, no. 6 (June 1962): 3–4, AHCVGC, box 35.

24. Crosby, *New York Herald Tribune*; Victor Gruen, "Urban Centers in Metropolitan Regions," speech delivered to New York Regional Plan Association, November 9, 1964, 12–13, AHCVGC, box 27; Lewis, "A New Downtown," 12.

25. "Center for Rochester," *Architectural Forum* (June 1962): 112.

26. William P. Larkin, "Midtown Plaza . . . One Answer to Downtown's Problems," *Chain Store Age* (August 1962): 5, AHCVGC, box 17.

27. Lewis, "A New Downtown," 13; "The Midtown Plaza Clock," c. 1961, AHCVGC, box 51.

28. Larkin, "Midtown Plaza," 2–7. Rochester, as the first New York municipality to make use of a 1950 state bill authorizing state assistance for urban road building, was able to construct the ring road.

29. Pat Brasley, "Kennedy, PPR, Tactics Held Keys for Democrats," *Rochester Democrat and Chronicle*, November 12, 1961; Jean Utter, "Four Council Candidates Trade Barbs on TV," *Rochester Democrat and Chronicle*, November 5, 1961. Dem. Pirrelo and Rep. Barry exchanged the barbs over Midtown.

30. See David Schuyler, *A City Transformed: Redevelopment, Race, and Suburbanization in Lancaster, Pennsylvania, 1940–1980* (University Park: Pennsylvania State University Press, 2002), 90–119.

31. The population of Minneapolis dropped from 492,370 to 482,872 while the entire metropolitan area grew from 911,077 to 1,482,030; the African American population increased from 4,646 to 11,817. *Census of the U.S. Population, 1940* (Washington, D.C.: U.S. Government Printing Office, 1940), tables 35, 36; *Census of the US Population, 1960* (Washington, D.C.: U.S. Government Printing Office, 1960), tables 44, 45.

32. See June Manning Thomas, "Detroit: The Centrifugal City," in Gregory Squires, ed., *Unequal Partnerships: The Political Economy of Redevelopment in Postwar America* (Brunswick, N.J.: Rutgers University Press, 1989), 144–45.

33. In 1940 the city population was 177,662, the county population was 225,521; by 1960 the numbers had increased to 356,268 and 538,495 respectively; *Fifteenth Census of the U.S. Population*, vols. 1–3 (Washington, D.C.: U.S. Government Printing Office, 1960).

34. David Rabe, "Merchant's Quest for Quality" *New Haven Register*, October 9, 1969, New Haven Colony Historical Society, Edward Malley Department Store file.

35. "Randhurst Center: Big Pinwheel on the Prairie," *Architectural Forum* (November 1962), AHCVGC, box 23; on Randhurst, *Shopping Center Age*, February 1962, November 1962, AHCVGC, box 35; "Anatomy of a New Project," *Architectural and Engineering News* (May 1962), AHCVGC, box 17.

36. "Mayor Schlaver Speaks at Randhurst Domestone Ceremony," *Mount Prospect Independent*, March 8, 1962, Mount Prospect Historical Society, Randhurst Shopping Center Archives, Mount Prospect, Ill..

37. "Randhurst," *Shopping Center Age*, November 1962; "Fall-Out Shelters Can Be Built Here," *Mount Prospect Herald*, August 10, 1961, 1, both in Mount Prospect Historical Society, Randhurst Shopping Center Archives, Mount Prospect, Ill.

38. Charles Hayes, "Suburbs: Cradle of Shopping Center," *Cook County Herald*, September 13, 1962; Joanne Koch, "Bands Greet Crowds at Randhurst's Debut," *Chicago Daily Tribune*, August 17, 1962, 1, both in Mount Prospect Historical Society, Randhurst Shopping Center Archives, Mount Prospect, Ill. Randhurst and Rochester's Midtown Plaza were featured side by side in the *World Book Encyclopedia, 1962 Year Book* under remedies for the problem of America's central cities.

39. See Herbert Gans, *The Urban Villagers* (New York: Free Press, 1961); Martin Anderson, *The Federal Bulldozer: A Critical Analysis of Urban Renewal, 1949–1962* (Cambridge, Mass.: MIT Press, 1964); Jane Jacobs, "Downtown Is for People," in Editors of Fortune, *The Exploding Metropolis* (Garden City, N.Y.: Doubleday, 1958) 157–84; and Jane Jacobs, *The Death and Life of Great American Cities* (New York: Random House, 1961) 350.

40. Gruen, *Heart of Our Cities*, 153–55.

41. Leonard Gordon, ed., *A City in Racial Crisis: The Case of Detroit Pre- and Post-the 1967 Riot* (Detroit: Wm. C. Brown, 1971), 119. The quote is from Dan Aldridge.

Conclusion: "Those Bastard Developments" and Gruen's Legacy

Note to epigraph: Victor Gruen, *Centers for the Urban Environment: Survival of the Cities* (New York: Van Nostrand, Reinhold, 1973), ix.

1. Gruen Associates continues to this day in Los Angeles. After Gruen left and sold his name to his partners, the company continued to thrive, especially after 1969, when it hired architect and firm partner Cesar Pelli as head of the design department. Among the projects completed were the Pacific Design Center; the Commons of Columbus, Ohio; San Bernadino Civic Center and downtown redevelopment; South Coast Plaza in Orange County; and the Museum Tower for the Museum of Modern Art. Pelli suggests that Gruen had been forced to retire because of his tight grip on the firm and his domineering personality. Author interview with Cesar Pelli, New Haven, Conn., March 5, 1998.

2. George E. Berkley, *Vienna and Its Jews: The Tragedy of Success, 1880s–1980s* (Cambridge, Mass.: Abt Books, 1988), 342; Harriet Pass Freidenreich, *Jewish Politics in Vienna, 1918–1938* (Bloomington: Indiana University Press, 1991), 207.

3. Author interview with Cesar Pelli. Pelli was speaking about Rudi Baumfeld.

4. Author interview with Peggy Gruen, Amherst, Mass., March 16, 1998.

5. Susanna Baird, "Fatherland, Victor Gruen—A Return Home, 1968–69," c. 1999, AHCVGC, Website.

6. Garret Eckbo to Victor Gruen, June 6, 1973, LoCVGC, Container 21.

7. HUD Award for Design Excellence, 1968, AMCVGC, box 14. "I had the great privilege of talking about Fresno, showing the movie at a special session of Mrs. Johnson's Beautification Committee at the White House." Victor Gruen to Karl Buckman, chairman, Redevelopment Agency of the City of Fresno, July 20, 1966, AHCVGC, box 8.

8. James Rouse to Victor Gruen, June 14, 1973, LoCVGC, box 22; "Cherry Hill Center Opening Crowd Put at 100,000," *Women's Wear Daily*, October 12, 1961; Joseph Mathewson, "Enclosed Malls Help New Shopping Centers Combat the Weather," *Wall Street Journal*, October 11, 1961; "Shopping Centers," *Architectural Record* (June 1962); "Cherry Hill," *Shopping Center Age* (January 1962), AHCVGC, box 17.

9. Johnson quoted in Walter Guzzardi, Jr., "An Architect of Environments," *Fortune* (January 1962): 138.

10. Some of the founding members of Gruen's Foundation were Ise Frank—wife of Walter Gropius—Jack Lemmon, Dion Neutra, Joanne Woodward, Art Siedenbaum, Stewart Udall, and Louis Redstone—another shopping center architect.

11. Gruen, *Centers for the Urban Environment*, 2–11.

12. Victor Gruen to Rachel Heimovics (freelance writer for *Encyclopedia Britannica*), May 10, 1972, 2, LoCVGC, box 21.

13. Gruen, *Centers for the Urban Environment*, 39.

14. Victor Gruen, "Shopping Centres, Why, Where, How?" February 28, 1978, speech before Third Annual European Conference of the International Council of Shopping Centres, London, LoCVGC, box 78; a version of the speech was reprinted as "The Sad Story of Shopping Centers," *Town and Country Planning* 46, nos. 7–8 (July/August 1978): 350–53; Neil Pierce, "The Shopping Center and One Man's Shame," *Los Angeles Times*, October 22, 1978.

15. Victor Gruen to David Travers, May 19, 1967, LoCVGC, box 20.

16. Victor Gruen, "Is Progress a Crime?" c. 1976, 150–51, AHVGC, box 5.

17. Witold Rybczynski, "The New Downtowns: Shopping Malls," *Atlantic Monthly* 271, no. 5 (May 1993): 98.

18. See "Vienna Stops the Clock," *Newsweek*, March 20, 1972; "Vienna Hears the Sounds of Silence," *Washington Post*, January 15, 1972, Style Section, both in AHCVGC, box 11.

19. Wolf Von Eckardt, "The Urban Liberator: Victor Gruen and the Pedestrian Oasis," *Washington Post*, February 23, 1980, Style, Cityscape, B1.

20. Victor Gruen, interoffice communication to Mel Gooch, May 8, 1966, transcribed in Los Angeles May 12, 1966, LoCVGC, box 20; Victor Gruen to Rudi Baumfeld, July 17, 1969, 2–3, LoCVGC, box 11.

21. On Tehran project see folder in AHCVGC, box 11.

22. Von Eckardt, "Urban Liberator," B1.

Index

Acknowledgments

Victor Gruen lived a rich and complicated life. Writing the story of his career has been an equally complicated task, beginning almost nine years ago. The work has grown, with numerous changes in direction and focus, into this book. Writing and research is rarely an individual effort, and I am grateful for all the many institutions and people who have made this a valuable and enjoyable effort. I have received much support, guidance, and kindness from family, friends, and teachers who have helped me in numerous ways.

My greatest debt is to colleagues in the American Studies department at Yale University. I received wise comments on writing and history from Dolores Hayden, Johnny Faragher, Alex Garvin, Jon Butler, and Michael Denning. Parts of this book have been presented at various conferences. I appreciate the thoughtful comments by Richard Longstreth, Mark Rose, Stephen Stein, Alan Colquhoun, Rogers Smith, and Roger Horowitz. Additionally, Daniel Horowitz gave very helpful comments as a reader's report to the University of Pennsylvania Press. Most of all, my advisor and friend Jean-Christophe Agnew also inspired me. His enthusiasm for this topic has been more than I could have imagined when I began this project. From line edits and word choices to big ideas and historical questions, he has made the writing of this book more enjoyable and fruitful.

Several fellowships have supported me throughout this effort. I am grateful for grants or fellowships from the American Heritage Center at the University of Wyoming; Hagley Museum and Library; the Pew Program in Religion and American History; and the Institute for Social and Policy Studies Program on Race, Inequality, and Politics at Yale. This book never would have been completed without this financial support.

I appreciate the help of the staffs of many libraries where work on this project was undertaken. For most of my research on Gruen, I have relied on two collections of his papers at the Library of Congress and the American Heritage Center. The staff at both institutions have been helpful and attentive. A travel grant from the American Heritage Center first piqued my interest in Victor Gruen. In addition, I have relied on corporate records at Dayton-Hudson's and the records of Strawbridge and Clothier at the Hagley Museum and Library. Mall managers at Northland, Hillsdale, Old Orchard, Woodmar, and Randhurst generously allowed me to dig through their old files.

People who knew Victor Gruen shared their memories of him with me. I am indebted to Michael Gruen and Peggy Gruen and to Charles Blau, Kenneth Champlin, Rod Kirkland, Howard Landau, Cesar Pelli, and Jerome Rappoport for taking time to talk with me.

Guiding my manuscript into a book was editor Bob Lockhart at the University of Pennsylvania Press. He has given this book his utmost attention and care. Without his encouragement, enthusiasm, and guiding hand, this book probably never would have been completed. Additionally, the meticulous editorial comments by Lauren Osborne and Alison Anderson improved much of my writing.

Numerous friends and colleagues have helped me in numerous ways with this project. I am deeply indebted to Hilary Anderson, Matthew Babcock, Brian Barth, Jen Briggs, Rob Campbell, Aimee Feinberg, John Fisher, Brigid Globenksy, Cathy Gudis, Andrew and Allegra Hogan, Ted Liazos, Kate Masur, Marina Moskowitz, Jen Owens, Jessica Smith, Emily Sollie, and Eric Steadman for all that they have done. My deepest thanks go to Gay Wierdsma for helping in large and small ways.

Finally, my family has been a constant source of lightness and support throughout this process. My brother Todd has taught me many lessons of fortitude, perspective, and laughter. My brother Brian has always been a great friend—giving me a place to stay in DC, meeting me for tennis or coffee, and speculating with me about America. My parents, Mark and Helen Hardwick, have given me much to be thankful for.